Mary Rhinelander McCarl
Birmingham
+
Glouceds

$19.95

2.iii.99

Hackers Art Bods -
N.4.

BURT FRANKLIN: BIBLIOGRAPHY & REFERENCE SERIES 279
Art History & Art Reference Series 23

THE PICTORIAL PRESS

NOTE.

Some of the chapters of this book in a condensed form were published a few years ago in the *Illustrated London News*, and my acknowledgments are due to the proprietors of that journal for permission to reprint such of the woodcuts as accompanied the text in that form. I have also to thank them for their courtesy in allowing me to use several other engravings from the *Illustrated London News*, including some from the early numbers, which must now be reckoned among the curiosities of the Pictorial Press.

M. J.

HEADING OF 'THE JACOBITE'S JOURNAL,' 1747.

(*Supposed to be Drawn by Hogarth.*)

(*See page 197.*)

THE
PICTORIAL PRESS
ITS ORIGIN AND PROGRESS

BY

MASON JACKSON

BURT FRANKLIN
NEW YORK

Published by BURT FRANKLIN
235 East 44th St., New York, N.Y. 10017
Originally Published: London, 1885
Reprinted: 1969
Printed in the U.S.A.

Library of Congress Card Catalog No.: 69-18619
Burt Franklin: Bibliography and Reference Series 279
Art History and Art Reference Series 23

CONTENTS.

PAGE

CHAPTER I. 1

The Pictorial Taste Universal—The Early 'News-books'
—Development of the Newspaper Press—General use of Newspapers—Establishment of Illustrated Journals—Wandering
Ballad-Singers the First Newsvendors—The *English Mercurie*
of 1588—The Abolition of the Star Chamber and its Effect
on the Press.

CHAPTER II. 8

Illustrated Broadsides—Sir Francis Drake's Operations
against the Spaniards—Papers of News in the Reign of
James I.—The first Periodical Newspaper published in
England—Illustrated Tracts relating to Storms and Floods—
Remarkable Murders favourite subjects with the early News-
writers—Murder of the Rev. Mr. Storre—Murder in
Cornwall—Apparition of Three Skeletons—Visions in the
Air—Attempt on the Life of the Duke of Buckingham—
Fall of Meteors at Bawlkin Green, Berkshire—The *Swedish
Intelligencer*—Passage of the River Leck by Gustavus
Adolphus—The Sallee Rovers—The *Weekly News* of 1638,
an Illustrated Paper—The Irish Rebellion of 1641—The
Plague in London—Murder on board an English Ship—The
Earl of Strafford—His Execution on Tower Hill—Arch-
bishop Laud—A Burlesque Play about him—Attack by the
Mob on Lambeth Palace—Caricature of the Devil offering
Laud a Cardinal's Hat.

CHAPTER III. 63

Ben Jonson's Ridicule of the Early Newspapers—Fond-
ness of the Old News-Writers for the Marvellous—The
Smithfield Ghost—The Wonderful Whale—The Newbury
Witch—Satirical Tracts and Caricatures at the Commence-

ment of the Civil War—Religion Tossed in a Blanket—
Caricatures of the Pope and the Bishops—Pluralists and Patentees—Taylor, the Water Poet—*Mercurius Aulicus*—Activity of the Pamphleteers—Welshmen Satirised—Satires on
Prince Rupert—On the King and Queen—The Ladies' Parliament—Illustrated Tracts relating to Social and Political
Subjects—Sir Kenelm Digby's Duel—The King entertained by
the City of London, 1641—Executions in 1641—The Liquor
Traffic and Sunday Closing in 1641—Abuses of the Ecclesiastical Courts—Ritualism and Nunneries in 1641—Truths
enforced by Lieing—Stage Players and the Plague in 1641—
Bartholomew Fair in 1641—Destruction of Charing Cross and
Cheapside Cross—Strange Apparition—Method of enforcing
their Views adopted by the Puritan Pamphleteers—Parodies
of Roundhead Sermons—Matthew Hopkins the Witch-finder
—The *Welsh Post* of 1643—William Lilly the Astrologer—
Three Suns seen in London on the King's Birthday.

CHAPTER IV.   108

The Civil War—Flying Sheets of News—Disturbance at
Kingston-on-Thames—Plot against London—Riotous Pro-
ceedings at York, and Conspiracy in Edinburgh—The House
of Commons—The Royal Standard raised at Nottingham—
Battle of Edgehill—Prince Rupert—The Lord Mayor of
London—*Mercurius Civicus*—The *Scottish Dove*—The *Flying
Post*—The *Kingdomes Weekly Post*—Cruelties of the Cavaliers
—The 'Levellers'—The King's Escape from Oxford—Funeral
of the Earl of Essex—The Great Seal Broken—Fairfax—
Cromwell—Sea Fight in the Channel—The Prince of Wales's
Squadron—Mutiny at Norwich—Siege of Colchester—Exe-
cution of Sir Charles Lucas—The King at Carisbrooke Castle
—Execution of the King—Confession of Richard Brandon.

CHAPTER V.   .   .   .   .   ,   .   .   .   153

Decrease of Newspapers after the Civil War—*Mercurius
Democritus*—The *Faithful Post*—The *Politique Post*—Broad-
sides for the People—The Hollow Tree at Hampstead—
Prodigious Monster taken in Spain—The Restoration—Trial
of the Regicides—Execution of the Regicides—Licenser of
the Press appointed—Popular Taste for the Supernatural
—Apparition in the Air in Holland—Revival of *Mercurius
Civicus*—Murder of Archbishop Sharpe—The *Loyal Pro-
testant*—Frost Fair on the Thames—Monmouth's Rebellion
—The Bloody Assizes—Funeral of Queen Mary, Consort of
William III.—Increase of Newspapers after the Revolution.

PAGE

CHAPTER VI. 180

Constant Attempts at Illustrated News—Increase of
Caricatures—The *Postman*, 1704—Fiery Apparition in the
Air, seen in London—Caricature against the Jacobites—The
South-Sea Bubble—Eclipse of the Sun, 1724—The *Grub
Street Journal* an Illustrated Paper—The *Daily Post*—
Admiral Vernon's Attack on Porto Bello—The *Penny London
Post*—Henry Fielding and the *Jacobite's Journal*—*Owen's
Weekly Chronicle*—*Lloyd's Evening Post*, and the Trial of
Lord Byron for the Murder of Mr. Chaworth—The *St.
James's Chronicle*—Illustrated Account of a Strange Wild
Beast seen in France—The *Gentleman's Journal* of Anthony
Motteux—The *Gentleman's Magazine* of Edward Cave—The
London Magazine—The *Scot's Magazine*.

CHAPTER VII. 219

Revival of Wood-engraving by Thomas Bewick—The
Observer started, 1791—The *Times* an Illustrated Paper—
Illustrations of News in the *Observer*—St. Helena and
Napoleon Bonaparte—Abraham Thornton and the 'Assize
of Battle'—Mr. William Clement and Illustrated Journalism
—The Cato Street Conspiracy—Trial of Queen Caroline—
The House of Commons in 1821—Coronation of George IV.
—Royal Visits to Ireland and Scotland—Murder of Mr.
Weare—Illustrations of the Murder in the *Morning Chronicle*,
the *Observer*, and the *Englishman*—*Bell's Life in London*—
Prize-Fight at Warwick—Liston as 'Paul Pry'—'Gallery
of Comicalities,' &c.—*Pierce Egan's Life in London*—Death
of the Duke of York—Death of Mr. Canning—Opening of
Hammersmith Bridge, 1827—Mr. Gurney's Steam Coach—
The Thames Tunnel—The Murder in the Red Barn—The
Siamese Twins—Death of George IV.—Opening of New
London Bridge, 1831—Coronation of William IV. and Queen
Adelaide—Fieschi's Infernal Machine—Funeral of William
IV.—Queen Victoria's First Visit to the City—Coronation
and Marriage of the Queen—Christening of the Prince of
Wales—The *Weekly Chronicle*—The Greenacre Murder—
Mr. Cocking and his Parachute—The Courtney Riots at
Canterbury—Burning of the Tower of London, 1841—The
Sunday Times—Burning of the Houses of Parliament, 1834—
The *Champion*—The *Weekly Herald*—The *Magnet*—Re-
moving the Body of Napoleon I.—The *Penny Magazine*—
Charles Knight—Humorous Journalism of the Victorian
Era.

PAGE

CHAPTER VIII. 284

The *Illustrated London News* — The Early Numbers — The Burning of Hamburg — Facetious Advertisements — Bal Masque at Buckingham Palace — Attempted Assassination of the Queen — The Queen's First Trip by Railway — First Royal Visit to Scotland — Political Portraits — R. Cobden — Lord John Russell — Benjamin Disraeli — The French Revolution, 1848 — The Great Exhibition, 1851 — The Crimean War — Coloured Pictures — Christmas Numbers — Herbert Ingram — The *Pictorial Times* — Other Illustrated Journals.

CHAPTER IX. 315

How an Illustrated Newspaper is Produced — Wood-Engraving — Boxwood — Blocks for Illustrated Newspapers — Rapid Sketching — Drawing on the Block — Method of Dividing the Block for Engraving — Electrotyping — Development of the Printing Machine — Printing Woodcuts — Machinery for Folding Newspapers — Special Artists — Their Dangers and Difficulties — Their Adventures in War and Peace.

CHAPTER X. 355

Artists who have assisted in founding the Pictorial Press — Sir John Gilbert, R.A., G. H. Thomas, and others — Wood-Engraving and its Connexion with the Pictorial Press — Other Methods of producing Illustrations — Wood-Engraving in England before and after Bewick's time — Its wide Diffusion owing to the kindred Art of Printing — The resources of the Art developed by Pictorial Newspapers — Conclusion. Newspapers a Necessity of Civilised Life — The *Acta Diurna* of the Romans — Early Newspapers in Venice, Germany, and the Low Countries — List of Illustrated Newspapers published Abroad.

THE PICTORIAL PRESS:

ITS ORIGIN AND PROGRESS.

CHAPTER I.

The Pictorial Taste Universal—The Early 'News-books'—Development
of the Newspaper Press—General use of Newspapers—Establishment
of Illustrated Journals—Wandering Ballad Singers the First Newsvendors—The *English Mercurie* of 1588—The Abolition of the Star
Chamber and its Effect on the Press.

THE inherent love of pictorial representation in all races
of men and in every age is manifest by the frequent
attempts made to depict natural objects, under the most
unfavourable circumstances and with the slenderest means.
The rude drawing scratched on the smooth bone of an
animal by the cave-dweller of pre-historic times, the painted
rocks of the Mexican forests, and the cave-paintings of the
Bushmen, are all evidences of this deeply-rooted passion.
The child of civilised life looks with delight on his picture-
book long before he can make out the letters of the alphabet,
and the untutored Esquimaux treasures up the stray number
of an illustrated newspaper left in his hut by the crew of
some whaling ship, though he cannot understand one word
of the printed page. But the pictures speak a universal
language, which requires no teaching to comprehend.

When the printing-press came into use this love of
pictures had a wide field for development. Some of the first

books printed in England were illustrated with woodcuts,
and many of the tracts, or ' News-books,' which preceded
regular newspapers, were adorned with rude engravings. It
mattered not how graphic was the pen, its work was deemed
incomplete without the aid of the pencil. It often happened
that the pen was none the better for the fellowship, but the
public taste was not fastidious, and the work sufficed for the
occasion. In tracing the origin and progress of pictorial
journalism we shall find in 'the abstracts and brief chronicles
of the time' many curious illustrations of contemporary
history. The subject is not without interest now that the
illustrated newspaper has become a prominent feature in the
journalism of every country.

The development of the newspaper press and its unre-
stricted use as the exponent of public opinion is one of the
most interesting signs of modern progress. When we consider the liberty of thought and action that prevails in our
own day, it is difficult to believe that our forefathers were
liable to the pillory and other degrading punishments when
they ventured to publish their opinions without first obtaining
the sanction of the ruling powers. We are accustomed to
the daily exercise of the right which cost Prynne his ears
and brought fines and imprisonment on Defoe. Newspapers
have become almost as necessary to our daily life as bread
itself. The mind demands its breakfast as well as the body ;
and to many a busy man the loss of his morning paper
would be as great a deprivation as the want of his usual
matutinal meal.

In London, and in all our great centres of population, the
newspaper has become the unfailing accompaniment of the
City man's journey to business. At the railway stations
journals of every kind tempt the loitering passenger, while
the illustrated papers appeal to him in a language of their
own. Whether in the railway carriage, the omnibus, or the
steam-boat, the newspaper is eagerly conned, and its contents
form the food of conversation. Most of these newspapers
are cast aside at the end of the twenty minutes' or half hour's

journey; and then, at second hand, they amuse the leisure moments of the railway porter, or, better still, they are collected together, and perhaps serve to solace the sick poor during many lingering hours in hospitals and refuges. Day by day the demand is made, and the supply is ready. The printing-machine never sleeps and is never tired. Its voice is one of the voices of the night—most unmusical, yet with a mysterious meaning. The daily newspaper, so potent in diffusing the light of knowledge, is itself the offspring of darkness. The busy brains and active fingers which create it turn night into day in the execution of their quickly recurring tasks, and with unflagging energy they labour on, that the slumbering world may be properly amused and instructed when it wakes.

The intelligent foreigner who happens to reach our southern coast on a Monday morning in summer or autumn, and travels to London by one of the early trains, is astonished, when the train stops, to see most of the gentlemen rush from the carriages and surround a small boy, whom they appear to hustle and threaten with violent gesticulations. The boy appears to buy off the hostility of his assailants by dealing out to each a paper, which he takes from a large bundle under his arm, and with which the appeased passenger returns to his carriage. Cries of '*Times! Daily News! Telegraph! Standard!*—Here, give us one—anything!' reach the ears of the wondering stranger, who beholds the boy at length take refuge in an empty railway carriage on the opposite side of the platform, and from that place of vantage he continues to deal out the mysterious papers. After a time the intelligent foreigner learns that these are the London papers of that morning, which are sent out to meet the trains, and are eagerly bought by the gentlemen who have been spending from Saturday to Monday at the seaside, and, having fasted from all newspapers during that time, they are now of course famishing for news. Such is their eagerness that politics are thrown to the winds. The Conservative will put up with a Liberal newspaper rather than have none at all; and he whose ill luck or inertness has left him without the coveted sheet is glad to borrow of his neighbour, that he may not be walking in the darkness of ignorance when he arrives at his place of business. As the train moves off, the intelligent foreigner, if he thrusts his head out of the carriage window, may behold in the distance the newsboy pensively counting his gains and endeavouring to make his receipts tally with the number of papers that have vanished.

One of the most remarkable phases of newspaper history has been the establishment of illustrated journals. Though this idea, in an immature form, is as old as the newspaper itself, yet it was never fully developed till the late Mr. Herbert Ingram brought out the *Illustrated London News* in 1842. Since that time the removal of the newspaper stamp and the repeal of the paper duty have imparted a freedom and a vigour to newspaper enterprise previously unknown. Journals of all kinds have sprung into existence, and cheapness has become the rule. Penny and even halfpenny papers compete with the leading journals in activity and enterprise. No expense is spared in obtaining the earliest and most authentic intelligence. Correspondents are sent to every part of the world where any information is to be gleaned, and the presence of the newspaper 'Special' is now expected at every great event. Each class has its organ, and 'he who runs may read.'

When we consider the immense amount of printed matter that is published every day by the newspapers, we cannot but wonder at the public appetite. And this appetite is fed from one year to another upon a diet that is only varied when there occurs a war, a revolution, an unusually disastrous shipwreck, or a murder of uncommon atrocity. Then the monotony of ordinary life gives place to the temporary excitement. There is a run upon the newspapers, which are as susceptible as barometers, and rise or fall according to the state of public feeling. The calamities of nations and the misfortunes of individuals are sources of profit and prosperity to the newspaper.

It was a happy idea to gather together the principal events of the week, to illustrate them with authentic pictures, and place them before the public in the form of a pictorial newspaper. Considering the great cost of production, and the restrictions under which newspapers lay at that time, to say nothing of the difficulty of bringing out news with appropriate illustrations, so that both should be fresh, the *Illustrated London News* was a bold undertaking. Like most things that are successful, it soon had many imitators, and there are now few large cities in the civilised world that have not their illustrated newspapers.

But the full development of illustrated journalism was immediately preceded by many significant symptoms. Several of the then existing newspapers, on the occurrence of any unusual or interesting event, introduced into their pages rough woodcut illustrations. A great fire—a remarkable murder—a fatal balloon ascent—these were the subjects seized upon at the moment to satisfy the public craving for illustrated news. All this seems to have been the working of an impulse or instinct which existed even before the days of newspapers; for, as I shall presently show, attempts were made to illustrate the news of the hour in tracts or 'Newsbooks' before the beginning of regular newspapers in England. The idea of illustrated journalism may be traced from the earliest years of the seventeenth century to 1842, the date of the first number of the *Illustrated London News*. The art of wood-engraving had fallen very low in the seventeenth century, and the illustrations to be found in early newspapers are mostly of a very rude description; but they show the existence of a germ which eventually grew into full and flourishing life.

The English newspaper, like many other great inventions, was a thing of gradual growth. The news that was sung or recited by wandering ballad-singers at the village cross, or in the court-yard of the squire's mansion, and the written newsletter furnished to the wealthy aristocracy, were the precursors of the early news-books and the periodical sheets of news.

As the art of printing extended, many of the productions of
the press assumed the character of *news* to attract readers.
Sermons, satires, and travels, were all put forward under the
name of *news*, and sometimes a single grain of truth was
deemed sufficient to leaven a whole bushel of fiction. Most
of these publications were small tracts, and published at
irregular intervals. Some of them were adorned with engravings on the title-pages, which show that even at this early
period the authors or printers of these papers were imbued
with the pictorial spirit. The idea of illustrating current
events had already taken root, and we find examples of it
long before the establishment of regular newspapers.

The earliest form of the newspaper is known to have
come into existence during times of war and tumult, and it
was for a long time believed that the first English newspaper
was brought forth under similar circumstances. But when
the *English Mercurie* of 1588 was proved to be a forgery, the
enthusiast in newspaper history received a heavy blow and
sad discouragement. It seemed so highly probable, when
this country was threatened with the descent of the Spanish
Armada, that something like a newspaper might have sprung
into existence, that people were only too ready to adopt the
imposture. When the whole nation was greatly excited and
anxious to learn something about the reality of their danger,
nothing was more natural than for the sagacious minister of
Queen Elizabeth to appeal to the people through the printing-
press, and by its means endeavour to calm the public mind
by circulating printed sheets of intelligence, ' for the contradiction of false reports.' But we were compelled to admit
that Lord Burleigh had missed his opportunity, and neglected to use the most powerful means for exciting the
patriotism or allaying the fears of his countrymen. The
author of this remarkable imposition showed great skill and
acuteness in constructing his false newspaper, and fixing the
date of its supposed publication. The forgery has been attributed to Lord Hardwick ; but what were his motives it is
difficult to understand. Unlike Chatterton and Ireland, he

never brought his imposture before the world, and if he intended it merely for an antiquarian *jeu-d'esprit* he had the enjoyment of the joke entirely to himself.

The abolition of the Star Chamber, in 1641, was an important event for the press of this country. The so-called newspapers then began to print English news and discuss home affairs, no longer dreading the fines, imprisonments, and mutilations, that had been so liberally dispensed by that obnoxious tribunal. There was not, however, any considerable increase in the number of newspapers till the Civil War reached its height. During that remarkable contest many hundreds of tracts and newspapers were published, some of them numbered consecutively and published at regular intervals; but the great majority bore no continuous title, and treated of one subject only. During the reigns of Charles II. and James II. the press was more or less under a censorship, from which it was not emancipated till the seventh year of William III. Lord Macaulay dates the commencement of English newspapers from this period, when a great many new journals made their appearance. They included political news amongst their contents; and they more nearly resembled in character, but not in appearance, what we now understand by a newspaper than anything that had preceded them. This press revival was not accompanied by any corresponding activity in the direction of pictorial illustration. Art of every kind was in a low condition in England at this time. Even if the art of popular illustration had been better understood, the means of production were exceedingly limited. Newspapers multiplied greatly, but illustrated journalism had to struggle with difficulties, and its existence was only made known by the occasional appearance of a rough woodcut or an indifferent copper-plate.

CHAPTER II.

Illustrated Broadsides — Sir Francis Drake's Operations against the Spaniards — Papers of News in the Reign of James I. — The first Periodical Newspaper published in England — Illustrated Tracts relating to Storms and Floods — Remarkable Murders favourite subjects with the early Newswriters — Murder of the Rev. Mr. Storre — Murder in Cornwall — Apparition of Three Skeletons — Visions in the Air — Attempt on the Life of the Duke of Buckingham — Fall of Meteors at Bawlkin Green, Berkshire — The *Swedish Intelligencer* — Passage of the River Leck by Gustavus Adolphus — The Sallee Rovers — The *Weekly News* of 1638, an Illustrated Paper — The Irish Rebellion of 1641 — The Plague in London — Murder on board an English Ship — The Earl of Strafford — His Execution on Tower Hill — Archbishop Laud — A Burlesque Play about him — Attack by the Mob on Lambeth Palace — Caricature of the Devil offering Laud a Cardinal's Hat.

BEFORE, and for a long time after, the general use of newspapers, illustrated broadsides were published relating to particular events, or satirising the vices and follies of the period. In a broadside adorned with a woodcut representing Death and Time, and entitled, *The Doleful Dance, and Song of Death,* allusion is made to the 'Fatal Assizes' of Oxford, when three hundred persons, including the High Sheriff, died of a distemper, which was supposed to have originated among the prisoners. A sheet of a later date refers to the Spanish Armada and the Gunpowder Plot; while a third, entitled, *Tittle-Tattle,* &c., satirises the gossiping habits of the fair sex, and contains many illustrations of manners, costume, and character. Such were the publications that did duty for newspapers in the days of Queen Elizabeth, whose subjects, however, were not left wholly without information as to passing events. In 1587 there was published an illustrated tract giving an account of the doings of Sir Francis Drake,

who was employed by Queen Elizabeth to harass the Spaniards in their harbours, and hinder them in their preparations for invading England. These operations, which Drake
himself described as 'singeing the King of Spain's beard,'
delayed the sailing of the Armada, and gave Elizabeth time
to prepare for defence. The tract referred to is entitled, ' *The
true and perfect Newes of the worthy and valiant exploytes per-*

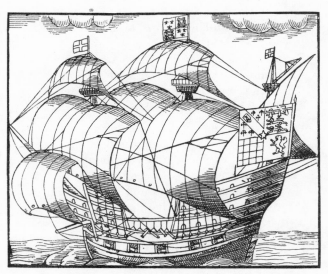

THE VALIANT EXPLOITS OF SIR FRANCIS DRAKE, 1587.

*formed and done by that valiant Knight Syr Frauncis Drake ;
Not only at Sancto Domingo, and Carthagena, but also nowe at
Cales, and upon the Coast of Spayne,* 1587. *Printed at London,
by J. Charlewood, for Thomas Hackett.'* There is an account,
in verse, written by one Thomas Greepe, of the doings of Sir
Francis Drake and other sea captains. The author tells his
reader, 'Here hast thou, gentle Reader, set forth unto thee
the most worthy and valiant exploytes and enterpryses, lately
atchieved and done by that valiant Knight Syr Frauncis Drake
& others not pend in lofty verse, nor curiously handled, but
playnly and truly, so that it may be well understood of the

Reader.' There is no attempt made to illustrate the events related in the tract, but on the title-page there is a wood-cut of a ship in full sail, which was perhaps intended to represent the admiral's own vessel. I have reproduced it on a reduced scale, as an early specimen of marine draughtsman-ship.

Thomas Greepe commences his poem with the following rhapsody :—

'Triumph, O England, and rejoice,
     And prayse thy God incessantly
For this thy Queene, that pearle of choyce,
     Which God doth blesse with victory !
          In countryes strange, both farre and neere,
          All raging foes her force doth feare.

Yee worthy wights that doo delighte
     To heare of Novels strange and rare,
What valors, woone by a famous knight,
     May please you marke I shall declare.
          Such rare exploytes performde and done
          As none the like hath ever woone.'

He gives a list of the ships under Drake's command :—

'Twenty-five ships were then preparde,
     Fifteene Pinnaces, brave and fine,
Well furnished for his safe garde,
     Preventing foes that would him tyne.
          With Masters good and Marriners rare
          As ever tooke charge, I dare compare.

     *   *   *   *   *   *   *

The *Bonaventure*, a ship royall,
     Cheefe Admirall then of the fleete,
Sir Frauncis Drake, cheefe Generall,
     As by desertes he was most meete.
          Most worthy Captaynes of hand and heart
          In this boon voyage then tooke hys part.

The *Primrose* next, Vice-Admirall,
  Appoynted by thyre best device,
Captayne Frobisher, Vice-Generall—
  A valiant Captayne, ware and wyse.
    Captayne Carelell they did ordayne
    Lieftenant-Generall on the mayne.'

The poem thus winds up :—

' God save our Queene of merry England,
  His sacred word long to maintaine ;
Her Graces Navie and royall bande,
  Through his good Grace, may long remaine.
    Lord blesse her counsell, and keepe them aye
    With all true subjects night and day.
        Finis, quoth Thomas Greepe.'

This curious poem is supplemented by a letter, written by Sir Francis Drake, ' To the right reverende, godly, learned Father, my very good friend, M. John Fox, preacher of the word of God.' This was John Fox, the Martyrologist, who died in 1587. The letter proceeds : ' Mister Fox, whereas we have had of late such happy successe against the Spanyardes, I do assure myselfe that you have faithfully remembered us in your good prayers, and therefore I have not forgotten, breefly to make you partaker thereof. The 19. of Aprill we arrived within the road of Calles, where we found very many shipping, but amongst the rest 32 of exceeding burden, lade and to be laden with provision, and prepared to furnish the King's Navie, intended with all speede against England, the which when we had boorded, and also furnished our severall ships with provision as we thought sufficient, wee burnt; and although by the space of two dayes and two nights that we continued there, we were still endangered, both with thundering shott from the towne, and assailed with the roaring Cannons of twelve galleys; yet we suncke two of them, and one great Argosey, and still avoyded them with very small hurt, and so at our departure

we brought away foure ships of provision, to the great
terror of our enemies, and honour to ourselves, as it may
appeare by a most curteous Letter written unto me with a
Flagge of truce by Duke Petro, Generall of the Galleys.
But whereas it is most certayne that the king doth not onely
make speedy preparation in Spayne, but likewise expected a
very great Fleete from the Straytes, and divers other places,
that should joyne with his forces to invade England ; we
purpose to sette apart all feare of danger, and by Gods
furtherance to proceed by all the good means we can devise
to prevent their coming ; wherefore I shall desire you to
continue faithfull in remembrance of us in your prayers that
our purpose may take that good effect, as God may be glori-
fied, his Church, our Queene and country, preserved, and
these enemies of the trueth utterly vanquished, that we may
have continuall peace in Israel.   Fro aboord her Majesties
good ship the *Elizabeth Bonaventure.*

'Your loving freende, and faythfull Sonne in Christ Jesus,

'FRAUNCIS DRAKE.'

In the reign of James I. papers of news began to be published, but they only appeared occasionally, and were chiefly
devoted to foreign intelligence.   In 1619 we have 'Newes
out of Holland,' followed by others in 1620, 1621, and 1622.
These occasional tracts were afterwards converted into a
regular weekly publication, entitled the '*Weekly News,*'
printed by J. D. for Nichs. Bourne and T. Archer.   This
was the first periodical newspaper published in England.
But long before this many illustrated tracts and pamphlets
were published relating to events of recent occurrence.   In
one dated 1607 occurs the earliest instance I have met with
of an attempt to illustrate the news of the day.   It is entitled
'*Wofull Newes from Wales, or the lamentable loss of divers
Villages and Parishes (by a strange and wonderful Floud)
within the Countye of Monmouth in Wales : which happened
in January last past, 1607, whereby a great number of his
Majesties subjects inhabiting in these parts are utterly undone.*'

The writer of this news-book describes the flood, and then, taking it for his text, preaches a sermon upon it. It is printed in Old English, and is plentifully interspersed with pious exhortations and scriptural references. It has on the title a woodcut, a fac-simile of which is given on the next page.

This interesting little tract has a preface, in which the author explains the difficulty he felt in producing it in the short time that was allowed him for the purpose :—' Reader, when these newes were brought, and an importunitie used to me that I would give the same forme, and bestow an exhortation on them, I was unwilling, both in regard of that short space (of lesse than one day which was limited to undertake the matter) and also in respect of the usual unfaithfulness of men ordinarily in reporting of such accidents as these bee ; whereby it often falleth out that the relation of them reapeth much discredit. But when I could not have these just excuses taken, I began and finished this businesse, as the shorte space wold permit me.'

The old story of the child washed away in a cradle, so often related as having occurred in great floods, and which Mr. Millais has immortalised in one of his pictures, is here told probably for the first time :—' Another little childe is affirmed to have bene cast upon land in a Cradle, in which was nothing but a Catte, the which was discerned, as it came floating to the shore, to leape still from one side of the Cradle unto the other, even as if she had been appointed steersman to preserve the small barke from the waves' furie.'

Another tract of the same date is illustrated with a woodcut similar to the one here copied, but it has in addition several more figures, including a cradle with a child in it floating on the water. This tract is entitled ' *A true report of certaine wonderful overflowings of waters now lately in Summersetshire, Norfolk, and other places in England, destroying many thousands of men, women, and children, overthrowing and bearing downe whole townes and villages, and drowning infinite numbers of sheepe and other cattle.*' It is written in the

GREAT FLOOD IN MONMOUTHSHIRE, 1607.

same sermonising style, beginning by calling men to repent, and to take warning from these signs of God's anger. Then follows the narrative. The inundation was caused by an irruption of the sea, and many incidents are related of the flood. Here the cradle·story is again told:—'An infant likewise was found swimming in a cradle, some mile or two fro' ye place where it was known to be kept, and so was preserved; for the cradle was not of wicker, as ours are here, but of strong, thicke bordes, closely joynted together, and that saved the infant's life.' This narrative of the Somersetshire flood was reprinted in another tract with '*An Addition of other and more strange Accidents happening by these Flouds, and brought to light since the first publishing of this Booke.*' This second edition is illustrated with the identical woodcut that is used in the tract relating the floods in Wales. The two tracts recounting the Somersetshire floods were 'printed at London by W. I. for Edward White, and are to be sold at the signe of the Gunne, at the North doore of Paules.' That describing the flood in Wales was 'printed for W. W., and are to be sold in Paules Church-yarde at the sign of the Grey-hound.' In those days printers frequently combined the functions of engraver and printer; and as regards the tracts under notice, we must conclude that the printer supplied each of his customers with the same woodcut, or that the booksellers of the time were in the habit of lending their woodcuts to each other.

Storms, floods, and burnings were favourite themes with the early newswriters, and several illustrated tracts exist describing such calamities. They are more or less interspersed with pious exhortations, but the narrative is rarely allowed to flag, and every incident is minutely described. There is '*Woeful newes from the West parts of England of the burning of Tiverton,*' 1612; and a small quarto pamphlet of 1613, printed in old English, affords another good example of this kind of news. It is entitled—it will be observed how fond the old newswriters were of alliterative titles—'*The Wonders of this windie winter, by terrible stormes and tempests,*

*to he losse of lives and goods of many thousands of men, women,
and children. The like by Sea and Land hath not been seene nor
heard of in this age of the world.   London.   Printed by G. Eld
for John Wright, and are to be sold at his Shop neere Christ-
Church dore.   1613.'*   On the title-page is a woodcut, a copy
of which is annexed.

GREAT STORM, 1613.

The tract opens very much in the manner of a sermon,
and declares the dreadful occurrences related are intended
to 'move sinful mankind to repentance and newnesse of
life.' It then goes on to describe 'that within these three
fore-passed months of October, November, and December,
the devouring gulfes of the Sea hath swallowed up above
two hundred saile of ships, as well of our own Country as of

neighbouring Nations, with great store of passengers, seafaring men, and owners of the same, adventuring their dear lives in the managing of the aforesaid ships, with all their goods, and merchandizes, making for our country all lost; yea, all, I say, in these three fore-passed months, hath been lost and drenched in the deep vaults of this watery world, a thing both lamentable and fearfull, that in so short a time, nay, in a small part of the yeare, even in an instant, so many heavy mischances should happen, and so many worthy vessels of adventure miscarrie, which had bin sufficient (if goodspeed had prevailed) to have inricht a whole Citie and bettered a kingdome; but such is the will of God, and such is His just indignation against us.

'By certification from men of good accompt and calling, it is reported and knowne for truth, that in the month of October last, a fleete of fourteene sayle of ships making from Newcastle towards London, laden with sea-coale and other commodities of those parts, had their passage, by the tyranny of the windes, most untimely stopt, and violently caste into the ocean's wombe, in which ships were perished to the number of a hundred and forty seafaring men, besides other passengers, both of men and women, which at that time made their watery graves in the deepe sea. This first strooke feare into the hearts of people, which hath been since seconded with many calamities, which lieth heavy upon the heart of the reporter.' The writer then goes on to relate that between 'Dover and Calice there hath been found floating upon the waters in one weeke of fowle weather above seven hundred drowned persons of divers nations, as of English, Dutch, French, and Spanish, with parts and parcels of many splitted ships.' Further details are given at great length, and in rather a wordy manner. For instance, the writer describes the great number of women who are made widows by the disasters at sea, 'besides fatherlesse children and children fatherlesse.' Several examples are related of the force of the wind. 'A man and his wife riding over Maidenhead Bridge upon one horse, by the fierceness of the

c

wind, were blowne beside, and there drowned both horse and all. God be merciful unto us and preserve us from all such like mischances. The like mishap befell in November last unto two Yorkshire men, as it is verified by some gentlemen of the Inns of Court and Chancery, which knew the parties, the one of them a tanner, named Francis Browne, the other a clothier, called Richard Smith, both dwelling in a towne neere Wakefield side called Thorby ; which two countriemen falling out upon small occassions wilfully purposed to come up to London, and their put their causes of themselves to the Lawes tryall ; yet notwithstanding came they up together, where in riding over a bridge about Bedfordshire, and con- ferring of their inward grudges, they were blowne both beside into the river, where, by the fierceness of the windes, they were most lamentably drowned, both horse and men ; and thus by sodaine death ended their malice, to the fear and amazement of all such as well could witness their envious proceedings. These and such like accidents may be fearful examples for the world to behold, especially for rich men, shewing to them the certaintie of life and goods subject to the chances of death and fortune, according to the saying of a worthy philosopher,

> " Full little thinks the man at morning sun
> What hap to him befalls ere day be done." '

A great many other instances are related of the fury of the tempests, all of which the writer feels certain ' have been laid upon us for our sinnes ;' and winds up with a pious exhortation to take warning.

Another tract of the same character and date, also printed in black letter, has a larger and more elaborate woodcut on the title-page, representing sinking ships, the shore strewed with dead bodies, and on the outside of a church tower the devil is seen throwing down the broken steeple. The following is the address to the reader :—
' Reader, I do here present unto thee and to thy under-standing (if thou hast any) some part of the lamentable

FLOODS AND TEMPESTS, 1613

losses and unrecoverable mischances that have happened by
occassion of these late blustering stormes of winde, and an
innumerable deal of rayne, the which a great many thousands have too true cause to beleeve, because they are sharers
in the misfortunes that this outragious weather hath caused.
Now, if thou hast sustained no loss thyselfe, perhaps thou
wilt not beleeve these things to be true that I have written ;
but if thou wilt or doest beleeve, then pray to God that it
will please Him to give them patience that are loosers, and
humilitie that are winners, and give God thanks that he
hath so blessed thee that thou hast no share in these mis-
haps. But if thou wilt not beleeve, goe and looke, or else
remaine still in thy unbeliefe.' A copy of the woodcut is
given on the preceding page.

Another pamphlet, of 1613, has the annexed woodcut,
and is entitled ' *Lamentable Newes, shewing the Wonderful
Deliverance of Maister Edmond Pet, Sayler, and Maister of a
Ship, dwelling in Seething-lane, in London, neere Barking
Church ; with other strange things lately hapned concerning
those great windes and tempestuous weather, both at Sea and
Lande. Imprinted at London by T. C., for William Barley,
dwelling over against Cree Church, neere Algate. 1613.'* It
describes the wreck of a Newcastle ship on the east coast,
and how 'Maister Pet,' after being exposed to the winds and
waves for forty-eight hours, was rescued by a Dutch man-of-
war, he being the only survivor from his ship. It will be
seen the woodcut represents two seamen lowering what
appears to be an arm-chair into the sea. This was probably
the artist's notion of the safest and most comfortable way to
rescue shipwrecked persons. The same tract relates other
occurrences during the stormy weather, such as 'A man
neere Bedford, being thaching a house, was blowne off
and kild; trees blown up by the rootes, houses and
chimnies quite blown downe,' &c. 'All which is for our
sinnes.'

Remarkable murders were even more favourite subjects
with the early news-writers than storms and floods, a par-

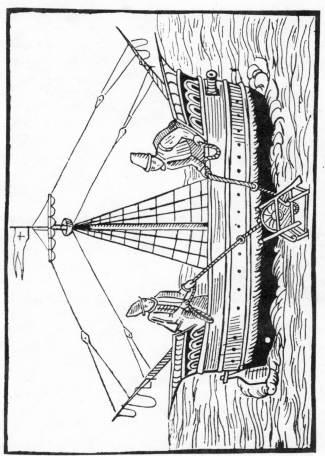

RESCUE OF EDMUND PET, MARINER, 1613.

tiality that has continued down to our own time. A tract of
1613 is devoted to the details of ' Three Bloodie Murders,'
but it is mainly taken up with an account of the murder of
the Rev. William Storre, of Market Rasen, Lincolnshire.
The full title runs thus :—' *Three Bloodie Murders. The first
committed by Francis Cartwright upon William Storre, M.
Arts Minister and Preacher at Market Rasen in the countie of
Lincolne. The second committed by Elizabeth James on the
body of her Mayde, in the Parish of Egham in Surrie : who
was condemned for the same fact at Sainte Margaret hill in
Southwark, the 2 of July* 1613, *and lieth in the White Lion
till her deliverie ; discovered by a dombe Mayde and her Dogge.
The third committed upon a stranger very lately near Highgate
foure mile from London, very strangely found out by a Dogge.
Also the 2 of July* 1613.'

The circumstances relating to the murder of the Rev.
William Storre are given at great length and with much
minuteness :—' Not long since, there happened some contro-
versey between the Lords and the rest of the inhabitants of
Market Raisin in the Countie of Lincolne concerning the
Commons and Libertie in the Towne Fields ; and the matter
being mooted by one of them in the Church immediately
after evening prayer on a Sabaoth day, divers hot intem-
perate speeches passed among them ; whereupon their
Minister, whose name was Mr. Storre, much disliking so
indiscreete a course, wished them to have respect both to
the time and place where they were : And further advised,
seeing the cause in hand concerned a multitude, (amongst
whom, some of the least government would always be the
readiest to speake) that they would therefore make choice
of two or three of the fittest and most substantial men, to
answere and undertake for all the rest. This motion seemed
to please them well, and therefore they intreated him, that
he would first, as a man indifferent speake what he thought
concerning the cause. But he not wishing to intermeddle
in that matter, twice or thrice denied their request ; and the
rather, for that there was present one Francis Cartwright, a

young man of an unbridled humour, the only Sonne and Heire to one of the same Lordes of the Towne, betwixt whom and himselfe, there was growne no small unkindnesse. Yet in the end being pressed thereunto by their importunities with the consent of both the parties he delivered his opinion, useing therein such discretion and reasons to confirme the same that they could not directly except against him. Notwithstanding, seeing him incline more to the right of the Freeholders and the rest of the Commons than to favour their intended purpose, they seemed to dislike his speaches, and to cavill at the same.

'Young Cartwright standing by, not able any longer to contain himselfe tooke occassion hereupon to breake forthe abruptly into these wordes: The Priest deserveth a good Fee, he speaketh so like a Lawyer. Maister Storre having often aforetime had experience of his hotte stomacke and hastinesse as well towards others as himselfe, thought it best to reply little against him for that present.' The Rev. Mr. Storre's forbearance was of no avail, for next day young Cartwright took occasion to renew the quarrel, and in the public market-place 'proclaymed that Storre was a scurvie, lowsie, paltrie Priest; that whoever sayd he was his friend or spake in his cause, was a Rogue and a Rascall, that he would (but for the Law) cut his Throat, tear out his Heart, and hang his Quarters on the May-pole.' These sanguinary threats caused Mr. Storre to seek the protection of the Magistrates; and he afterwards preached a sermon containing words which young Cartwright thought were purposely directed against him, so that he 'more and more thirsted for revenge.'

'About a week after, he espied Mr. Storre walking about eight of the clocke in the morning alone, by the south side of the Towne in his cloake, went to a cutler's shop, and tooke out of the same a short sword, formerly provided and made very sharpe for that purpose, and presently overtooke him.' The young man attacked the clergyman, and the pamphlet gives a minute account of the dreadful wounds he inflicted

upon him until 'A Mayde coming that way by occassion of
businesse, cried out, whereupon he fledde.'

The clergyman died of the frightful wounds he received,
and the murderer was taken and carried before a justice,
'where, either for lacke of their due information of the
truth, or by the corrupt and favourable affection of the

MURDER OF THE REV MR. STORRE, 1613.

magistrate, or both, there was a very slender bayle taken,
and the malefactor by this flight sent away.'   Cartwright's
friends 'laboured by corrupt dealing and wrong information'
to procure his pardon; but so barbarous a murder could not
be hushed up, and the culprit eventually 'fled beyonde the
seas.'

On the title-page of the pamphlet is a woodcut representing
the murder of the Rev. Mr. Storre, which is copied above.

The two other murders are not related at such great length, and are not illustrated.

This is the earliest example I have met with of a kind of illustrated news that is very popular even in our own day. From the pains taken to describe all the circumstances of the crime and its consequences, the author evidently regarded it as a subject of the highest interest, and worthy of all the elaboration he was capable of bestowing upon it.

There is a very curious and rare tract of the date of

NEWS FROM PENRHYN IN CORNWALL, 1618.

1618, which describes the circumstances of another remarkable murder. It is entitled '*News from Perin (Penrhyn), in Cornwall, of a most Bloody and unexampled Murther very lately committed by a Father on his owne sonne (who was lately returned from the Indyes), at the instigation of a mercilesse Step Mother, together with their severall most wretched endes, being all performed in the Month of September last, Anno* 1618.' On the title-page is a woodcut representing the discovery of the murder, which is reprinted in the body of the pamphlet. Another woodcut illustrates a scene before the murder is committed, where the son hands his bag of treasure to his step-mother. The story is a very minute history of a scapegrace son, who, after various adventures, returns to his father's house a penitent and reformed man. Many years having elapsed, the son is not recognised by his father, who has married a second wife and is in straitened circumstances. The son begs a night's lodging and resolves not to make himself known till next morning. In the meantime, to show that he will be able to recompense his host and hostess for their hospitality, he gives the latter a bag of gold and jewels to take care of for him till the morrow. The woman, excited by the possession of the gold, thinks how easy it would be to relieve themselves from their embarrassments by murdering their guest and keeping possession of his treasure. She urges her husband to do the deed. After many refusals he consents, and the father murders his own son. In the morning it is made known to him who his victim is, and, in a fit of remorse and despair, he kills himself; upon which the guilty wife also commits suicide, and the tract thus winds up :— 'And to the end it may be a warning to all covetous step mothers, and a content for all easie Fathers to avoyde the like hereafter. At the entreaty of divers Gentlemen in the Countrey, It is as neere the life as Pen and Incke could draw it out, thus put in Print.'

William Lillo, the author of *George Barnwell*, is said to have founded his play of ' Fatal Curiosity ' on this tract. Lillo was a prosperous London jeweller and a successful dramatic author. He depicted the harrowing details of this tragic story with great power; and the agonies of old Wilmot, the father, constitute one of the most appalling and affecting incidents of the drama.

A curious black-letter tract of 1616, which is illustrated with a fearful apparition of three skéletons, is entitled, ' *Miraculous Newes from the cittie of Holdt, in the Lord-ship of Munster (in Germany), the twentieth of September last past 1616, wherein there were plainly beheld three dead bodyes rise out of their Graves, admonishing the people of Judgements to*

come.' The truth of this miraculous news is vouched for by
' divers worthy Persons and Burgimasters of the same citty,'
whose names are given. This miraculous appearance was
preceded by a fearful tempest of thunder and lightning.
' When this great tempest of thunder and lightning was
ceased, there was heard throughout all the parts and places
of the citty a most hideous and dolefull clamour or outcry,
striking terror into all the people, yet no man could perceive
whence it came, or where this clamour should bee. The
people came over all the citty after the noise, but could not
finde it; for when they were at one corner of the citty they
then heard it at another; and when they were come to that
other corner there it seemed to them to be in the middle of
the citty; and to them that were in the middest it seemed
farther off. So that all heard it, but none could find where
it was, or from whence it came.

' At length the people assembling in the churchyard
behelde there so strange and incredible judgements sent by
the Lord, that for the most part the beholders fell flatt on
their faces to the ground, crying loude unto the Lord for
mercy. For there they beheld coming out of their graves
three most ghostly and fearfull dead bodyes.

1.

' Whereof the first that was seen to arise out of the earth,
seemed very white, cleane, and cleere, who opening his
mouth and beating his handes together spake thus:
" Blessed be God in the highest Heaven, that our release-
ment is come, for we have wayted many a hundred yeare for
this time." The people hearing this fell upon their knees
and prayed unto the Lord with weeping and great lamentation, saying: O Lord beholde us with thy merciful eyes, and
let us not be overwhelmed or smothered in our sinnes.

2.

' The second dead man that arose out of the earth caused
farre greater feare and trembling then the former, for the

beholders saw him altogether from the toppe to the toe, like
unto a burning fire; he likewise opened his mouth, and
wringing his handes, and tearing his haire, cryed with a
loude voyce: Repent yee, Repent yee; Almighty God hath
taken his chastising rodde in hand, to punish the people for
their sinnes, for their great wealth, for their great talke or
presumptious wordes, for their pompe, and for their pride:
The which the Lord will no longer suffer nor endure, for the
cry and complaint of these sinnes is asended up into his eares;

MIRACULOUS NEWS FROM MUNSTER IN GERMANY, 1616.

Wherefore hee will destroy you with a suddaine sicknesse,
and fiery Pestilence, so that you shall not have so much time
as one houre, to utter one worde, to call upon God.

3.

' After this fiery apparition and threatening speech ended,
there appeared likewise rising out of the grave a third dead
man, grinding and gnashing his teeth together, striking his
handes the one against the other, and crying with a most
fearful and hideous voyce, insomuch that it seemed to all the
multitude there present, that the earth would certainly have
rent in sunder; and spake that all the people plainly heard

and understood his wordes, which were these; Woe, woe, woe, to the wicked; this is the time that wee have long attended and looked for; wherefore (ye people) looke to it, and beware lest the great day of the Lord come upon you suddainly, and fall upon you unprovided; for the time of his comming is neerer than you thinke.

'After the uttering of these wordes, the three dead Bodyes vanished and the Graves were shut againe, the heavens became cleere, the Tempest ceased, and all the people being released of their present horror and feare, rejoyced, and assembling themselves together, gave glory and laude, and praise unto the Lord for his Fatherly mercy and unspeakable goodnesse, in the mitigation of his furie, and withdrawing his heavy hand for the present. And thereupon appointed a sett day of supplications, prayers, and fasting, with true and unfained Repentance to be proclaimed, and observed.'

This account is supplemented by an 'apology,' setting forth that men must not be incredulous because they hear of miraculous occurrences—that God is able to bring back the age of miracles, &c. The writer evidently thought his readers might require to be strengthened by argument before they could place implicit faith in his narrative, and so he takes some pains in his 'apology' to convince them that however unnatural and uncommon may be the appearances he relates, the wickedness of the world was a sufficient justification for this and other extraordinary events. A copy of the woodcut that illustrates this curious production is shown on the preceding page.

In 1620 Nathaniel Butter printed an illustrated tract entitled ' *Good Newes to Christendome, sent to a Venetian in Ligorne, from a Merchant in Alexandria, Discovering a Wonderfull and Strange Apparition, visibly seene for many dayes together in Arabia over the place where the supposed Tombe of Mahomet (the Turkish Prophet) is inclosed; By which the learned Arabians prognosticate the Reducing and Calling of the great Turke to Christianitie. With many other Notable Accidents: But the most remarkable is the miraculous rayning of Bloud*

'GOOD NEWES TO CHRISTENDOME,' 1620.

about Rome.' This tract, which is very long and discursive, relates, among other things, the apparition of a woman in the air, with a book in her hand, being the same apparition that is described at great length in a tract of 1642, which I shall quote hereafter. In the tract under notice there is a woodcut representing an army in the clouds—the clouds raining blood over a city; a woman with sword and book; and a crowd of men below watching the aerial phenomenon. The writer, in winding up his narrative, thus addresses his reader:—' If you cannot beleeve it as truth, yet to make that use of it as if it were true; and then shall you know, there is but one way to happiness, and all the predictions, prophesies, visions, apparitions, comets, inundations, stormes, tempests, famine, warre, alteration, and subversion of kingdomes, with all the cabinet of mysteries, tend to this end that *premium* and *pœna* be the mastering curbs of the world; that is, that God hath a *Magazine* of judgements to inflict on the obstinate sinner with punishments: and a store-house of mercy to support the penitent soule with comfort.'

In 1627 we come upon a very curious and literal example of illustrated news. In that year Charles I., having declared war against France, fitted out an expedition of a hundred sail and an army of 7000 men for the support of the Protestant cause in that country. The King's favourite, the self-confident and vainglorious Duke of Buckingham, took the command of the expedition, although he was totally unfit for that position. He was personally brave, but possessed no other quality of a commander. He had no knowledge or experience of the art of war, and was too proud and presumptuous to be guided by the advice of others. The expedition was destined for Rochelle, then in possession of the Huguenots; but Buckingham went to sea without any understanding with his allies; and, when he anchored off Rochelle, he was refused admission to the town. He then directed his course to the neighbouring Isle of Rhè, where he succeeded in landing his men under the fire of his ships, and defeated a small French force commanded by the governor of the island. Instead of immediately following up his success, Buckingham allowed the French commander to secure and strengthen the fortress of St. Martin; and when he did advance he foolishly left the enemy in possession of another fort in his rear. He besieged the Castle of St. Martin for many weeks, and then led his men to storm the place without having made a single breach in the walls. They were repulsed at all points with considerable loss, and attempted to retreat to their ships; but Marshal Schomberg with a French army had thrown himself between the Duke and the fleet, and had put a strong corps and artillery into the fort of La Prèe, which Buckingham had left in his rear. No precautions whatever had been taken, and they suffered great loss before they could re-embark. The expedition was a total failure, and Buckingham returned to England beaten and disgraced.

While the Duke of Buckingham was besieging the citadel of St. Martin, an attempt was made, or was said to have been made, upon his life by a French Papist or Jesuit, with a thick four-edged knife. An account of the Duke's proceedings while in the Isle of Rhè appears to have been sent home, and was published probably with a view of influencing the people in his favour and showing to what dangers he was exposed in the national service. There is in the British Museum a tract entitled '*A Continued Journal of all the Proceedings of the Duke of Buckingham his Grace, in the Isle of Ree since the last day of July. With the names of the Noblemen as were drowned and taken in going to releeve the Fort. As also the Portraiture of the knife with which his Excellence should have been murdered, which very knife was brought over by Captaine Buckestone and delivered unto the Duchess of Buckingham her Grace on Monday night last. Published by Authoritie. London, Printed for Thomas Walkley, and are to be sold at his shop at the Eagle and Childe in Britaines Bursse, 1627.*' The following account is given of the intended assassination of the Duke:—

'Received the 27 of August.

'Here I have sent you all the remárkable Newes that I

have upon the last of *July.* There was taken by a *Perdue* of ours, in the night (a Frenchman), that was sent by *Monsieur de Thorax,* the Governour of the Citadell, with a full intent to kill my Lord Duke; and for the speedy effecting of the same he had prepared a strange and dangerous *Poynado,* which, although it was taken about him, he confidently denied that he came not with any intent to kill the *Duke* untill he came to the Tortures, which being presented before him he promised to discover all to my *Lord* if he would promise him life, the which he did, and doth so performe with him, like a noble and mercifull Generall.' The tract

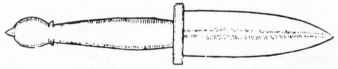

KNIFE INTENDED FOR THE ASSASSINATION OF THE DUKE OF BUCKINGHAM, 1627.

contains a large woodcut of a knife, a reduced copy of which is given above, and underneath the engraving is the following description :—' This is the true Portraiture of the poysoned knife, both in length and breadth, having foure edges, with which a Jesuited Vilaine was sent out of the Fort by Monsieur de Thorax, the Governour of that Island, with an intent to have killed his Excellence, but by God's providence was delivered. His Grace hath used the French so nobly in all respects that he rather deserved their love than any wayes to have his life thus treacherously sought after, under the pretence that it was a meritorious act. Which knife was brought over into England by Captaine Buckestone, and by him delivered unto the Dutches of Buckingham her Grace on Monday night last.'

Whether the attempt on Buckingham's life was a reality or was got up for the purpose of endearing the court favourite to all good Protestants, it foreshadowed his ultimate fate. In the following year, while he was at Portsmouth, and about to embark on a second expedition to Rochelle, he

D

was stabbed by Felton, who had served under him in the expedition to the Isle of Rhè.

Besides the subjects already noticed, the old news-writers delighted in signs and portents in the air, and failed not to improve the occasion whenever they met with a text so much to their liking. There was a fall of meteorites in 1628, which was chronicled at the time in an illustrated pamphlet, entitled, ' *Looke up and See Wonders: a miraculous Apparition in the Ayre, lately seen in Barke-shire, at Bawlkin Greene, neere Hatford, April 9th,* 1628.' The author, like his fellow-chroniclers, already quoted, regards the occurrence as a sign of Heaven's displeasure, and addresses his readers thus:—'So Benummed wee are in our Sences, that albeit God himselfe Holla in our Eares, wee by our wills are loath to heare him. His dreadfull Pursiuants of *Thunder and Lightning* terrifie vs so long as they haue vs in their fingers, but beeing off, wee dance and sing in the midst of our Follies.' He then goes on to tell how ' the foure great quarter-masters of the World (*the foure Elements*) . . . haue bin in ciuill Warres one against another. . . . As for *Fire,* it hath denied of late to warme vs, but at vnreasonable rates, and extreame hard conditions. But what talke I of this earthy nourishment of *fire?* How haue the *Fires* of Heauen (some few yeares past) gone beyond their bounds, and appeared in the shapes of Comets and Blazing Starres? . . . The *Aire* is the shop of Thunder and Lightning. In that, hath of late been held a Muster of terrible enemies and threatners of Vengeance, which the great Generall of the Field who Conducts and Commands all such Armies (*God Almighty, I meane*) auert from our Kingdome, and shoote the arrowes of his indignation some other way, vpon the bosomes of those that would confound his Gospell. . . . . . . Many windowes hath he set open in heauen, to shewe what Artillery hee has lying there, and many of our Kings haue trembled, when they were shewne vnto them. What blazing Starres (euen at Noone-dayes) in those times hung houering in the Aire? How many frightfull Ecclipses both of Sun and Moone? . . . . It is not for

man to dispute with God, why he has done this so often . . . .
but, with feare and trembling casting our eyes vp to Heauen,
let vs now behold him, bending his Fist onely, as lately he
did to the terrour and affrightment of all the Inhabitants
dwelling within a Towne in the County of Barkshire. . . . .
The name of the Towne is *Hatford*, some eight miles from
Oxford. Ouer this Towne, vpon Wensday being the ninth of
this instant Moneth of *April*, 1628, about fiue of the clocke
in the afternoone this miraculous, prodigious and fearefull
handy-worke of God was presented. . . . . The weather
was warme, and without any great shewe of distemperature,
only the skye waxed by degrees a little gloomy, yet not so
darkened but that the Sunne still and anon, by the power of
the brightnesse, brake through the thicke clouds. . . . .

'A gentle gale of wind then blowing from betweene the
West and *North-west*, in an instant was heard, first a hideous
rumbling in the *Ayre*, and presently after followed a strange
and fearefull peale of Thunder, running vp and downe these
parts of the *Countrey*, but it strake with the loudest violence,
and more furious tearing of the *Ayre*, about a place called
The White Horse Hill, than in any other. The whole order
of this *thunder*, carried a kind of Maiesticall state with it, for
it maintayned (*to the affrighted Beholders' seeming*) the fashion
of a fought Battaile.

'It beganne thus: First, for an onset, went off one great
Cannon as it were of *thunder* alone, like a warning peece to
the rest that were to follow. Then a little while after was
heard a second; and so by degrees a third, vntil the number
of 20 were discharged (or thereabouts) in very good order,
though in very great terror.

'In some little distance of time after this was audibly
heard the sound of a Drum beating a Retreate. Amongst
all these angry peales shot off from Heauen, this begat a
wonderful admiration, that at the end of the report of every
cracke, or *Cannon-thundering*, a hizzing noyse made way
through the *Ayre*, not vnlike the flying of *Bullets* from the
mouthes of great Ordnance; and by the iudgement of all the

terror-stricken witnesses they were *Thunder-bolts.* For one of them was seene by many people to fall at a place called *Bawlkin Greene,* being a mile and a half from *Hatford:* Which *Thunder-bolt* was by one Mistris *Greene* caused to be digged out of the ground, she being an eye-witnesse amongst many others, of the manner of the falling.

'The forme of the *Stone* is three-square, and picked in the end: In colour outwardly blackish, some-what like Iron: Crusted ouer with that blacknesse about the thicknesse of a shilling. Within it is soft, of a grey colour, mixed with some kind of minerall, shining like small peeces of glasse.

'This *Stone* brake in the fal: The whole peece is in weight nineteene pound and a halfe: The greater peece that fell off weigheth fiue pound, which with other small peeces being put together, make foure and twenty pound and better. . . .

'It is in the Countrey credibly reported that some other Thunder-stones haue bin found in other places: but for certainty there was one taken vp at *Letcombe,* and is now in the custody of the *Shriefe.*'

This curious account is illustrated with a quaint woodcut, in the foreground of which the thunder-bolt seen by Mistress Green is being ' digged out of the ground.'

Amongst the many publications relating to the victorious career of Gustavus Adolphus, king of Sweden, there was one entitled the *Swedish Intelligencer,* printed at London, in 1632, for Nathaniel Butter and Nicholas Bourne, both of them names associated with the first establishment of newspapers in England. The *Swedish Intelligencer* gives very full accounts of the exploits of Gustavus, and it is illustrated with his portrait, a bird's-eye view of the siege of Magdeburg, a plan showing how the King of Sweden and his army crossed the river Lech into Bavaria, and a plan or bird's-eye view of the battle of Lutzen, where Gustavus was killed. The portrait, the siege of Magdeburg, and the battle of Lutzen, are engraved on copper, but the passage of the Lech

FALL OF METEORS AT BAWLKIN GREEN, BERKSHIRE, APRIL 9, 1628.

is a woodcut. I have copied the latter, the others being
too elaborate for reproduction on a reduced scale. The
three last named are very curious as illustrations of war
news. Gustavus had crossed the Danube, and his troops
overspread the country between that river and the river
Lech. Field Marshal Tilly was in front of him, waiting for
reinforcements from the army of Wallenstein, in Bohemia,
and the junction of fresh levies raised in Bavaria, with
which he hoped to drive the invaders back across the
Danube. The account in the *Swedish Intelligencer* of this
celebrated passage of the River Lech is too long for quotation, but I give a condensed version of the circumstances
from other sources.

The Lech takes its rise among the mountains of the
Tyrol, and, after washing the walls of Landsberg and Augsburg, falls into the Danube at a short distance from the town
of Rain. The banks are broken and irregular, and the
channel uncertain. Nor are there many rivers of the same
size in Germany which can be compared with it in the
strength and rapidity of its current. The united forces of
Bavaria and the League, with this efficient means of defence
in front, extended their right wing towards the Danube and
their left towards Rain, while the banks of the river, as far
as the city of Augsburg, were observed by their patrols,
supported by detached bodies of infantry. Tilly had taken
the precaution of breaking down the bridges over the Lech,
and had thrown up fieldworks at points where he judged the
passage might be considered attended with fewest difficulties.
That the Swedes would attack him in his main position was
a pitch of daring to which, well as he was acquainted with
the enterprising spirit of the king, he could scarcely suspect
him of having yet attained. Such, however, was the full
determination of Gustavus. After he had reconnoitred the
course of the Lech for some miles, at the imminent peril of
his life, he fixed upon a point between Rain and Thier-
hauppen, where the river makes a sweep to the eastward, as
the spot for carrying his venturous design into effect. The

king's first intention was to throw a floating bridge over the stream, but the attempt was no sooner made than it was found to be rendered hopeless by the rapidity of the current. It was then imagined that tressels might be sunk, and firmly secured by weights in the bed of the river, on which the flooring of the bridge might afterwards be securely laid. The king approved of this plan, and workmen were commanded to prepare the necessary materials at the small village of Oberendorf, situated about half a mile from the spot. During the night of the 4th of April the work was entirely finished, the supports fixed in the stream, and the planks for forming the bridge brought down to the water's edge. The king had, in the meantime, ordered a trench to be dug along the bank of the river for the reception of bodies of musketeers, and several new batteries to be constructed close to the shore, the fire from which, as they were disposed along a convex line, necessarily crossed upon the opposite side; those upon the left hand of the Swedes playing upon the left of the enemy, and those on the right upon the wood held by the Bavarians. Another battery, slightly retired from the rest, directed its fire against the entrenchments occupied by Tilly's centre. By daybreak on the 5th, all necessary preparations having been made, the bridge was begun to be laid, and completed under the king's inspection. Three hundred Finland volunteers were the first who crossed, excited by the reward of ten crowns each to undertake the dangerous service of throwing up a slight work upon the other side for its protection. By four in the afternoon the Finlanders had finished their undertaking, having been protected from a close attack by the musketry of their own party and the batteries behind them, from which the king is said to have discharged more than sixty shots with his own hand, to encourage his gunners to charge their pieces more expeditiously. The work consisted merely of an embankment surrounded by a trench, but it was defended both by the direct and cross fire of the Swedes. As soon as it was completed, Gustavus, stationing himself with

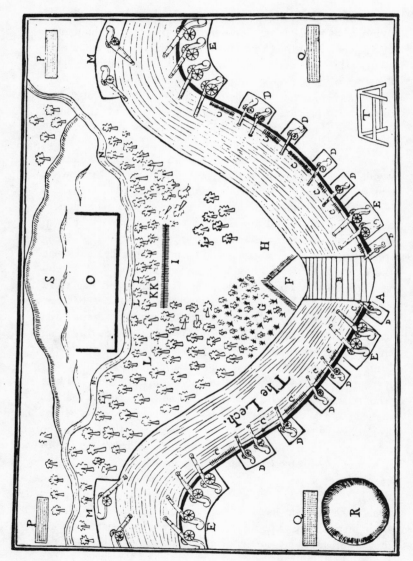

PASSAGE OF THE RIVER LECH, BY GUSTAVUS ADOLPHUS. FROM THE 'SWEDISH INTELLIGENCER,' 1632.

the King of Bohemia at the foot of the bridge, commanded Colonel Wrangle, with a chosen body of infantry and two or three field-pieces, to pass over, and after occupying the work, to station a number of musketeers in a bed of osiers upon the opposite side. The Swedes crossed the bridge with little loss, and after a short but desperate struggle the Imperialists were routed. The whole of the Swedish army was soon upon the eastern bank of the Lech, where the king, without troubling himself with the pursuit of the enemy, commanded his army to encamp, and ordered the customary thanksgivings to be offered for his victory.*

The account in the *Swedish Intelligencer* is wound up in these words: 'And this is the story of the King's bridge over the *Lech*, description whereof we have thought worthy to be here in Figure imparted unto you.' Then follows an 'Explanation of the Letters in the Figure of the *Bridge*,' given below the illustration. The engraving does not appear to have been entirely satisfactory to the author, for on its margin the following words are printed: 'Our Cutter hath made the Ordnance too long, and to lye too farre into the River. The Hole also marked with R, should have been on the right hand of the Bridge.'

REFERENCES TO PASSAGE OF THE RIVER LECH.

'A The King of Sweeden, and the King of Bohemia by him.
B The Bridge.
C A Trench or Brestworke, in which the Kings Musketeers were lodged, betwixt the severall Batteryes of the great Ordnance, which Musketeers are represented by the small stroakes made right forwards.
D Divers little Field-pieces.
E Plat-formes or Batteryes for the Kings greater Cannon.
F The Halfe-moone, with its Pallisadoe or Stocket, beyond the Bridge, and for the guard of it. It was scarcely bigge enough to lodge a hundred men in.
G A little Underwood, or low Bushy place.
H A plaice voyd of wood; which was a Bache, sometimes overflowne.
I A Brestworke for Tillyes Musketeers.
K K Tilly and Altringer; or the place where they were shot.
L The high wood where the Duke of Bavaria stood.
M Tilleyes great Batteryes to shoot down the Bridge.
N A small riveret running thorow the wood.
O Tillyes great Brestworke; not yet finished. Begun at sixe in the morning; and left off when he was shot.
P Some Horse-guards of Tillyes: layd scatteringly here and there all along the river from Rain to Augsburg.
Q The kings Horse-guards, and Horse-sentryes.
R A hole in the earth, or casual advantageable place; wherein some of the Kings Foot were lodged.
S The Hill behind Tillyes great worke.
T The fashion of the Tressels or Arches for the Kings Bridge.

* *Life of Gustavus Adolphus.* Family Library.

In 1636 the Sallee Rovers had become very troublesome,
and not only hindered British commerce, on the high seas,
but even infested the English coasts. They had captured and
carried into slavery many Englishmen, for whose release a
'Fleete of Shippes' was sent out in January, 1636. Assisted
by the Emperor of Morocco, the nest of pirates was destroyed
and the captives released. A full account of this expedition
is given in a curious pamphlet, entitled, '*A true Journal of
the Sally Fleet with the proceedings of the Voyage, published
by John Dunton, London, Mariner, Master of the Admirall
called the Leopard. Whereunto is annexed a List of Sally Captives names and the places where they dwell, and a Description of
the three Townes in a Card. London, printed by John Dawson
for Thomas Nicholes, and are to be sold at the Signe of the Bible
in Popes Head Alley*, 1637.' This tract is illustrated by a
large plan of Sallee, engraved on copper, with representations
of six English vessels of war on the sea. After minutely describing the proceedings of the voyage, and giving a long
list of the captives' names, the journalist winds up in these
words: 'All these good Shippes with the Captives are in
safety in England, we give God thanks. And bless King
Charles and all those that love him.'

At the end of the pamphlet is printed the authority for
its publication: 'Hampton Court, the 20. of October, 1637.
This Journall and Mappe may be printed.'

There is an illustrated pamphlet of this period which I
have not been able to see. It is entitled, '*Newes, and Strange
Newes from St. Christopher's of a Tempestuous Spirit, which is
called by the Indians a Hurrycano or Whirlwind; whereunto is
added the True and Last Relation (in verse) of the Dreadful
Accident which happened at Witticombe in Devonshire*, 21.
October, 1638.'

The *Weekly News*, begun in 1622, had been in existence
sixteen years when the idea of illustrating current events
seems to have occurred to its conductors; for in the number
for December 20, 1638, there is, besides the usual items of
foreign news, an account of a 'prodigious eruption of fire,

which exhaled in the middest of the ocean sea, over against
the Isle of Saint Michael, one of the Terceras, and the new
island which it hath made.' The text is illustrated by a full-
page engraving showing 'the island, its length and breadth,
and the places where the fire burst out.' I have not been
able to find a copy of the *Weekly News* for December 20,
1638, either in the British Museum or elsewhere. My
authority for the above statement is a letter in the *Times*
of October 13, 1868. As far as I have been able to ascertain,
no other illustrations were published in the *Weekly News*, so
that we must conclude the engraving of the 'prodigious
eruption of fire' was an experiment, which in its result was
not encouraging to the proprietor or conductors of the
journal.

When the Irish Rebellion of 1641 broke out, many news-
books were published describing the transactions in that
country, and several of them are illustrated. I may here
remark that the illustrations of events in these pamphlets, as
well as many of those contained in the numerous tracts published during the Civil War in England, appear to be works
of pure imagination, and were, probably, invented by the
artist just as a modern draughtsman would illustrate a work
of fiction. Others, again, were evidently old woodcuts executed for some other purpose. A few instances occur, however, where drawings have been made from actual scenes, and
sometimes maps and plans are given as illustrations of a
battle or a siege. This rising of the Roman Catholics in Ireland began with a massacre of the Protestants, and, according
to the tracts published at the time, the atrocities of recent wars
in Bulgaria and elsewhere were equalled in every way by the
Roman Catholics in Ireland in the seventeenth century. The
illustrations in these tracts are very coarse woodcuts. One
represents the arrest of a party of conspirators, and another
is a view of a town besieged, while a third gives a group of
prisoners supplicating for mercy. The best illustration that
I have met with of this Irish news is contained in a pamphlet
entitled, '*Approved, good and happy Newes from Ireland; Re-*

Rebel

Proteſt.

Ireland

TAKING OF THE CASTLE OF ARTAINE, IRELAND, 1641.

lating how the Castle of Artaine was taken from the Rebels, two of their Captaines kild, and one taken prisoner by the Protestants, with the arrival of 2000 foot, and 300 horse from England. Also a great skirmish between the Protestants and the Rebels at a place near Feleston, wherein the English obtained great renowne and victory : Whereunto is added a true relation of the great overthrow which the English gave the Rebels before Drogheda, sent in a letter bearing date the 27 of February to Sir Robert King, Knight, at Cecill house in the Strand. Printed by order of Parliament. London, Printed for John Wright 1641.' The woodcut on the title-page of this tract represents the taking of the castle of Artaine, but there is only the following very short paragraph relating to it :—' The last news from Ireland 7 March 1641. The 10 of February our men went to *Artaine* against a castle so called, which had before done some mischiefe, to some of our men, the enemy being in it. But the enemy fled before our second coming, and left the Castle, and a garrison was left in it by us.' The other news is related more at length, and one of the paragraphs runs thus :—' On the 13 a man was brought to our City, being taken by some of our scattering men scouting about our City, who confest without constraint, that he had killed an *Englishwoman* at a place called *Leslipson,* 6 Miles West of our City, and washed his hands in her bloud, being set on by the popish Priests so to doe; he was presently hanged, but dyed with much repentance and a protestant, which few do.' The concluding paragraph of this pamphlet shows the writer to have been a man of a commercial spirit :—' Tis to be feared that a famine is like to be in our City, in that still men come to us and provision is short, and none of yours that come to us bring any vittailes, great taxes are upon us, more than can be borne. He that had Butter, and Cheese; and Cloath, at between 6 and 14 shillings a yard here sent by any out of London might make a good trade of it. Cheshire Cheese is sould here for sixpence a pound already. Some of your Londoners are come hither (acquaintance of mine) that will send for such things, for great profit may be made by them

and quicke returne.' Annexed is a facsimile of the woodcut
representing the taking of the Castle of Artaine.

Several other pamphlets relating to the Irish Rebellion
are illustrated, but, with a few exceptions, the cuts bear very
little relation to the subject, and were probably not executed
for the purpose. One gives an account of a victory obtained
by the English at Dundalk in 1642, and it has a woodcut of
a man firing a cannon against a town, a copy of which is
appended.

VICTORY AT DUNDALK, 1642.

The description is in the following words:—'Newes from
Ireland. On Monday morning came three Gentlemen to our
City of Dublin from Sir Henry Tichbourne, who brought a
message to the state of a great and happy victory obtained
by the aforesaid Sir Henry Tichbourne with 2000 horse and
foot marched to Ardee, and there put 400 of the Rebels to
the sword, yet lost not one man of our side; from thence
upon the Saturday following, he mustered up his forces
against a place called Dundalke some 14 miles northward
from Tredath, where the enemy was 5000 strong, and well

fortified. At his first approach there issued out of the Towne 3000 of the Rebels who all presented themselves in Battallia, our Forlorne hopes of horse and foot had no sooner fired upon them, but they routed the Rebels. Captaine Marroe's Troope of horse setting on kiiled great store of the Rebels who thereupon retreated to the Towne, made fast the gates, and ran out at the other end to their boats beforehand provided : Our Army coming in fired the gates, entred, and killed those within. Captain Marroe followed the flying foe, and slew abundance of them upon the strand, and it is reported by them that if he had known the Fords and the River, he had cut them all off, if he had gained the other side of the River, but being a stranger, could not doe it (wanting a guide) without endangering the Troope. There was slaine of the Rebels in this sudden skirmish not less than 1100 besides what they took prisoners. Sir Philomy O'Neale fled with the rest of the Commanders; but 10 common soldiers were lost of our side. Sir Philomy O'Neale made speed away to a place called Newry, a chiefe garrison of the Rebels. Sir Henry Tichbourne hath sent 600 men more to Dublin, intending that place shall be the next he begins withall, which is granted, and tomorrow there goeth to him 500 men, if not 5000, for whose safety and prosperity in the meantime is the subject of our daily prayers that he may have as good success as in all his other designs from the first till this time ; for no man was ever so beloved by his souldiers, that protest to follow him while they can stand. We are in great hope he will recover the Newry very shortly ; it is credibly reported, that they got 20,000 pounds at least in pillage at Dundalke.'

In another pamphlet, dated 1642, there is an account of a battle at Kilrush, which is also illustrated with a woodcut. The circumstances are related in detail, but they are sufficiently set forth in the title, without further quotation :— 'Captaine Yarner's Relation of the Battaile fought at Kilrush upon the 15th day of Aprill, by my Lord of Ormond, who with 2500 Foot and 500 Horse, overthrew the

Lord Mountgarret's Army, consisting of 8000 Foot and 400 Horse, all well armed, and the choyce of eight Counties. Together with a Relation of the proceedings of our Army, from the second to the later end of Aprill, 1642.'

BATTLE OF KILRUSH, 1642.

Many other illustrated pamphlets relating to current events were published at this time. It would appear that in 1641 there was a visitation of the plague in London, and a tract of that date has reference to it. It is entitled :— '*London's Lamentation, or a fit admonishment for City and Country, wherein is described certain causes of this affliction and visitation of the Plague, yeare* 1641, *which the Lord hath been pleased to inflict upon us, and withall what means must be used to the Lord, to gain his mercy and favour, with an excellent spirituall medicine to be used for the preservative both of Body and Soule.*' The 'spiritual medicine' recommended is an earnest prayer to heaven at morning and evening and a daily service to the Lord. The writer endeavours to improve the occasion very much like a preacher in the pulpit and continues his exhortation thus :—' Now seeing it is apparent that sin is the cause of sicknesse : It may appear as plainly that prayer must be the best means to procure health and safety, let not our security and slothfulnesse give death opportunity, what man or woman will not seem to start, at the signe of the red Crosse, as they passe by to and fro in the streets ? And yet being gone they think no more on it. It may be, they will say, such a house is shut up, I saw the red crosse on the doore; but look on thine own guilty conscience, and thou shalt find thou hast a multitude of red crimson sinnes remaining in thee.' I have copied the illustration to this tract, and it will be seen that it is divided into two parts—one representing a funeral procession advancing to where men are digging two graves—the other showing

THE PLAGUE IN LONDON. 1641.

dead bodies dragged away on hurdles. The first is labelled 'London's Charity.' The second 'The Countrie's Crueltie.' This was perhaps intended to impress the reader in favour of the orderly burial of the dead in the city churchyards, a subject on which public opinion has very much changed since that time.

We have already noticed that the vicissitudes of the sea and the accidents of maritime life, which supply so much material to modern newspapers, were not less attractive to the early news-writers. There is a very circumstantial account of the voyage and wreck of a ship called the *Merchant Royall* in a pamphlet published in 1641. The engraving it

E

contains is the same block used by Thomas Greepe in 1587.
It is entitled, ' *Sad news from the seas, being a true relation of
the losse of that good Ship called the* Merchant Royall, *which
was cast away ten leagues from the Lands end, on Thursday
night, being the* 23 *of September last* 1641 *having in her a world
of Treasure, as this story following doth truly relate.*'   Another
illustrated pamphlet, dated 1642, contains a long and minute
narrative of how a certain ship called the *Coster* was
boarded by a native of Java, who, watching his opportunity,
murdered the captain and several of the crew, but who was
afterwards killed when assistance arrived from another ship.
There is a woodcut representing the murders, and the title
runs as follows :—'*A most Execrable and Barbarous murder
done by an East Indian Devil, or a native of Java-Major, in the
Road of Bantam, Aboard an English ship called the* Coster, *on
the* 22 *of October last,* 1641. *Wherein is shewed how the wicked
Villain came to the said ship and hid himselfe till it was very
dark, and then he murdered all the men that were aboard, except
the Cooke and three Boyes.   And lastly, how the murderer himselfe was justly requited.   Captain William Minor being an eye-
witnesse of this bloudy Massacre.   London : Printed for T.
Banks, July the* 18, 1642.'   The very full particulars given
in this pamphlet show how minute and circumstantial the
old news-writers were in their narratives.   It will be seen
by the following extracts that the story has an air of truth
given to it by careful attention to various .small matters of
detail :—

'On Friday the 22 of October last 1641 towards night
there came aboard an English ship called the *Coster*, in a
small Prow (or flat Boat with one paddle) a proper young
man, (a Java, which is as much as to say as a man born or
native of the Territory of Java.)   This man, (or devill in
mans shape) with a pretence to sell some Hews, (hatching
mischiefe in his damned minde,) did delay and trifle time,
because he would have the night more dark for him to do
his deeds of darknesse.   At last he sold 6 Hews for half a
Royall of 8 which is not much above two shillings.   There

came also another Java aboard, (with the like small Prow or Boat) to whom he gave the half Royall, sent him away and bade him make haste; he being asked for what the other Java went for, the answer was that he had sent him for more Hews and Goates to sell.

'Night being come, and very dark, (for it was the last night of the wane of the Moone) this inhumane dog staid lurking under the half deck having 2 Crests (or dangerous waving daggers) and a Buckler, of which he would have sold one and the Buckler with it, and as he was discoursing he took off one of the Crests hefts and put cloth about the tongue of the Blade, and made it sure fast: on the other Crest he rolled the handle with a fine linnen cloth to make it also sure from slipping in his hand; these things he did whilst the Master, Robert Start, Stephen Roberts, his mate, Hugh Rawlinson, Chirurgeon, William Perks, Steward, James Biggs, Gunner, and 3 Boys or Youths attending. At supper they were very merry, and this Caitiffe took notice of their carelessnesse of him to suffer him to sit on the quarter deck upon a Cot close by them.

'Supper being ended about 6 at night the Master went to his Cabin to rest, the Gunner asked leave to go ashore, (the ship riding but half a mile from landing.) Afterwards Robert Rawlinson and Perks walked upon the quarter deck; and the devilish Java perceiving the Master to be absent, he asked the Boyes where he was, who answered he was gone to sleepe. This question he demanded 3 or 4 times of the Boyes, and finding it to be so, he arose from the place where he sate, which was on the starboard side and went about the Table next the Mizzen Mast (where Roberts, Rawlings and Perks were walking) with his Target about his Neck for defence against Pikes, or the like; and his 2 Crests in his hand, and upon a sudden cries *a Muck*, which in that language is I hazard or run my death. Then first he stabd Roberts, secondly he stabd Rawlinson, thirdly Perks, all three at an instant. After that he let drive at the Boyes, but they leapd down, and ran forward into the forecastle,

where they found the Cooke, to whom the Boyes related
what had happened.'

Further details are given at great length, showing how
the savage continued his bloody work, and how he was
finally overpowered. The narrative thus winds up:—

'It is observable that of all these men that were thus
butchered, the Hel-hound did never stab any man twice,
so sure did he strike, nor did he pursue any man that kept

MURDERS ON BOARD AN ENGLISH SHIP, 1642.

clear of his stand under the quarter-deck. So there dyed in
all (in this bloody action) Robert Start, Master, Stephen
Roberts, his Mate, Hugh Rawlinson, Chirurgeon, William
Perks, Steward, Walter Rogers, Gunner's Mate, and Francis
Drake, Trumpeter of the *Mary*. And after the Muck, Java,
or Devill, had ended the first part of this bloody Tragedy,
there was only left in the ship, the Cooke, 3 Boyes, and one
John Taylor, that was almost dead with a shott he foolishly
made. So that 7 men were unfortunately lost (as you have
heard) and the Gunner escaped very narrowly through God's

merciful prevention, from the like of these related disasters and suddaine mischiefs, Good Lord deliver us.'

The engraving, like all those belonging to this period, is very rough; but it was evidently prepared specially for the occasion, and some care appears to have been taken to represent the '*Java*' as he is described. It is a genuine attempt to illustrate the story, and on that account is more interesting than some of the woodcuts in the early newspapers.

The Earl of Strafford, who was executed on Tower Hill, May 12, 1641, forms the subject of more than one illustrated tract of this period. In 1642 was published a curious pamphlet, consisting of an engraved title and eight pages of illustrations, representing the principal events of 1641–2. There are sixteen illustrations, exclusive of the title, two on each page. They are all etched on copper, and are done with some freedom and artistic ability. I shall have occasion to refer to this pamphlet hereafter; but at present I have copied the engraving entitled, 'The Earle of Strafford for treasonable practises beheaded on the Tower-hill.'

In this example of illustrated news the artist has faithfully represented the locality in his background, but there the truth of his pencil stops. Strafford himself, although his head is not yet severed from his body, lies at full length on the scaffold, and instead of the usual block used for decapitations the victim's head rests on an ordinary plank or thick piece of wood. There is no one standing on the scaffold but the executioner, whereas history asserts that the Earl was attended in his last moments by his brother, Sir George Wentworth, the Earl of Cleveland, and Archbishop Usher. These omissions, if they were noticed at all, were no doubt looked upon as trivial faults in the infancy of illustrated journalism, and before a truth-loving public had learnt to be satisfied with nothing less than 'sketches done on the spot.' What appears to be a more correct view of the execution was, however, published at the time. In the British Museum are two etchings by Hollar (single sheets,

1641), representing the trial and execution of the Earl of
Strafford. They both look as if they had been done from
sketches on the spot, that of the execution giving a correct
view of the Tower and the surrounding buildings, but they
are too crowded to admit of reproduction on a reduced
scale.

The taste of the time tolerated the publication of satires
and petty lampoons even upon dead men. Soon after

The Earle of Strafford for treasonable practises
beheaded on the Tower-hill

EXECUTION OF STRAFFORD, 1641.

Strafford's death a tract was published entitled '*A Description
of the Passage of Thomas, late Earle of Strafford, over the
River of Styx, with the Conference betwixt him, Charon, and
William Noy.*' There is a dialogue between Strafford and
Charon, of which the following is a specimen :—

'*Charon.*—In the name of Rhodomont what ayles me ?
I have tugged and tugged above these two hours, yet can
hardly steere one foot forward; either my dried nerves
deceive my arme, or my vexed Barke carries an unwonted
burden. From whence comest thou, Passenger ?

'*Strafford.*—From England.

'*Charon.*—From England ! Ha ! I was counsailed to

prepare myselfe, and trim up my boat. I should have work
enough they sayd ere be long from England, but trust me
thy burden alone outweighs many transported armies, were
all the expected numbers of thy weight poor Charon well
might sweat.

' *Strafford.*—I bear them all in one.

' *Charon.*—How? Bear them all in one, and thou shalt

STRAFFORD CROSSING THE STYX, 1641.

pay for them all in one, by the just soul of Rhodomont;
this was a fine plot indeed, sure this was some notable fellow
being alive, that hath a trick to cosen the devil being dead.
What is thy name?

' (Strafford sighs.)

' *Charon.*—Sigh not so deep. Take some of this Lethæan
water into thine hand, and soope it up; it will make thee
forget thy sorrows.

' *Strafford.*—My name is Wentworth, Strafford's late Earle.

'*Charon.*—Wentworth! O ho! Thou art hee who hath been so long expected by William Noy. He hath been any time these two months on the other side of the banke, expecting thy coming daily.'

Strafford gives Charon but one halfpenny for his fare, whereat the ferryman grumbles. Then ensues a conversation between Strafford and William Noy, part of which is in blank verse. The tract is illustrated with a woodcut, representing Strafford in the ferryman's boat with William Noy waiting his arrival on the opposite bank.

No man of his time appears to have excited the hostile notice of the press more than Archbishop Laud. The Archbishops of Canterbury had long been considered censors of the press by right of their dignity and office; and Laud exercised this power with unusual tyranny. The ferocious cruelty with which he carried out his prosecutions in the Star Chamber and Court of High Commission made his name odious, and his apparent preference for ceremonial religion contributed to render him still more unpopular. Men were put in the pillory, had their ears cut off, their noses slit, and were branded on the checks with S. S. (Sower of Sedition), and S. L. (Schismatical Libeller). They were heavily fined, were whipped through the streets, were thrown into prison; and all for printing and publishing opinions and sentiments unpleasing to Archbishop Laud, under whose rule this despotic cruelty became so prevalent that it was a common thing for men to speak of So-and-so as having been 'Star-Chambered.' No wonder, when the tide turned, that the long-pent-up indignation found a vent through the printing-press. Amongst the numerous tracts that were published after the suppression of the Star Chamber were many which held up Laud to public execration. He was reviled for his ambition, reproached for his cruelty, and caricatured for his Romish sympathies. During the four years between his fall and his execution, portraits of him and other illustrations relating to his career may be found in many pamphlets. I propose to introduce the reader to some of these, as examples of the kind of feeling that was excited by a man whose character and actions must have contributed not a little to bring about a convulsion which shook both the Church and the throne to their foundations. It must have been with a peculiar satisfaction that Prynne, one of the chief sufferers under Laud's rule, found himself armed with the authority of the House of Commons to despoil his old enemy. Probably a similar feeling caused many others to chuckle and rub their hands when they read, ' *A New Play called Canterburie's Change of Diet*, printed in 1641.' This is a small tract illustrated with woodcuts, and is written in the form of a

A BURLESQUE PLAY ABOUT ARCHBISHOP LAUD.   ACT I.   1641.

play. The persons represented are the Archbishop of Canterbury, a doctor of physic, a lawyer, a divine, a Jesuit, a carpenter and his wife. The doctor of physic is intended for either Dr. Alexander Leighton, or Dr. John Bastwick, both of whom had their ears cut off; the lawyer is Prynne; and the divine is meant for the Rev. Henry Burton, a London clergyman, who also suffered under Laud's administration. In the first act enter the Archbishop, the doctor, the lawyer, and the divine. Being seated, a variety of dishes are brought to the table, but Laud expresses himself dissatisfied with the fare placed before him and demands a more racy diet. He then calls in certain bishops, who enter armed with muskets, bandoleers, and swords. He cuts off the ears of the doctor, the lawyer, and the divine, and tells them he makes them an

example that others may be more careful to please his palate.
On the previous page is a copy of the cut which illustrates
the first act.

In the second act the Archbishop of Canterbury enters a

A BURLESQUE PLAY ABOUT ARCHBISHOP LAUD.   ACT II.

carpenter's yard by the waterside, and seeing a grindstone
he is about to sharpen his knife upon it, when he is interrupted by the carpenter who refuses to let him sharpen his

A BURLESQUE PLAY ABOUT ARCHBISHOP LAUD.   ACT III.

knife upon his grindstone, lest he should treat him (the
carpenter) as he had treated the others.   The carpenter then
holds the Archbishop's nose to the grindstone, and orders his
apprentice to turn with a will.   The bishop cries out,
'Hold! hold! such turning will soon deform my face.   O,

I bleed, I bleed, and am extremely sore.' The carpenter, however, rejoins, 'But who regarded "hold" before? Remember the cruelty you have used to others, whose bloud crieth out for vengeance. Were not their ears to them as pretious as your nostrils can be to you? If such dishes must be your fare, let me be your Cooke, I'll invent you rare sippets.' Then enters a Jesuit Confessor who washes the bishop's wounded face and binds it up with a cloth. There is also an illustration to this act which is here copied.

The rising of Prentifes and Sea-men on South=wark fide to affault the Arch-bifhops of Canter=burys House at Lambeth

ASSAULT ON LAMBETH PALACE, 1642.

In the third act the Archbishop and the Jesuit are represented in a great Cage (the Tower) while the carpenter and his wife, conversing together, agree that the two caged birds will sing very well together. The woodcut to this act represents a fool laughing at the prisoners.

There is a fourth act in which the King and his Jester hold a conversation about the Bishop and the confessor in the cage. There is no printer's or publisher's name to this play, only the date, 1641.

The pamphlet previously referred to as containing a picture of Strafford's execution, has also an engraving showing

how the tide of public feeling had set against Archbishop
Laud. The powerful Churchman had been impeached for
high treason; he was deprived of all the profits of his high
office and was imprisoned in the Tower. All his goods in
Lambeth Palace, including his books, were seized, and even
his Diary and private papers were taken from him by
Prynne, who acted under a warrant from the House of
Commons. The engraving under notice is entitled 'The
rising of Prentices and Sea-men on Southwark side to assault
the Archbishops of Canterburys House at Lambeth.'

In a tract entitled '*A Prophecie of the Life, Reigne, and
Death of William Laud, Archbishop of Canterbury,*' there is a
caricature of Laud seated on a throne or chair of state. A
pair of horns grow out of his forehead, and in front the
devil offers him a Cardinal's Hat. This business of the
Cardinal's Hat is alluded to by Laud himself, who says, 'At
Greenwich there came one to me seriously, and that avowed
ability to perform it, and offered me to be a Cardinal. I
went presently to the king, and acquainted him both with
the thing and the person.' This offer was afterwards
renewed: 'But,' says he, 'my answer again was, that
something dwelt within me which would not suffer that till
Rome were other than it is.' It would thus appear that the
Archbishop did not give a very decided refusal at first or the
offer would not have been repeated; and that circumstance,
if it were known at the time, must have strengthened the
opinion that he was favourably inclined towards the Church
of Rome. At all events, the offer must have been made
public, as this caricature shows.

Though Laud behaved with dignity and courage when
he came to bid farewell to the world, if we are to believe the
publications of the time, he was not above petitioning for
mercy, while any hope of life remained. In 1643 a pamphlet
was published with the following title, '*The Copy of the Petition presented to the Honourable Houses of Parliament by the
Lord Archbishop of Canterbury, wherein the said Archbishop
desires that he may not be transported beyond the Seas into New*

England with Master Peters in regard to his extraordinary age and weaknesse.' The petition is dated ' From the Tower of London this 6th of May 1643,' and in it the petitioner sets forth that out of a ' fervent zeal to Christianity ' he endeavoured to reconcile the principles of the Protestant and Roman Catholic religions, hoping that if he could effect this he might more easily draw the Queen into an adherence to the Protestant faith. He deplores that his endeavours were not successful, and he begs the honourable Parliament to

CARICATURE OF THE DEVIL OFFERING LAUD A CARDINAL'S HAT, 1644.

pardon his errors, and to ' looke upon him in mercy, and not permit or suffer your Petitioner to be transported, to endure the hazard of the Seas, and the long tediousnesse of Voyage into those trans-marine parts, and cold Countries, which would soon bring your Petitioners life to a period; but rather that your Petitioner may abide in his native country, untill your Petitioner shall pay the debt which is due from him to Nature, and so your Petitioner doth submit himselfe to your Honourable and grave Wisdoms for your Petitioners request and desire therein. And your Petitioner shall humbly pray &c.'

If Archbishop Laud was really the author of this petition he appears to have expected that his long imprisonment would end in banishment rather than death. He was beheaded on Tower Hill, January 10, 1645. There is a woodcut portrait of the Archbishop printed on the title-page of the petition.

ARCHBISHOP LAUD.

CHAPTER III.

Ben Jonson's Ridicule of the Early Newspapers—Fondness of the Old News-Writers for the Marvellous—The Smithfield Ghost—The Wonderful Whale—The Newbury Witch—Satirical Tracts and Caricatures at the Commencement of the Civil War—Religion Tossed in a Blanket—Caricatures of the Pope and the Bishops—Pluralists and Patentees—Taylor, the Water Poet—*Mercurius Aulicus*—Activity of the Pamphleteers—Welshmen Satirised—Satires on Prince Rupert—On the King and Queen—The Ladies' Parliament—Illustrated Tracts relating to Social and Political Subjects—Sir Kenelm Digby's Duel—The King entertained by the City of London, 1641—Executions in 1641—The Liquor Traffic and Sunday Closing in 1641—Abuses of the Ecclesiastical Courts—Ritualism and Nunneries in 1641—Truths enforced by Lieing—Stage Players and the Plague in 1641—Bartholomew Fair in 1641—Destruction of Charing Cross and Cheapside Cross—Strange Apparition—Method of Enforcing their Views adopted by the Puritan Pamphleteers—Parodies of Roundhead Sermons—Matthew Hopkins the Witch-finder—*The Welsh Post* of 1643—William Lilly the Astrologer—Three Suns seen in London on the King's Birthday.

WHEN Ben Jonson called the newspaper 'a weekly cheat to draw money,' and ridiculed the growing taste for news, he had some reason for satirising the journalism of the period. To satisfy the craving for news all kinds of impositions were freely circulated. Nothing was too wonderful for the credulity of the age, and people eagerly accepted what was placed before them, fully believing that whatever was in print must be true. It was not, however, till many years after Ben Jonson's death that the so-called newspapers put forward their full powers as purveyors of the marvellous. *Mercurius Democritus* was the *Punch* of that day. While he satirised men and things he laboured to satisfy the popular taste for the wonderful, as in the following account of a ghost that was said to haunt the neighbourhood of Smithfield :—' There is a great report of a ghoast that walks every Night amongst the Butchers at *Smithfield Barrs*, the *Shambles*, White-*Chappell*, and *Eastcheape*, in the habit of *Mallet*, the Lawyer, pulling the meat off the Butchers Tainters; many have adventured to strike at him with Cleavers and Chopping-knives, but cannot feel anything but Aire, every Saturday at night between 9 and 12, he

THE SMITHFIELD GHOST.   FROM ' MERCURIUS DEMOCRITUS,' 1654.

walks his stations, in this very habit as you see, doing more mischiefe to the *Butchers* than ever *Robin Goodfellow* did to the Country Hindes.'

Another example of the marvellous occurs in a tract entitled, ' *The Sea Wonder : a true and wonderful relation of a Whale pursued in the Sea, and incountered by multitudes of other Fishes as it was certified by divers Mariners of Weymouth, who, comming from France in the good ship called the* Bonaventure, *did shoote the said Whale, which making to Land did strike upon the Shore, within three miles of Weymouth, where being opened there was found in the belly of it a Romish Priest, with Pardon for divers Papists in England and Ireland, whose names are here inserted.'* Great pains appear to have been taken to give an air of truth to the narrative, which begins thus ·—'On the 19th of October being the Lord's Day the good Ship called the *Bonaventure* of *Weymouth* being bound for *England* was bringing home her Merchandise from *France* which was wines, linning cloth, and abundance of Wall-nuts,

THE WONDERFUL WHALE, 1645.

the day was very fair and no wind stirring, so that the ship for above three hours space lay hulling upon the Seas, being not able to move either one way nor other for want of wind, although she was full sayled and prepared to take the advantage of every gale.' The author gravely explains that the excitement of the fishes and their attacks on the whale were caused by their instinctively feeling the presence of the Popish Priest. Annexed is a copy of the woodcut on the title-page of this curious tract.

'*Newes, True Newes, Laudable Newes, Citie Newes, Country Newes; The World is Mad, or it is a Mad World my Masters especially now when in the Antipodes these things are come to*

F

pass.' Such is the lengthy title of a pamphlet containing an
imaginary account of things at the Antipodes, and illustrated
with a fanciful woodcut on the title-page. Then we have
news from Boston in New England of a strange and prodigious birth of a child with two heads, also illustrated.
Mercurius Democritus, besides such waggeries as giving an
account of 'a sight seen in the air by a blind philosopher,'
communicates '*Many strange wonders out of the World, in the
Moon, the Antipodes, Maggy Land, Tenebris, Fary-Land, Green-
land, and other adjacent countries. Published for the right
understanding of all the Mad-merry-people of Great Bedlam.*'
Another example of the wonderful stories put forth to entertain the multitude relates to the discovery and punishment
of a witch during the civil war. It occurs in a pamphlet
entitled '*A most Certain, Strange and true Discovery of a
Witch, being taken by some of the Parliament Forces, as she
was standing on a small planck-board and sayling on it over the
River of Newbury.*' The illustration is of the rudest description, and the story is told in a breathless sort of way, without
a full stop in the whole narrative :—

'A part of the Army marching through Newbury, some
of the Souldiers being scattered by the reason of their loyter-
ing by the way, in gathering Nuts, Apples, Plummes, Black-
berries, and the like, one of them by chance in clambring up
a tree, being pursued by his fellow or comrade in waggish
merriment, jesting one with another, espied on the river
being there adjacent, a tall, lean, slender woman, as he supposed, to his amazement, and great terrour, treading of the
water with her feet, with as much ease and firmnesse as if
one should walk or trample on the earth, wherewith he softly
calls, and beckoned to his fellows to behold it, and with all
possible speed that could be to obscure them from her sight,
who as conveniently as they could they did observe, this
could be no little amazement unto them you may think to
see a woman dance upon the water, nor could all their sights
be deluded, though perhaps one might, but coming nearer to
the shore, they could perceive there was a planke or deale

overshadowed with a little shallow water that she stood upon,
the which did beare her up, anon rode by some of the commanders who were eye witnesses, as well as they, and were
as much astonished as they could be, still too and fro she
fleeted on the water, the boord standing firm boult upright,
indeed I have both heard and read of many that in tempests
and on rivers by casualty have become shipwracked, or cast
overboard, where catching empty barrells, rudders, boards, or
planks have made good shift by the assisting Providence of
God to get on shore, but not in this womans kind to stand
upon the board, turning and winding it which way she
pleased, making it pastime to her, as little thinking who
perceived her tricks, or that she did imagine that they were
the last she ever should show, as we have heard the swan
sing before her death, so did this devilish woman, as after
plainly it appeared make sport before her death, at last
having sufficiently been upon the water, he that deceived
her alway did so then, blinding her that she could not, at
her landing see the ambush that was laid for her, coming
upon the shore, she gave the board a push, which they
plainly perceived, and crossed the river, they searched after
her but could not find her she being landed the Commanders
beholding her, gave orders to lay hold on her, and bring her
to them straight, the which some were fearful, but one being
more venturous than other some, boldly went to her and
seized on her by the arms, demanding what she was? but
the woman no whit replying any words unto them, they
brought her to the Commanders, to whom though mightily
she was urged she did reply as little; so consulting with
themselves what should be done with her, being it so apparently appeared she was a *witch*, being loth to let her goe
& as loth to carry her with them, so they resolved with themselves, to make a shot at her, and gave order to a couple of
their souldiers that were approved good marksmen, to charge
and shoot her straight, which they prepared to doe ; so setting her boult upright against a mud bank or wall ; two of
the souldiers according to their command made themselves

ready, where having taken aime gave fire and shot at her,
but with a deriding and loud laughter at them she caught
their bullets in her hands and chew'd them, which was a
stronger testimony than the water, that she was the same
that their imaginations thought her for to be, so resolving
with themselves if either fire or sword or halter were sufficient for to make an end of her, one set his Carbine close
unto her brest ; where discharging, the bullet back rebounded
like a ball, and narrowly he mist it in his face that was the
shooter ; this so enraged the Gentleman, that one drew out

THE NEWBURY WITCH, 1643.

his sword and manfully run at her with all the force his
strength had power to make, but it prevailed no more than
did the shot, the woman still though speechless, yet in a
most contemptible way of scorn, still laughing at them,
which did the more exhaust their furie against her life, yet
one amongst the rest had heard that piercing or drawing
bloud from forth the veins that crosse the temples of the
head, it would prevail against the strongest sorcery, and
quell the force of Witchcraft, which was allowed for triall ;
the woman hearing this knew then the Devill had left her
and her power was gone, wherefore she began alowd to cry,
and roare, tearing her haire, and making pitious moan, which

in these words expressed were : And is it come to passe that
I must die indeed ? Why then his Excellency the Earle of
Essex shall be fortunate and win the field, after which no
more words could be got from her ; wherewith they immediately discharged a Pistoll underneath her ear, at which
she straight sunk down and died, leaving her legacy of a
detested carcasse to the wormes, her soul we ought not to
judge of, though the evils of her wicked life and death can
scape no censure.'

On the outbreak of the great Civil War an immense
number of tracts and pamphlets were published relating to
social and political questions, many of which were illustrated.
Satire was a weapon freely used, and many hard hits were
made, the point and bitterness of which cannot now be
understood. Caricatures, which are generally supposed to
have made their appearance in England at a much later
date, are of frequent occurrence. The wonderful and supernatural were freely dealt in, and many tracts were published
which were not strictly news, yet had some reference to
public men and passing events. The woodcuts in the tracts
and pamphlets of this period were frequently repeated, being
sometimes used where they had no relation to the subject
treated.

The minds of men being much exercised on questions of
religion at this time, it was to be expected that the subject
would not escape the notice of the satirist. Accordingly,
many tracts were published relating to religious matters,
some of which are illustrated with woodcut caricatures.
There is one of the date of 1641 containing a woodcut of
four men tossing Religion (represented by a Bible) in a
blanket. The writer condemns the numberless sects which
were perplexing men's minds and tearing the Church
asunder :—

'Religion is made a Hotch potch, and as it were tossed
in a Blanquet, and too many places of England too much
Amsterdamnified by several opinions. Religion is now become
the common discourse and Table-talke in every Taverne and

Ale-house, where a man shall hardly find five together in one minde, and yet every one presumes hee is in the right. The Booke of Common prayer which was established by Act of Parliament by that good and Godly King Edward the sixth, and after reestablished by another Parliament by that

RELIGION TOSSED IN A BLANKET, 1641.

unparaled and peerlesse princesse Queen Elizabeth, and continued since in the happy Raignes of two gracious kings in the church of England for the service of God these ninetie yeares; yet one would have it to be cast out now, holding it to be a false worship; another is angrie at the vestments and habits of the Ministry; one will not kneel, another will not stand, one will sit downe, one will not bowe, another will not be uncovered, one holds all good manners to be popery, another that all decencie is superstitious, another that railes are Romish (which is false for the papists have no railes in their churches, nor anything so convenient). One foolishly assumes and presumes to save himselfe and some of his Neighbours too, by his good workes; another will be saved by a bare and lazie Faith that will do no work at all, and thus religion is puft and blowne to and fro with every wind of doctrine, and as it were tost in a Blanquet; but of this more largely hereafter in another part which will

CARICATURE OF THE POPE, 1643.

suddenly be printed, till when and ever it shall be my hearty prayers that as there is but one Shepheard, that is God in his gracious goodnesse and mercie would make us all one sheepfold.'

The shafts of satire were frequently aimed at the Pope and the Bishops. One caricature represents the Pope seated, while a unicorn tumbles the triple crown from his head. The same woodcut illustrates a '*Letter from the Devil to the Pope of Rome.*' Another tract has a representation of the Pope riding upon a seven-headed monster and holding in his hand a scroll on which are the words 'Estote proditores' —'Betraye your Country.' This advice he is giving to a

cavalier, a bishop, and a monk, and at the same time three
devils are represented as leaving him and entering into
them. This cut, which is repeated in other pamphlets, is
curious as an early specimen of caricature, but its meaning is
now lost.

The Bishops were treated with as little ceremony as the

CARICATURE OF THE BISHOPS, 1642.

Pope. In one caricature four of them are represented as
falling to the earth, with the following lines underneath the
woodcut :—

> ' The tottering prelates, with their trumpery all,
>   Shall moulder downe, like elder from the wall.'

In a pamphlet called *The Decoy Duck*, printed in 1642,

there is a quaint woodcut caricature and a satirical account of how the Bishops of Durham, Lichfield, Norwich, Asaph, Bath, Hereford, Oxford, Ely, Gloucester, Peterborough, and Llandaff were decoyed and deceived by the Bishop of Lincoln (Bishop Williams). I have copied the woodcut, but no quotation from the pamphlet would be understood unless given at great length. It doubtless refers to the charge of high treason against the twelve Bishops.

The abuses of the Established Church in an age when the spirit of dissent was strong were pretty sure to attract the notice of the satirical writer and the caricaturist. Accordingly, we find representations of the pluralist holding a church in each hand and one on each shoulder; while the non-resident clergyman was compared to the locust :—' The Locust is given to spoile and devoure greene things ; it was one of the plagues of Egypt. Non-residents devoure the tithes of many parishes in this kingdome ; and they are not to be numbered amongst the least of those plagues that God inflicts upon us for our sins. The Locusts caused Pharaoh and his servants to cry unto Moses that he would entreat the Lord to take them away; and our Non-Residents cause all good people to cry mightily unto God, to the King's Majesty, and to the Honourable House of Parliament, to reform them or remove them ; that there may not be any carelesse Non-Resident in all the coasts of England . . . . Some of our carelesse Non-Residents have a cure of soules in one place and live in another, like fugitive Captaines forsake their Ensigne and Company at Barwick, and flee to Dover ; who being with Jonah commanded for Nineveh, flee to Tarshish ; being placed in the Country they run to the Cathedrals, they leave their charge as the Ostrich doth her eggs in the earth and sands, forgetting that either the foot may crush them or that the wild beast may break them, or at the best they leave their Congregations, as the Cuckoo doth her eggs to be hatched of a sparrow or some other bird.'

The following woodcut is copied from a pamphlet entitled

'*A Purge for Pluralities, showing the unlawfulnesse of men to have two Livings, or the Downefall of Double Benifices.*'

The abuse of the Crown's prerogative in the granting of patents and monopolies was very frequent in the reigns of

THE PLURALIST, 1642.

Elizabeth and James, and was not diminished under Charles the First.   The practice did not fail to attract the notice of the satirical writers of the day, and caricature laid hold on the ' Projectors and Patentees,' and held them up to ridicule. '*A Dialogue or accidental discourse betwixt Mr. Alderman Abell,*' *and Richard Kilvert, the two maine Projectors for Wine,* 1641, contains a woodcut showing 'The manner and forme how Projectors and Patentees have rode a Tylting in a Parliament time.' The wit of the illustration is a little obscure to the modern reader, but at the time of its publication it was no doubt understood, and relished accordingly. The pamphlet describes how Messrs. Abell and Kilvert laid their heads together to obtain the patent for wine ; how they put the patent in force, and how, after the tide turned against them, they reviled one another.

As the excitement of the Civil War increased, political animosity rose to a red heat. Cavaliers and Roundheads belaboured each other in many a merciless pamphlet, to which they often endeavoured to give additional bitterness by woodcut caricatures. Prominent individuals, such as Prince Rupert, became marks for the satirist's wit. Even the throne itself did not escape, and it was broadly hinted that the Protestant king was unduly influenced by the Roman Catholic queen. The curious subject of the growth of caricature might be illustrated by numerous examples from the publications of this period, but it will be sufficient to refer to two or three more woodcut satires of this date.

The distractions of the times were epitomised by John Taylor, the Water Poet, in an illustrated rhyming pamphlet, published in 1642. It is entitled, '*Mad Fashions, Od Fashions, all out of Fashion; or the Emblems of these distracted Times.*'

The author compares England to the engraving on his title-page, where everything is represented upside down:—

> ' The Picture that is printed on the front
> Is like this Kingdome if you look upon 't;
> For if you well doe note it as it is,
> It is a Transform'd Metamorphasis.
> This Monstrous Picture plainly doth declare
> This land (quite out of order) out of square.
> His Breeches on his shoulders doe appeare,
> His doublet on his lower parts doth weare.

His Boots and Spurs upon his Armes and Hands,
His Gloves upon his feet (whereon he stands)
The church o'erturned (a lamentable show)
The Candlestick above, the light below,
The Coney hunts the Dogge, the Rat the Cat,
The Horse doth whip the Cart (I pray marke that)
The Wheelbarrow doth drive the man (Oh Base)
And Eeles and Gudgeons flie a mighty pace.

EMBLEMS OF THE DISTRACTED TIMES, 1642.

And sure this is a Monster of strange fashion
That doth surpasse all Ovids transformation.
And this is England's case this very day,
All things are turned the clean contrary way;
For now, as when a Royall Parliament,
(With King, and Peers, and Commons whole consent)
Have almost sate two years, with paines and Cares,
And charge, to free us from our Griefes and fears,
For when many a worthy Lord and Knight,
And good Esquire (for King and Countrey's Right)

Have spent so much time with great Toyle and Heede
All England's vicious garden how to weed,
So like a wildernesse 'twas over run,
That though much better hath been done; All is not done.'

The Water Poet sided with the Cavalier party, and verse and prose flowed plentifully from his pen in favour of the Royal cause. His effusions provoked many replies, one of which is entitled, ' *No Mercurius Aquaticus, but a Cable-Rope, double twisted for John Tayler, the Water Poet; who escaping drowning in a Paper - Wherry - Voyage, is reserved for another day, as followeth, viz.*'
Then follows the subjoined woodcut, with verses underneath. The hint that the poet was born to be hanged because he had escaped from drowning refers to his having undertaken to sail from London to Queenborough in a boat made of brown paper. In this foolhardy exploit Taylor and a friend who was with him nearly lost their lives. The tract under notice affords a good specimen of the sort of language used by the partisans of each faction against their opponents: ' I should be loathe to foule my fingers with any base Pamphlets that comes from Oxford, if the venom of their malicious spleens were darted against my particular self : But when through my sides they wound the honour of the Parliament and our Armies abroad, I cannot but set Pen to paper, and pay them back again in their own kinde. And who d'ye think I should meet abroad for a *Rogue-in-Print* but one of our City Water-rats, the doughty John Taylor, who according to the knavish custom, changes his name upon every new paper-designe ? Sometimes he calls himself *Thorney Ailo, Mercurius Aquaticus,* and now he entitles himself No MERCURIUS AULICUS. I thought I had lately sent *rope* enough for all the Parrots in Oxford ; But I perceive they will be prattling still ; and therefore I must unmaske the Mysterious Masters of the science of railing. There are three grand paper conspirators well known by the name of *Mercurius Aulicus, George Naworth,* and reverend Master

John Tayler the water-tankard, by whose sprinklings in this
great dearth of Wit and Honesty the University is cherished
and kept in credit.   These three are they which pumpe and
Pimpe about with their Prostitute Noddles in the behalf of
Popery, Murder, and Rebellion against the state; they are
Liars in all elements, *Aulicus* for Land-lies, *Tayler* for Water,
and hungry *George Naworth* for all between Heaven and
Earth, where I doubt not but to see them all meet together
to take their farewell of the world, where the *Parrots* will

PREDICTED FATE OF JOHN TAYLOR THE WATER POET, 1644.

find *Ropes* made of stronger Lines than mine, and such as
will *non-plus* the very primest Wits in the University.'
    The pamphleteer goes on to give the Water-Poet what he
doubtless considered a thorough drubbing, and at the end he
leaves him ' to the Gallows, the proper cure for such Rebels.'
The words ' London ' and ' Oxford ' on the woodcut have
reference to another voyage which the Water-Poet performed
in a sculler's boat between those places.
    Mercurius Aulicus was the organ of the Court party, and
was published at Oxford.   A curious satire upon this Court
paper was printed in 1645, entitled, *Newes from Smith the
Oxford Jaylor.*   It consists of a dialogue between the author
and the ' Oxford Jaylor,' and sets forth that ' Mercurius
Aulicus ' was sentenced, by a jury of women, ' to stand in the

pillory three market-days in Oxford, for his lies, libels, and deceitful glozings ; ' to have a written paper over his head announcing his shame ; to beg forgiveness of ' Mercurius Brittanicus ; ' to be prevented from writing any more libels for one year. 'That before two months' expiration he be cut of the simples, and his braines be taken out, washt in white

MERCURIUS AULICUS IN THE PILLORY, 1645.

wine, and put in againe.' 'That for every morning during the said time he have one mess of stewd broth made of the interlinings of fower Court Parazites, and the braines of 26 Oxford Widgins boyld in the water of forgetfulnesse.' 'That he may never hereafter have so much as one graine of wit left him in his empty Hogshead (his brains being taken out and washed as before is ordered) to scandalize those whom if he had any grace he is bound to honour.' There is a wood-cut of *Mercurius Aulicus* in the pillory, which is supposed to

represent Sir John Birkenhead, who acquired the title of the
Loyal Poet, and suffered several imprisonments. This cut
was used on several other occasions.

The troubles of the times are constantly indicated in the
pamphlets of the period. In one the State is represented as a
two-headed serpent, with these lines underneath the engraving :

'This double-headed serpent is a wonder,
  It draws two ways and tears the womb in sunder ;
  The wofull emblem of a troubled State
  Where civill warres doe threat to ruinate.'

SQUARE CAPS TURNED INTO ROUND HEADS, 1642.

The partisans of the Parliament faction appear to have
been much more active pamphleteers than the Cavaliers.
'*Square Caps turned into Round Heads, or the Bishop's Vindication and the Brownist's conviction, being a Dialogue between
Time and Opinion; showing the folly of the one and the worthi-
nesse of the other*,' is a tract with an illustration representing
Opinion turning a wheel, on which are five square caps and
five round heads, while Time, with his scythe and hour-
glass, holds converse with Opinion. Under the woodcut are
the following lines :—

'Time doth Opinion call unto accompt,
  Who turns the Bishop's downe and Roundheads mount ;
  Upon her lofty wheels their Noddles are,
  But her Camelion feedeth on his aire.'

'*Cornucopia, or Room for a Ram head, wherein is described the dignity of the Ram head above the Roundhead or Rattlehead*,' is another tract, with a woodcut caricature representing a woman attempting to saw the horns from a man's head. The letterpress consists of a dialogue between a man and his wife, wherein the man humorously praises horns. It was a favourite joke to represent the Puritan as a '*cuckoldy* Roundhead.'

Another satirical pamphlet has a woodcut representing

CARICATURE, 1642.

Cavaliers and Roundheads exciting their dogs to fight. It is entitled, '*A Dialogue or rather a Parly between Prince Rupert's Dogge whose name is Puddle, and Tobie's Dog whose name is Pepper, &c. Whereunto is added the challenge which Prince Griffin's Dog, called Towzer, hath sent to Prince Rupert's Dog Puddle, in the behalfe of honest Pepper, Tobie's Dog. Moreover, the said Prince Griffin is newly gone to Oxford to lay the wager, and to make up the Match.*' In this satire, which is very highly flavoured, both Cavaliers and Roundheads are pelted with very vigorous epithets, but in the end the Roundhead dog is converted by his opponent, and seals his recantation in a very striking manner.

There is a tirade against the Jesuits entitled, '*A Peece of ordnance invented by a Jesuite, for Cowards that fight by Whisperings, and raise jealousies to overthrow both Church and State, which with the help of a private Ensign in the Cabbinet Councell, or Westminster Hall is able to doe more mischiefe at twentie miles distance, than a whole Regiment of stout Souldiers, at Musket-shot. Which grievance is by way of Remonstrance*

CARICATURE, 1643.

humbly presented to the consideration of the Parliament.' This tract has a woodcut of a man firing a cannon formed of the figure of a man.

'*Hell's Hurlie-Burlie, or a Fierce contention between the Pope and the Devill,*' is illustrated ; and there is a pamphlet, with a woodcut, entitled, '*The Devill's White Boyes: A Mixture of Malicious Malignants, with their much evill and manifold practises against the Kingdome and Parliament, with a bottom-lesse Sack-full of Knavery, Popery, Prelacy, Policy, Treachery, Malignant Trumpery, Conspiricies, and Cruelties, filled to the top by the Malignants, laid on the shoulders of Time, and now by Time emptied forth, and poured out, to show the Truth, and shame the Devill.* Beneath the woodcut are the following verses :—

> ' Malignants are the Divell's Agents still,
>   The Sack is *England,* which they strive to fill
>   With misery and mischief, and this Sack
>   Full stufft is laid upon Times aged back ;
>   *Time* pours it out now in an angry mood
>   That all their knaveries may be understood.'

On the cut itself are printed the lines :—

' *Time* now at the last pours out much knavery,
   The Devill holds down fast to hinder the discovery.'

CARICATURE, 1644.

The Welshman came in for a share of the satirist's wit at the commencement of the Civil War. He generally figures under the name of ' Ap Shinkin,' and is made to speak English much the same as the Scottish Highlander does in Scott's novels. *' The Welsh mans Postures, or the true manner how her doe exercise her company of Souldiers in her own Country in a warlike manners,'* is a satire of a very broad character, and is illustrated with a woodcut representing men exercising with the pike. Shinkin is also ridiculed for the share he took in the battle of Edgehill, the first important engagement in the Civil War. There is an illustrated tract with the following title : ' *The Welsh mans Complements : or the true manner how Shinkin wood his Sweetheart Maudlin after his return from Kenton Battaile.* Also *Fair Maudlin's reply and answer to all Shinkin's Welch complements, full of merry wit and pleasant mirth.*' The ' merry wit ' is certainly not refined, and the ' pleasant mirth ' is founded on Shinkin's supposed hasty departure from the neighbourhood of the fight. The woodcut represents Shinkin and Maudlin in conversation.

Prince Rupert is often the mark for the satirist's wit. In '*Rupert's Sumpter, and private Cabinet rifled, and a Discovery of a Pack of his Jewels, by way of Dialogue between Mercurius Brittanicus and Mercurius Aulicus,*' there is a discussion as to the Prince's merits and demerits, and he is charged with aiming at the crown. Both the King and Queen were brought under the caricaturist's lash. In 1644 there was an illustrated pamphlet published, representing the King, Queen, and a bishop, with the following title : ' *The Sussex Picture, or an Answer to the Sea-gull.*' The address to the reader is headed : ' The Sceptre's Submission, the Distaffs Triumph, and the Crosiers Combination. Reader, If thou hast view'd that stately Picture, which was lately sent up to the Parliament by Collonel Morley, and was taken in a Flemish Ship upon the Sussex Shore ; Thou hast beheld therein the weaker sexe triumphing over the stronger, and by the help of a Miter, thou hast seen a Scepter doing homage to the Distaffe. If thou hast never seen the Originall, yet here is to be seen a poore, rude, counterfeit of the chief part in it ; use thy judgement freely, and impartially : let both the Peèce itself, and that which is said by both sides, in judgement thereupon, be put into one equal ballance. If the Dutch Author be not to undergo censure, as if he intended an English Storie, yet neither art thou to be censured for doubting his intention, or for standing amazed at his phancie. Shadows which are not fashioned by some certain, neer, interposing body present nothing to the eye, and therefore work nothing upon the understanding. The language of a picture is to be borrowed from the veritie of the matter, if that be wanting, neither the Art of the Limner nor the imagination of the spectator can supply its vocall organs.' This caricature may have referred to the influence which the Roman Catholic Queen was supposed to exercise over the Protestant king under clerical guidance.

Charles I. summoned a Parliament at Oxford in 1644, consisting of such members of both Houses as were devoted

THE PARLIAMENT OF LADIES, 1644.

to his interests. There exists a satirical tract ridiculing this Parliament, and, in fact, representing it as a Parliament of old women. The tract is entitled '*An exact Diurnall of the Parliament of Laydes,*' and is illustrated with a woodcut. It sets forth that 'Countesses and other Ladies (on Monday morning early in a Prosopopia) being met in Mary Maudlins Hall in Oxford, they first made choyce of their speaker; and it was agreed by all that the Lady Oboney should have the chaire, the Lady Rivers was made Chancellor, Nurse Windham High Constable, the Countess of Derby High Treasurer, and the Countess of Essex High Chamberlain. These Ladies having all taken their places, Mrs. Powell was appointed cheefe Clerk to the House, and Mrs. Peele Chaire Lady to the Close Committee, and Moll Cut-Purse was made Sergeant at Arms.' Prince Rupert and others are tried and sentenced for various crimes, but the ladies afterwards relent, and pardon all the prisoners brought before them. I give on the preceding page a reduced copy of the rough woodcut which illustrates this curious burlesque.

A writer of much verbosity satirised the Assembly of

CARICATURE, 1644.

Divines at Westminster in another illustrated pamphlet, printed 'by Martin Claw-Clergy for Bartholomew Bang-Priest, and sold in Toleration-street, at the sign of the Subject's Liberty, opposite to Persecuting Court.' The author states on the title-page that his production displays 'many witty Synodian Conceits both pleasant and commodious,' and adorns his work with the above curious engraving, which probably had some reference to a Papal Bull, but at this distance of time we look in vain for the point and meaning of many of these old caricatures.

Having glanced at the satirical side of illustrated journalism at the epoch of the Civil War, I will quote two or three examples relating to the social and political condition of the country before entering upon the stirring events of that time.

A great variety of subjects are embraced in this section. There are accounts of apparitions, signs and portents in the heavens, monstrous births, duels and murders, criminal trials and executions, besides many tracts relating to the vices and follies of the age. One of the first illustrated pamphlets we come to in this division of our subject describes a duel fought in vindication of the good name of King Charles I. The pamphlet is entitled, '*Sir Kenelme Digby's Honour maintained by a most couragious Combat which he fought with the Lord Mount le Ros, who by base and slanderous words reviled our King. Also the true relation how he went to the King of France, who kindly intreated and sent two hundred men to guard him so far as Flanders. And now he is returned from Banishment, and to his eternal honour lives in England.*' This is a tract written by an undoubted Royalist. It begins in praise of valour, which is divided into three kinds—that which is allied to rashness, that which is born of the fear of death, and temperate or true valour. It describes how Sir Kenelme Digby was dining with a French lord, who, having toasted most of the kings of Christendom, then proposed the health of the most arrant coward in the world; and on Sir Kenelme inquiring who that was, he was told, after he had drunk the toast, that it was meant for the King of England : ' At which the good knight seemed very much discontent, knowing in what nature his Soveraigne was wronged ; yet very wisely did he seem to pass it by untill dinner being ended, then did he desire the same lord the next day to· come and dine with him, who promised him upon his honour that he would.'

The next day the French Lord repaired to Sir Kenelme's lodgings, where an entertainment befitting his rank was provided : ' Neither did Sir Kenelme seem to remember the former daies discontent, but was very frolic and merry, and in

the midst of dinner time desired them all to be bare, for he
would beginne a health to the bravest king in the world. The
French Lord asked whom that was, Sir Kenelme made answer
that when it had gone about he should know; well, about it
went and then Sir Kenelme said that it was the health of the
bravest king in the world, which is the King of England,
my royal Master, for although my body be banished from

SIR KENELM DIGBY'S DUEL, 1641.

him, yet is my heart loyally linkt; the French Lord at those
words seemed to laugh repeating the same words before
mentioned, then was Sir Kenelme throughly moved in the
behalf of our Soveraigne King Charles whereupon he whis-
pered the Lord in the eare, telling of him how that twice he
had reviled the best King in the world in the hearing of me
which am his faithful subject, wherefore for satisfaction I
require a single combate of you, where either you shall pay
your life for your sawcinesse, or I will sacrifice mine in the

behalfe of my King. The French Lord being of a resolute spirit condescended: to fight, the place was appointed, dinner being ended, they both arise from table and privately went together, being in field off they pluckt their doublets, and out they draw their weapons.

' Mars would have bashful beene to have seene himselfe by Noble Digby there excelled, long work with the contemptible French Lord, he would not make, for fear lest any should lye in ambush and so he might hazard his own life, wherefore in four bouts he run his rapier into the French Lords brest till it came out of his throat againe, which so soon as he had done, away he fled to the Court of France, and made all knowne to the King thereof, who said the proudest Lord in France should not dare to revile his brother King.

' A guard was presently chosen to conduct Sir Kenelme into Flanders, which they did, where he tooke shipping for England, where he now is, where in peace and quietnesse may he still remaine.

' As for the French Lord he was paid according to his desert, and may all be so rewarded which shall dare to revile the Lords anointed, who suffers by other Nations, for the clemency he hath shown to his own Nation, *sed beati sunt pacifici,* but blessed is the peace maker; good king for thy patience in this world there are Crownes of immortal glory laid in store for thee in the world to come, there thall not traitors dare to show their faces, nor shall perplexity proceed from the great care of ruling of a kingdome, in the meanwhile may more such Noble Digbies increase to rebuke all cursing *Achitophels* and reviling *Rabshakey's.*

' Let God arise and then shall the enemies of our gracious King be sure to be scattered.

> ' Now I conclude commanding fame to show
> Brave Digby's worthy deed, that all may know
> He lov'd his king, may all so loyal prove
> And like this Digby to their king show love.'

Many portraits of Charles I. were published in tracts

about this time.   One of the best is contained in a poetical
welcome to the King on his return from Scotland. '*King
Charles his Entertainment and Londons Loyaltie,*' 1641, contains a precept issued by the Lord Mayor, directing how the
aldermen and citizens shall meet the King, on his return
from Scotland, at Shoreditch Church, and conduct him to the
Guildhall to a banquet, and afterwards to Westminster.

CITY TRUMPETER, 1641.

There is also a a very spirited woodcut of a City trumpeter
in this pamphlet, which is copied above. City entertain-
ments to sovereigns and princes have always been fruitful
occasions for illustrated newspapers.

The wholesale executions that used to take place at this
period would astonish the modern newspaper reader. Sometimes as many as twenty-four persons were executed in one
day at Tyburn. '*A Coppy of the Prisoners judgement condemned to dy, from Nugate on Monday the* 13 *of December,*
1641,' gives an account of eight Jesuits and several other

prisoners who were executed. A descriptive list is given of the condemned, and amongst them are the following:—

' Charles James, an handsome gentile young man, was convicted for Robery and Burglary.

' John Hodskins, a fine Scholler, a pretty fellow, yet wanted grace.

' John Davis, a lusty stout personable man.

' Francis Middlefield, a pretty youth, and a good Scholler, convicted of felonie.'

Several highwaymen, horse-stealers, and coiners, are also included in this gloomy list, which is adorned with a wood-cut of an execution.

The regulation of the licensed victuallers' trade and the Sunday closing movement appear to have been as troublesome questions in the seventeenth century as they are now. As early as 1641 the publican was uttering the complaints which he still continues to utter. In a pamphlet of that date there is a dialogue between a tapster and a cook, which sets forth the grievances of both these worthies. The pamphlet is entitled, ' *The Lamentable Complaints of Nick Froth the Tapster and Rulerost the Cook, concerning the restraint lately set forth against drinking, potting, and piping on the Sabbath day, and against selling meate.*' The publican expresses himself thus:—

' I much wonder Master Rulerost why my trade should be put downe, it being so necessary in a commonwealth; why the noble art of drinking, it is the soul of all good fellowship, the marrow of a Poet's Minervs, it makes a man as valiant as Hercules though he were as cowardly as a Frenchman; besides I could prove it necessary for any man sometimes to be drunk, for suppose you should kill a man when you are drunk, you shall never be hanged for it untill you are sober; therefore I think it good for a man to be always drunk; and besides it is the kindliest companion, and friendliest sin of all the seven, for most sins leave a man by some accident or other, before his death, but this will never forsake him till the breath be out of his body ; and lastly a full bowle of strong beere will drown all sorrows.'

To which master Cook rejoins:—' Master Nick, you are mistaken, your trade is not put downe as you seem to say; what is done is done to a good intent; to the end that poor men that worke hard all the weeke for a little money, should not spend it all on the Sunday while they should be at some church, and so consequently there will not be so many Beggars.'

Froth—'Alack you know all my profit doth arise onely on Sundays, let them but allow me that privilege, and

THE COMPLAINT OF THE LICENSED VICTUALLERS, 1641.

abridge me all the weeke besides; S'foot, I could have so scowered my young sparks up for a penny a demy can, or a halfe pint, heapt with froth. I got more by uttering half a Barrell in time of Divine service, than I could by a whole Barrell at any other time, for my customers were glad to take anything for money, and think themselves much ingaged to me; but now the case is altered.'

Cook—'Truly Master Froth you are a man of a light constitution, and not so much to be blamed as I that am more solid: O what will become of me! I now think of the lusty Sirloines of roast Beefe which I with much policy divided into an innumerable company of demy slices, by which, with my provident wife, I used to make eighteene pence of that which cost me but a groat (provided that I sold it in service time,) I could tell you too, how I used my halfe cans and my Bloomsbury Pots, when occasion served; and my Smoak which I sold dearer than any Apothecary doth his Physick; but those happy days are now past, and therefore no more of that." '

This pamphlet is illustrated with a woodcut showing the Cook and Tapster in confabulation, while in the background joints are roasting, and guests are seated in boxes, refreshing themselves with ' half-cans and Bloomsbury pots.'

The abuses of the Ecclesiastical Courts did not escape the notice of the seventeenth-century pamphleteers. Doctors' Commons and the Proctors were quizzed in an illustrated pamphlet, wherein 'Sponge, the Proctor,' and 'Hunter, the Parator,' hold a long conversation, and express their opinion that the only way to make men live in quietness is to beggar them with long suits and large fees. Other evil-doers were shown up in a similar manner. A certain Edward Finch, Vicar of Christ-church, London, gave so much offence to the parishioners by his manner of life that a petition was presented to Parliament on the subject. The petitioners said they were offended by their Vicar's 'frequent and unreasonable bowings' before the altar, and by his 'scandalous life and conversation.' They set forth in the petition that they are 'troubled in their church with singing, organs, and other Instruments of Musicke, not understood by them, whereby they are greatly distracted in the service of God, the same being altogether unprofitable, and no way tending to their spirituall edification.' The Vicar is charged with drunkenness and incontinence—with exacting unreasonable fees—with being a non-resident; and the evidence in support of the petition shows that on one occasion he went to Hammersmith in a coach with certain loose companions and spent the day in a manner unfit for a clergyman. He is proved to

have attempted to administer the Sacrament to a dying
woman while he was in a state of drunkenness, and to have
been guilty of many other disgraceful acts.   The House of
Commons passed a vote of censure on this graceless Ritualist;
and the petition setting forth his misdeeds was printed and
published, illustrated with a woodcut showing the journey to
Hammersmith in a coach.   Notwithstanding the condemnation of Parliament, the Rev. Edward Finch continued in his

Ed Finch
his Perambulations.

away for hamerſmith

EVIL DOINGS OF THE REV. EDWARD FINCH, 1641.

evil courses, and conducted his 'life and conversation' much
the same as before.

From the 'perambulations' of a Ritualistic clergyman we
come to a nunnery, in a pamphlet published in 1641, entitled,
' *The Arminian Nunnery, or a briefe description and relation of
the late erected Monasticall Place, called the Arminian Nunnery
at Little Gidding, in Huntingdonshire.*'   The writer of this
pamphlet gives a minute and by no means 'brief' description
of the institution, which he evidently believes to be Roman
Catholic, or a stepping-stone to it, though the 'Deacon' who
attended him on his visit assured him to the contrary.   He,
however, sets down all the tapers and crosses, the bowings

and prostrations, as so many proofs of idolatry, and marvels
that, in a settled Church government, the Bishops should
suffer any such institutions to exist; particularly that Archbishop Laud, professing to be such an 'Anti-Papist and
enemy to superstition and idolatry, should permit this inno-
vation and connive at such canting betwixt the barke and
the tree in matter of Religion.' While censuring the prelates for their criminal slothfulness, the writer gave his
countrymen the benefit of his own acuteness and energy,
and published his description, illustrated with an engraving

NUNNERY AT LITTLE GIDDING, HUNTINGDONSHIRE, 1641.

representing one of the nuns, with a portion of the nunnery
in the background.

The next illustrated pamphlet we come to is a curious
attempt on the part of its author to satirise his literary contemporaries for the falsehoods contained in their writings,
and he burlesques their productions by relating many things
as lies which, however, he means to be understood as truths.
It is called ' *The Liar, or a contradiction to those who in the
titles of their Books affirmed them to be true, when they were
false; although mine are all true yet I term them lyes. Veritas
Veritatis.*'

' There was an Englishman which travelled to the Swedish

Army, and began to relate very strange passages which he
had seen here in England, thinking that travellers might lye
by authority; for said he in the County of Berke, at a place
called Abingdon, when the Earle of Strafford lost his head,
was such thundering and lightning, and earthquakes, that it
is almost incredible.   Surely I think it is incredible indeed,
for I know 'tis no such matter.

'He told too that the very same day that my Lord Archbishop of Canterbury was committed to the Tower, there was

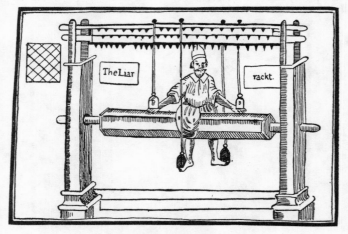

THE LIAR ON THE RACK, 1641.

a child born in the County of Somerset with a Mitre on its
head, a marke on his breast like a Crucifix, and many other
strange things which were there seene.'   Having invented
the travelling Englishman for a mouth-piece and selected the
Swedish army for an audience, the writer goes on to relate
many other strange things, which, though told as lies, are
evidently intended to be taken as truths.

'They heard him with patience till he had made an end
of his lying, and then they asked him whether yea or nay he
saw these things he spake of, he presently swore all the oaths
of God that he saw these things with his own natural eyes,

which he had reported, and he would maintaine it, though
he spent his dearest blood in the doeing of it; well, they
heard his protestations, and made a full account that they
would prove his constancie whether he would be a Martyr
yea or nay, in the meane time they horsed him, and this was
the manner of it.

'There was a great high thing raised to the height of
twelve or fourteen yards, made of Iron, whereon he was
seated, with two great weights on his toes, and the like on
his hands where he sate in great paine, if he should chance
to ease himselfe upwards, there were sharp nailes over his
head which would prick him, thus he sate and thus he suffered, till they had sufficiently made a laughing stock of
him; well, when he had suffered enough they let him
downe.'

There is a woodcut representing the lying traveller on
his 'horse,' and the tract winds up thus :—

'Gentle Reader, I have heere related under the name of
lies nothing but true tales, for if a man doth now speake
truth he shall be sure to smart for it now-a-daies, either here
or in other places : read gentlie and buy willingly.'

When the Plague visited London in 1641 the theatres
were closed and the players were thrown out of employment. This state of things is discussed in a dialogue
between 'Cane of the Fortune and Reed of the Friars,' in a
tract illustrated with a woodcut which was frequently used
afterwards in broadsides. Bartholomew Fair, which was
proclaimed for the last time in 1855, was in all its glory in
the days of Charles I. A contemporary tract gives a
graphic description of the fair, and is illustrated with a
woodcut representing a man swallowing a serpent. This
probably represented a picture hung outside one of the
shows. The title of the tract is, '*Bartholomew Faire, or
Variety of Fancies, where you may find a faire of wares and all
to please your mind; with the several enormities and mis-
demeanours which are there seen and acted.*' The fair is
described as beginning 'on the twenty-fourth day of

H

August, and is then of so vast an extent that it is contained in no lesse than four several parishes, namely, Christ Church, Great and Little Saint Bartholomew's, and Saint Sepulchre's. Hither resort people of all sorts, High and Low, Rich and Poore, from cities, townes, and countreys; of all sects, Papists, Atheists, Anabaptists, and Brownists, and of all conditions, good and bad, virtuous and vitious.' It is said to be 'full of gold and silver-drawers; just as Lent is to the Fishmonger so is Bartholomew Faire to the Pick-

A BARTHOLOMEW FAIR WONDER, 1641.

pocket; it is his high harvest, which is never bad but when his cart goes up Holborn.

'It is remarkable and worth your observation to behold and hear the strange sights and confused noise in the Faire. Here a knave in a fool's coat, with a trumpet sounding, or on a drum beating, invites you and would fain perswade you to see his puppets; there a rogue like a wild woodman, or in an Antick shape like an incubus, desires your company, to view his motion; on the other side Hocus Pocus, with three yards of tape or ribbin in's hand, shewing his art of Legerdemain, to the admiration and astonishment of a company of cockoloaches. Amongst these you shall see a gray goose cap (as wise as the rest), with a what do ye lacke in his mouth, stand in his boothe, shaking a rattle, or scraping on a fiddle, with which children are so taken, that they presently cry out for these fopperies; and all these together make such a distracted noise that you would think Babell were not comparable to it. Here there are also your gamesters in action, some turning of a whimsey, others throwing for pewter, who can quickly dissolve a round shilling into a three-halfpenny saucer. Long Lane at this time looks very faire, and puts out her best cloaths, with the wrong side outward, so turned for their better turning off. And Cloth Faire is now in great request; well fare the ale-houses therein; yet better may a man fare (but at a dearer rate) in the pig market, alias Pasty-nooke, or Pye Corner, where pigges are all hours of the day on the stalls piping hot, and would cry (if they could speak) come eate me.'

In 1641 an order of Parliament directed the removal of idolatrous pictures from churches and the demolition of crosses in the streets. It must have been on the passing of this order that ' *The Doleful lamentation of Cheapside Cross,*' with a woodcut of the Cross, was published, 1641. Also, '*A Dialogue between the Crosse in Cheap and Charing Crosse,*' 1641, which has also a woodcut representing the two crosses, while a Brownist and an Anabaptist converse about their demolition. It was not, however, till 1643 that Charing Cross and Cheapside Cross were demolished. ' *The Downfall of Dagon, or the taking down of Cheapside Crosse this second of May,* 1643,' is a mock lamentation for the destruction of the Cross on account of its being a symbol of idolatry. The Cross itself is made to describe its history and to lament its errors. Divers reasons are given for its demolition, and the tract concludes in these words: ' And so this Tuesday it is a taking down with a great deal of judgement and discretion, and foure Companies of the Traine Bands of the City to guard and defend those that are about the worke, and to keep others from domineering, and so I leave it to be made levell with the ground this second day of May 1643.' The tract is illustrated with a woodcut representing the demolition of the Cross; and, as the day of publication is the day after the event, the persons concerned in its production must have been unusually prompt and energetic. The destruction of Cheapside and Charing Crosses is also recorded, under the date of 1643, in '*A Sight of the Transactions of these latter yeares Emblemized with Ingraven Plates, which men may read without Spectacles.*'

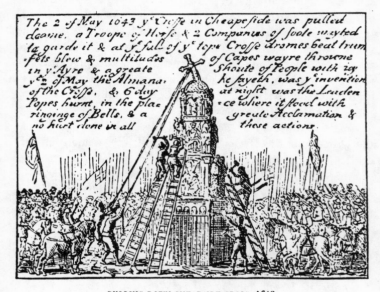

The 2 of May 1643 yᵉ Croſſe in Cheapeſide was pulled deowne. a Troope of Horſe & 2 Companies of foote wayted to garde it & at ẛ full of yᵉ topᵉ Croſſe dromes beat trum -fets blew & multitudes of Capes wayre throwne in yᵉ Ayre & a greate Shoute of People with zg ẛᵉᵈ of May the Almana· he ẛayeth, was yᵉ invention of the Croſſe. & 6 day at night was the London Popes burnt, in the plaᵉ -ce where it ẛtood with rinoinge of Bells. & a greate Acclamation & no hurt done in all these actions.

PULLING DOWN CHEAPSIDE CROSS, 1643.

This pamphlet contains a reprint of the etched plates previously mentioned, together with six others, one of which represents the pulling down of Cheapside Cross, and a summary of the transactions of the reign of Charles I., in which occurs the following passage :—'Cheapside Crosse, Charing Crosse, and all other crosses, in and about London utterly demolished and pulled down, and that abominable and blasphemous book of tolerating sports and pastimes on the Lord's daies, voted to be burnt, and shortly after accordingly burnt, together with many crucifixes and popish trinckets and trumperies in the very same place where Cheapside Crosse stood.' I have copied the plate representing the demolition of Cheapside Cross.

The affairs of Turkey would seem to have had an interest for the English public in the seventeenth century, if we may judge from a pamphlet printed in 1642, with the following lengthy title:—'*Strange and Miraculous Newes from Turkie, sent to our English Ambassadour resident at Constantinople, of a woman which was seen in the Firmament with a Book in her hand at* Medina Talnabi, *where Mahomet's Tomb is. Also several visions of armed men appearing in the Ayre for one and twenty dayes together. With a prophetical interpretation made by a Mahomedan Priest, who lost his life in the maintenance thereof. London, printed for Hugh Perry neere Ivy Bridge in the Strand June* 13, 1642.' There is a woodcut of the apparition, and a lengthy description, passages from which I have extracted:—

'There came newes to Constantinople of a strange Apparition or Vision, which was seene at *Medina Talnabi* in Arabia, whereat Mahomet their great Prophet was buried. To visit whose Tombe the Turkes used to goe in Pilgrimage, but they must first goe to *Mecha*, which is some few dayes journey off, and there they take a ticket from the Grand Seigniors Beglerbeg, else they are not allowed to go to Medina.

'This Vision continued three weeks together, which terrified the whole country, for that no man could discover the truth thereof.

'About the 20 of *September* there fell so great a Tempest and so fearful a Thunder about midnight, as the Heavens were darkened, and those that were awake were almost distracted, but the Vapours being disperst, and the Element cleere, the people might read in Arabian characters these words in the Firmament, *O Why will you believe in Lies.* Betweene two and three in the morning there was seen a woman in white compassed about with the Sun, having a cheerfull countenance, holding in her hand a

Booke, coming from the Northeast, opposite against her
were Armies of *Turkes, Persians, Arabians,* and other Ma-
hometans, ranged in order of Battaile, and ready to charge
her, but she kept her standing, and onely opened the Booke,
at the sight whereof the Armies fled, and presently all the
lamps about Mahomet's Tombe went out, for as soon as ever
the Vision vanished (which was commonly an hour before
sunne rising) a murmuring Wind was heard, whereunto they

STRANGE VISION IN THE AIR, 1642.

imputed the extinguishing of the lamps.   The antient pil-
grims of Mahomet's Race, who after they have visited this
place, never use to cut their haire, were much amazed, for
that they could not conceive the meaning of this vision, only
one of the *Dervices,* which is a strict religious order among
the *Turkes* like unto the Cappuchins amongst the Papists,
and live in contemplation, stepped up very boldly and made
a speech unto the Company which incensed them much

against him, so as the poore Priest for his plain dealing lost his life, as you shall hereafter heare.'

Then follows the speech of the Dervish to the Turks, who became so incensed that they put him to death, 'the poore man crying to the last gaspe, O thou woman with the Booke save me, and so he died. At which time there was a fearefull tempest.'

It seems to have been a favourite method amongst the Puritan pamphleteers of inducing belief in a particular creed or doctrine by setting forth the awful consequences arising from adherence to an opposite faith. Thus, in 1645, in the parish of Kirkham, a Popish gentlewoman was said to have become the mother of a child without a head, because she wished she might bear a child without a head rather than her offspring should become a Roundhead. Again, it was related that in Scotland a woman wished she might become the mother of a monster rather than her child should receive the rites of the Church of England. Accordingly, the child was born with two heads, long donkey-like ears, &c. In all these cases the pamphlets recording these extraordinary occurrences are illustrated. The apparitions of deceased persons were also used as a means of enforcing certain views. For example, in 1642, the ghosts of King James, the Marquis of Hamilton, George Eglisham, and the Duke of Buckingham, were made to hold a conversation, wherein Buckingham was charged with having caused the deaths of the others by poison. Buckingham confesses his guilt and promises to weep repentant tears. This pamphlet is also illustrated. The sermons of the Roundhead preachers were sometimes parodied, as in the case of a humorous pamphlet entitled, '*A Seasonable Lecture, or a most learned Oration; disburthened from Henry Walker, a most judicious quondam ironmonger, &c.*' There is a woodcut to this pamphlet representing a person holding forth from a tub to several others who are listening to him. In '*A Glasse for the Times*, 1648,' there is a woodcut representing the 'Orthodox true Minister' preaching in a church, while the 'Seducer, or False Prophet,' is holding forth to people in the open air; and the reader is instructed as to the difference between true ministers and false teachers.

Amongst the numerous executions that took place about the beginning of the Civil War, some of the sufferers belonged to the Roman Catholic Religion, and went to the gallows for conscience sake. In 1643 a certain Father Bell, a Romish priest, was hanged; and a few days after the execution a pamphlet was published, entitled '*The Confession, Obstinacy, and Ignorance of Father Bell, a Romish Priest, wherein is declared the manner of his Tryall, Condemnation, and Execution on Munday December* 11, 1643.' There is a woodcut of the execution of Father Bell, and an account of his behaviour on the occasion, his speech at the gallows, and his disputatious conversation with the Sheriff.

Though many persons were put to death for witchcraft during the Long Parliament, I have met with no illustrated record of any such event. Matthew Hopkins was 'witch-finder general' at this time, and he had a flourishing trade. He had a regular system for finding out witches; but it appears that it must have been called in question, for the objections to his system and his answers thereto were delivered to the Judges of Assize for the County of Norfolk in 1647. A pamphlet of that date contains a full account of Hopkins's rules for finding witches, and it is illustrated with a woodcut representing the interior of a house, with the witch-finder, two witches seated, and surrounded by their imps in the shapes of animals.

The Welsh Post of 1643 is a curious illustrated pamphlet which relates the news of the Civil War in language such as was supposed to be used by a Welshman speaking English. It begins thus:—'Whereas there hath beene many Tiurnals and Passages, the truth whereof hath beene much suspected, so tat her doth not be certaine to heare the true report of her pretherns proceeding; her hath terefore chosen to herselfe a fery true Printer (tat do scorne to print lie) to print a weekly Tiurnall for her dear Countryman of Whales to understand te fery truth marke you me tat now, for ferily her will not lye truly, but tell her to pare naked truth.' The news from Oxford is that 'te kings forces are fery weake there, and that the Countrey are fery glad of

HOPKINS, THE WITCHFINDER, 1647.

it, because of teir intollerable trouble and charge.' There is also news from Northamptonshire, Cheshire, Gloucester, Plymouth, Yorkshire, &c., all related in the same language.

The Welsh Plunderer is another pamphlet, with a woodcut of a Cavalier, which is probably intended for Prince Rupert. It contains a rambling protestation from 'Shinkin' of his loyalty, and states what he will do in case Prince Rupert should visit Wales.

William Lilly, the Astrologer, found a rich field for the exercise of his gifts during the progress of the Civil War. He was employed by both Royalists and Roundheads; and it is said he was even consulted by the King about signing the propositions of the Parliament. His advice was also sought respecting the King's projected escape from Carisbrook Castle. He kept his name before the public by publishing various almanacs and tracts, in one of which, *The Starry Messenger*, 1645, he gives an account of a strange apparition of three suns seen in London on the King's birthday. This is preceded by a long list of similar appearances, from the time of Christ to his own time, and the remarkable events which followed. In high-flown language, mixed with the jargon of astrology he vaguely hints at great events impending :—' I am clearly of opinion, These Sights, as well as many others, were caused by those tutelary Angels, who, by Gods permission, and under him, have the Government of the English Commonwealth. They are sensible of those many impending Miseries now too plentifully amongst us. Their conference with man now, as in the days of old, very few attain unto, it being a blessing sought after by many, attained unto by few : And yet there are some of opinion there lives in the world some, and of those some, a small Party in England, that know more than they utter, and either by Vision, or verball Colloquie, have the knowledge of future events, yea, even from the blessed Angels :'—which is as much as to say, I, William Lilly, am one of the favoured few ! Come to me and I will teach you wisdom—I will unfold to you the mysterious future ! The tract is illustrated with a woodcut ; and a later tract published by Lilly contains an engraving of the three suns, together with a further exposition of his views on the subject :—' God many wayes in these last times (though not by prophecy) yet discovers and signifies his intentions unto us, and especially in and at those times when his heavy judgments are imminent upon us; witnesse the many and frequent Appearances of severall Prodigies seen in this Kingdom of England within these four or five years, the like whereof for number are not recorded in any, either ancient or modern History, so that I might weary the reader, should I but mention the severall Letters which from sundry parts of this Kingdom have come to my hands, some men-

THREE SUNS SEEN IN LONDON ON THE KING'S BIRTHDAY, 1648.

tioning strange sights in the ayre; others men fighting therein; others Guns shooting; others relating of three moons; others the apparition of two suns; some sending me letters, and including therein some part of that Corn which was rained down from heaven, &c. I forbear all further discourse hereof, assuring the kingdom, these Prodigies are the Premonitions, and assumed infallible Messengers of Gods wrath against the whole Kingdom, for our wicked transgressions, &c. God give us peace and grace to repent.'

CHAPTER IV.

The Civil War—Flying Sheets of News—Disturbance at Kingston-on-
Thames—Plot against London—Riotous Proceedings at York, and
Conspiracy in Edinburgh—The House of Commons—The Royal
Standard raised at Nottingham—Battle of Edgehill—Prince Rupert
—The Lord Mayor of London—*Mercurius Civicus*—*The Scottish
Dove*—*The Flying Post*—*The Kingdomes Weekly Post*—Cruelties of
the Cavaliers—The 'Levellers'—The King's Escape from Oxford—
Funeral of the Earl of Essex—The Great Seal Broken—Fairfax—
Cromwell—Sea Fight in the Channel—The Prince of Wales's Squad-
ron—Mutiny at Norwich—Siege of Colchester—Execution of Sir
Charles Lucas—The King at Carisbrooke Castle—Execution of the
King—Confession of Richard Brandon.

THE discontent which had been growing for so many years,
and which had been strengthened and inflamed by the acts
of Charles I. and his advisers in violating the principles of
the Constitution, had now arrived at the point of rebellion.
At the commencement of the Civil War the excitement was
increased and sustained by the publication of flying sheets of
news. Although the practice of publishing regular periodical papers had commenced, numerous fugitive tracts and
pamphlets continued to be printed relating to particular
events. Some of these papers were illustrated with woodcuts evidently executed on the spur of the moment, while
others appear to have been taken from other sources and
adapted to the occasion. An example of this latter kind
occurs in a tract of 1642, which strikingly illustrates the
state of the times:—

*'A true Relation of the late Hurleyburly at Kingston upon
Thames on Wednesday the 12th of January caused by Collonell
Lundsford and the rest of his company, and the Towne fearing
they would rise up in Rebellion, one cam speedily to declare it at*

London, *upon which the Traine Band were raised and caused to watch all night for the safety of the City.'* On the title-page is a woodcut of an officer and a soldier, which, however, was evidently not executed for this special occasion, the officer being in the costume of the preceding reign. A facsimile of it is subjoined. The tract describes the commotion made in Kingston by the appearance of Colonel Lundsford and three hundred troopers, who, 'about the middle of the Towne, went in to drink, and continued there part of that day, swagger-

HURLEYBURLEY AT KINGSTON-ON-THAMES, 1642.

ing, and swearing blasphemous Oathes (which filled the Towne with feares) and some amongst the rest, to frighten the Towne, swore bitter Oathes that they should see bloody times ere long.'

A tract of the same date refers to a reported conspiracy of the same Colonel Lundsford:—'*A terrible plot against London and Westminster discovered, showing how Colonell Lunsford the Papist, that should have bin Lieutenant in the Tower, should in a Conspiracy among the Jesuits and other Papists*

*have blowne up the City of London, placing the pieces of Ordi-
nance against it.   Also how the papists with their forces should
have risen against Westminster, and burnt downe the parliament
house.   Likewise how by this Conspiracy the Arch-bishop of*
Canterbury *should have been transported into France, and how*

CAPTAIN VAUL, THAT CRUEL TYRANT, 1642.

*Bishop Wren with many other Bishops and popish Doctors
should have bin conducted with him thither, where Canterbury
should have bin Sainted, and Wren made Cardinall.   With an
exact Relation of the chiefe Cause of the Apprentices rising in
Armes to defend the City of London from their treachery, Describing most succinctly the singular mercy of God towards us in
defending this Kingdome from the manifold Plots of the Papists*

and their *Treacherous Conspiracies.*' On the last page is a
woodcut of a Cavalier in a hat and feathers, entitled 'Captaine
Vaul that cruell Tyrant.' As there is no mention of this
person in the pamphlet it was perhaps a well-known nick-
name of Colonel Lundsford. I annex a copy of this cut.
The same cut appears in a tract entitled '*Terrible Newes from
York*,' detailing certain riotous proceedings in that city, where
it is given as 'Mr. Holk, chief Agent in the uproar.' Its
first appearance, however, is in an account of a '*Bloody Conspiracy at Edinburgh;*' and, from its frequent use, this rough
woodcut must have been regarded as a good, bold representation of a truculent soldier, suitable for the times.

While the King and the House of Commons were contending for the upper hand there was published '*A Perfect
Diurnall of the Passages in Parliament,*' illustrated with a
woodcut of the House of Commons, with Mr. Speaker in the
chair. This is used as a heading to several numbers of the
same *Diurnall*, and sundry varieties of it are printed as headings to other reports of Parliament. This old woodcut has
been often copied, but my examples of illustrated journalism
would not be complete unless I introduced it here.

The printing-presses that are said to have been carried
by both armies during the Civil War must have been used
solely for the printing of Proclamations, General Orders, and
suchlike documents. It seems to be an ascertained fact that
Cromwell's soldiers set up a printing-press in Scotland, and
printed a newspaper; but it is not so certain that the armies
of Charles I. and of the Parliament issued printed 'news'
from whatever town they chanced to occupy at the time. It
does not follow that because a tract is entitled *News from
Hull* it was actually printed at that place. On the contrary,
I have found nearly all the tracts I have examined bear
the imprints of London printers. *The News from the North,
The Last printed News from Chichester*, &c., were all sent up
to London, and there printed and published.

In the words of Hume, 'The open signal of discord and
civil war throughout the kingdom' was made at Nottingham

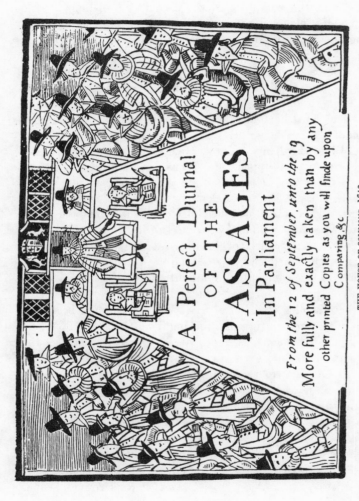

A Perfect Diurnal OF THE PASSAGES In Parliament

From the 12 of September, unto the 19
More fully and exactly taken than by any
other printed Copies as you will finde upon
Comparing, &c

THE HOUSE OF COMMONS, 1642.

on August 22, 1642, when the King erected his Royal standard and appealed to the loyalty of his subjects to support his authority by arms. Historians differ as to the precise day when this formal declaration of hostilities took place. Clarendon and Hume both fix it on the *25th* of August, while Rushworth gives the *22nd* as the date. The latter view is confirmed by a contemporary pamphlet, which gives an account of the raising of the Standard, and is illustrated with a woodcut representing the event. This pamphlet was written in the interest of the Parliament and against the King's party; but his Majesty is referred to in the most respectful language, as is generally the case in the pamphlets of the time. At the beginning of the struggle frequent hopes were expressed that the King would consent to be guided by the Parliament, while his Cavalier adherents were represented as his real enemies. The pamphlet referred to has the following title :—

'*A true and exact Relation of the manner of his Majesties setting up of His Standard at* Nottingham *on Munday the* 22 *of August,* 1642.

'*First, the forme of the Standard, as it is here figured, and who were present at the advancing of it.*

'*Secondly, the danger of setting up of former standards, and the damage which ensued thereon.*

'*Thirdly, a relation of all the Standards that ever were set up by any King.*

'*Fourthly, the names of those knights who are appointed to be the King's Standard-bearers, with the forces that are appointed to guard it.*

'*Fifthly, the manner of the Kings comming first to Coventry.*

'*Sixthly, the Cavalieres resolution and dangerous threats which they have uttered, if the King concludes a peace without them, or hearkens unto his great Councill the Parliament; moreover how they have shared and divided London amongst themselves already. London, printed for T. Coles,* 1642.'

The account of this interesting historical event is given in these words: 'Munday being the 22 of August in the

I

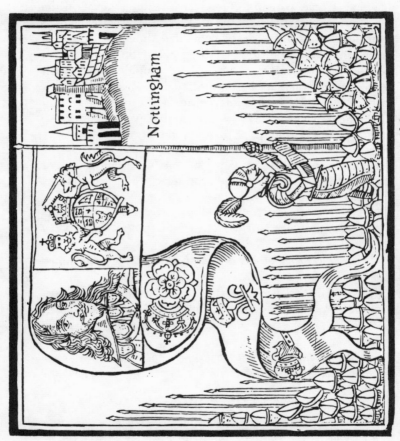

Nottingham

RAISING THE ROYAL STANDARD AT NOTTINGHAM, 1642.

morning, his Majesty left his forces before Coventry, and with some Lords and others in company rode to Leicester, where he dined that day at the Abbey House, the Countesse of Devonshire's house; however, so many printed intelligences doe falsely, though with much confidence aver (much like their other relations) that the king was with his Army in the field, at the time of the battell between them and the Lord Brookes forces, which was not untill the day following. Presently after dinner the King againe tooke horse, and with his company rode to Nottingham, where was great preparation for the setting up of the Standard that day as was formerly appointed. Not long after the Kings coming to towne, the Standard was taken out of the Castle, and carried into the field a little on the back side of the Castle wall. The likenesse of the Standard it is much of the fashion of the City Streamers used at the Lord Mayor's Show, having about 20 supporters, and is to be carried after the same way; on the top of it hangs a bloody flag, the Kings Armes quartered, with a hand pointing to the Crowne which stands above with this Motto: *Give Cæsar his due.* The names of those Knights Baronets who were appointed to beare the Standard, viz. The chiefe was Sir *Thomas Brookes*, Sir *Arthur Hopton*, Sir *Francis Wortley*, and Sir *Robert Darlington.*

' Likewise there was three troop of Horse appointed to waite upon the Standard, and to beare the same backwards and forwards with about sixe hundred foot Souldiers. It was conducted to the field in great state, his Majesty, the Prince, Prince *Robert* (whom his Majesty hath lately made a Knight of the Garter), going along with divers other Lords and Gentlemen of his Majesties traine, beside great company of Horse and Foot, in all to the number of about two thousand, who came more to see the manner of the thing than any waie to offer assistance to his Majesty, as did afterwards evidently appear, for that upon the taking downe of the Standard, there were not above thirty of the trained bands that offered to come in to his Majesty, which, because their numbers were so inconsiderable his Majesty refused to accept of.

'So soon as the Standard was set up, and his Majesty and the other Lords placed about it, a Herauld at Armes made ready to proclaim a Proclamation declaring the Ground and Cause of his Majesties setting up his Standard namely to suppress the pretended Rebellion of the Earle of Essex in raysing forces against him, to which he required the aid and assistance of all his loving subjects. But before the Trumpeters could sound to make Proclamation his Majesty called to view the said Proclamation ; which being given him he privately read the same over to himselfe, and seeming to dislike some passages therein called for Penne and Inke, and with his owne hand crossed out and altered the same in diverse places, (a thing well worthy the noting) and then gave it the Herauld, who proclaymed the same to the people, though with some difficulty after his Majesties corrections ; after the reading whereof, the whole multitude threw up their hats, with other suchlike expressions, *God Save the King.* Not long after the reading of the said Proclamation, it being towards night, the Standard was taken downe, and again carried into the castle, with the like state as it was brought into the field. And the next day it was again set up, and his Majesty came along with it, and made proclamation as the day before, and the like also was done on Wednesday, his Majesty being also present. But since that it hath been set up with lesse ceremony, there being not a hundred persons as are yet heard of that have offered themselves to his Majesty since the first setting up of his Standard.

'Since which time his gracious Majesty hath pleased to send some propositions to both Houses of Parliament ; and hath employed the Earle of Dorset, the Earle of Southampton, and Sir John Culpeper, and Sir William Uvedall to deliver his Majesties minde to the honourable Houses of Parliament for a fair Treaty and accommodation of Peace, and that all differences and mistakes might be ended, and all hostile manner of warre to cease in our Land and that it might be sent over to Ireland upon which report the Cavaliers which are about the Country are very desperate to heare that his

Majesty will hearken to an accommodation of peace, or to apply or comply with his Parliament ; telling his Majesty that it is dishonourable to stoop to his Subjects, and if his Majesty doth, they will either hang themselves, or kill and murther themselves, and doth vow private revenge to this Kingdome, if they do now misse of their hopes and enterprises, for they say they are sure to overcome us whom they called Roundheads, and call our Souldiers nothing else but a company of Shrove-Tuesday boyes, and idle headed prentices, who run away from their Masters under pretence of having this opportunity to get liberty from their hard service and cruelty. It is truly reported that the Cavaliers are all desperately bent against the City of London, and the inhabitants; they have already within themselves shared and divided it ; some have allotted to themselves Gracious Street, others Lumbard Street, then others have shared Cheapside, and Pauls-Church-yard, others do determine to seize upon the rich Aldermens houses and Persons, others to whom they owe or are indebted to by bond, or bill, or book, doe resolve when they come into the City to seize upon those persons first, to whom they are indebted, and to cut their throats, and then to seize upon Usurer or others, and to cut his throat for that money, so say they, we shall be both at once out of debt and have money to boot ; these are the resolutions of the Cavaliers who doth but looke for such an advantage, so full of cruelty and malice they are, which God in his infinite and blessed mercy protect both our King and Kingdome from ; and that their own swords may returne into their own bosoms that wish and long for such a day.'

Then follows a notification from both Houses of Parliament that none shall proclaim the setting up of the King's Standard ; and whoever shall suffer loss or damage through the Cavaliers shall receive reparation.

According to Clarendon, the Royal Standard was set up under the most ill-omened and depressing circumstances : ' There was not one regiment of foot yet brought hither, so that the train-bands which the sheriff had drawn together

were all the strength the King had for his person and the
guard of the Standard. There appeared no conflux of men
in obedience to the proclamation; the arms and ammunition
were not yet come from York, and a general sadness covered
the whole town. The Standard was blown down the same

PRINCE RUPERT, GENERAL OF THE KING'S HORSE, 1643.

night it had been set up, by a very strong and unruly wind,
and could not be fixed again in a day or two, till the tempest
was allayed. This was the melancholy state of the King's
affairs when the Standard was set up.'

Soon after the King had unfurled his Standard at Nottingham the battle of Edgehill was fought, and an illustrated
tract relates how the inhabitants of Kenton, a village near
the battle-field, were disturbed at night by strange noises and
the appearance of apparitions after the battle. The name of

Prince Rupert begins to appear in the narratives of events, and his portrait frequently occurs in the illustrated sheets of this period. This dashing and impetuous Cavalier, whose rash courage excited the admiration of the Royalists, was regarded by the Roundheads as a cruel and bloodthirsty enemy, and he was often denounced by the Puritan preachers. In 1643 there was a pamphlet published called ' *The Bloody Prince ; or, a Declaration of the Most Cruell Practises of Prince Rupert and the rest of the Cavaliers in fighting against God and the true Ministers of his Church.*' Facing the title is a woodcut representing Prince Rupert on his charger, with the towns of Birmingham and Daventry in the background, both of which places were the scenes of conflict during the war, the former having been taken, partially burnt, and a heavy fine inflicted on the inhabitants by Prince Rupert.

The City of London having taken the side of the Parliament, was naturally inclined to honour its chief magistrate when he was found to be an active and energetic promoter of its views. Isaac Pennington was Lord Mayor in 1643, and his portrait was published in a laudatory pamphlet, entitled '*A True Declaration, and just Commendation of the great and incomparable care of the Right Honourable Isaac Pennington.*' His Lordship is styled the Atlas of the city, bearing the weight and management of all civil affairs on his shoulders, and he is much commended for his great care in superintending the building of the fortifications round London under the direction of the Parliament. 'And herein,' says the writer, ' your honour hath shewed yourselfe an excellent Magistrate complying with the Parliament in all matters that concerne the publicke administration of the Commonweale ; so that you have lookt upon the present state of this Citie and Religion with the cleare eye of justice; you have heard of the great pressures which the country hath endured by the cruelty of the Cavaliers ; you have to the discouragement of malignants on the shoulders of fortitude, bore and suffered their false aspersions . . . . Your Honour hath in your present Magistracie walked uprightly, having clean and pure hands; nay, strong hands; for your Honour hath been the

chiefest raiser and promoter of the workes and fortifications
round about the Citie of London: you saw the times were
dangerous, and that the King's Cavaliers gaped after nothing
more than to get London, and make it a prey to the supplying

ISAAC PENNINGTON, LORD MAYOR OF LONDON, 1643

of their necessities.'   I have copied the portrait of the
man who was thus distinguished by his fellow-citizens, not
merely as an example of illustrated news, but as showing
what a Lord Mayor of London looked like in Charles I.'s
time.

It was in the City of London, and during the second
year of the Civil War, that the first illustrated newspaper
came into existence. *The Weekly News* had attempted on

only one occasion to illustrate the news of the day, but the *Mercurius Civicus* frequently gave illustrations, and it is therefore entitled to be ranked as the first illustrated newspaper. It is true that most of the engravings it contains are portraits, and sometimes the same woodcut is used to represent more than one person. Besides portraits of the King and Queen, there are portraits of the chief generals and commanders engaged in the war. There are Prince Rupert, the Lord General, Sir Thomas Fairfax, the Marquis of Huntley, Sir Edward Deering, General Lesley, Lord Inchiquin, Lord Digby, Sir W. Waller, the Earl of

CHARLES I. AND HIS QUEEN, FROM ' MERCURIUS CIVICUS,' 1643.

Warwick, and others. *' The Mercurius Civicus, London's Intelligencer, or Truth impartially related from thence to the whole kingdom, to prevent misinformation, from Thursday July 13 to Thursday July 20, 1643,'* is the full title of No. 8; and it is curious to notice ·how nearly a portion of the title— *London's Intelligencer*—corresponds to the *London News.* It was a peculiar feature of the early newspapers that they were announced as being published ' to prevent misinformation,' or for the ' correction of false reports'—not so much for the diffusion of truth as for the correction of falsehood.

On the front page of Number 8 of the *Mercurius Civicus* are small portraits of Charles I. and his Queen, engraved on wood. Over the woodcut is a sort of table of contents, thus:—' The King and Queen conjoyned, the Kentish news related, our Forces are united, A publique Fast appointed.' On the preceding page is given a facsimile of the cut of the King and Queen.

Similar portraits occur in other numbers, as well as several ornamental letters; but there is in Number 11 a

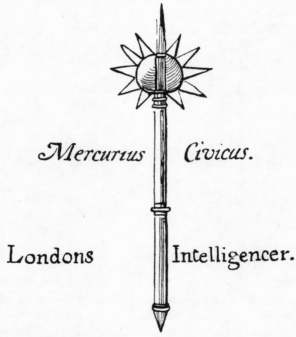

Mercurius   Civicus.

Londons   Intelligencer.

WEAPON CALLED A ROUNDHEAD, FROM 'MERCURIUS CIVICUS,' 1643.

very interesting illustration of the news of the hour.   It is a woodcut of a weapon said to be intended for use against the Roundheads, and the following account is given of it:—' In the Danish Ship lately taken by the Earle of Warwicke, near Newcastle, were found Armes compleat for 5000 foot and for 500 horse, 500 barrels of Gunpowder, Great store of Match and Lead, beside a thousand of those weapons which the Papists call Round-heads, for that with them they intended to bring the Round-heads into subjection. Many such weapons were long since found in divers Papists' houses in Lancashire; it is a weapon with an ovall or round top, stuck full of iron spikes. The forme whereof for better satisfaction is here set downe.' Then follows a representation of the weapon, of which a facsimile is given on the opposite page. The same cut is reprinted in other numbers.

In another number it is related that ' the Manchestrians have lately taken from severall Papists in that County many desperate weapons which they call Round-heads.' No. 22

PORTRAIT OF PRINCE RUPERT, FROM ' MERCURIUS CIVICUS,' 1644.

has a portrait of a Cavalier in hat and feather, intended probably for Prince Maurice, as there is in the body of the number an allusion to a report of his death. In No. 42 there is a portrait of Prince Rupert and the following summary on the title-page:—' Prince Rupert's forces routed near Stratford-on-Avon. Generall King's Army dispersed by the Scots. Himselfe wounded and fled to Yorke. Banbury Castle besieged by Colonell Cromwell.' I give a copy of Prince Rupert's portrait, which is made to do duty for the Marquis of Newcastle in another number. This practice of making the same woodcut pass for the portraits of different individuals savours somewhat of impudence on the part of the editor, and shows a cool reliance on the good nature or the obtuseness of his readers.

In the number of the *Mercurius Civicus* for April 11, 1644, there is a curious woodcut representing the 'Oxford Junta in Council,' with the following paragraph referring to it :—' The news from his Excellencies generall Roundezvous at Ailsbury on Good-Fryday next, will no doubt cause the Oxonian Papists to whip themselves before the time, and to make the Oxford Junto to recall their late votes.' The lady and gentleman in the balcony were probably intended for

THE OXFORD JUNTA IN COUNCIL, FROM 'MERCURIUS CIVICUS,' 1644.

the King and Queen. There is more variety in this number of *Mercurius Civicus* than in any I have seen. In the war news there is the taking of Waltam House, in Hampshire ; the taking of numerous men and horses at Christchurch, in Dorsetshire ; then comes a paragraph stating that ' On Munday last, April 8, there were ten men and two women executed at Tyburne for the severall offences for which they were condemned the last weeke at the Sessions in the Old Bayley.' Mention is made of a fight between the Scots Army and the Marquis of Newcastle's forces near Hilton ; the gathering of the King's forces in the neighbourhood of Marlborough, and an announcement that the Parliament intend to draw all their forces together, and, if possible, by fighting a decisive action 'to put a speedy end to these miserable distractions.' The trial of Archbishop Laud was at this time going on, and reference is made to his appearance before the House of Peers. Two Welshmen were taken into custody for talking in Welsh, while they were crossing the river from Westminster to Southwark, about firing the city in several places, they not knowing that the waterman understood their language. It is stated that a solemn day of thanksgiving had been observed in London for the victory obtained over Sir Ralph Hopton's forces, and an ordinance was read in the churches exhorting the citizens to contribute all their strength to bring the contest to a final issue. There is also some account of recent fires in the city, which are attributed to the treachery of Cavaliers and Malignants. 'But,' says the writer, 'which way soever these sad accidents are brought to passe, they may afford the whole City this caution : that if the firing of some few houses be so dreadful and fearfull, as I am sure this appeared to those that beheld them, notwithstanding they had all means convenient to quench them, and the multitude being industrious to set their hands to the worke : O how terrible would it be to see your houses set on fire by the enemy, and the cruell souldiers, instead of bringing buckets of water, should stand with their drawne swords threatening the death of those that should offer to quench the flame ? Poore Ireland can give ample testimony of this.' From Yorkshire there is news that Fairfax had taken Cawood Castle ; from Banbury that the Royalist garrison was withdrawn from that place, and 'that the Carriers of Banbury and Southam were robbed the last weeke neere Tossiter in Northamptonshire by divers of the Cavaliers Forces.' In the number for April 25, 1644, there is a figure of the King armed with a sword, and with this inscription :—'Fire and sword again menaced by his Majesty.' During the first years of the Civil War the newspapers contained many portraits of the King, some of which were carefully engraved on copper.

It is noticeable that the *Mercurius Civicus* and other

papers published during the Civil War were in the habit of
including on their title-pages a summary of the contents of
the number. Sometimes it was put in the form of rhyme, as—

> ' Tewkesbury is taken
> Yorke walls are well shaken.'

HEADING TO THE ' SCOTTISH DOVE,' 1644.

The *Scottish Dove* frequently indulged in these rhyming
summaries. On the title-page of Number 39 for July 13,
1644, the following lines are printed :—

> ' Rupert and Newcastle wholly Routed
> Rupert and Newcastle's jarres undoubted ;
> Newcastle fled to Sea, Rupert to the King,
> Give God the Glory heavenly praises sing.
> A day of thankes the parliament hath set,
> Lord Gray with some of Hasting's troops hath met.
> From Oswestree Middleton the siege did raise
> And Barnstaples defence, doth Essex praise ;
> The Queen Pendennis Castle liketh best.
> The King uncertain where to take his rest.'

The *Scottish Dove* was a small quarto numbered and paged consecutively like the *Mercurius Civicus*. On the front page of every number was printed a woodcut of a dove bearing an olive-branch in its mouth, and at the side of the woodcut was usually printed the rhyming summary. I annex a facsimile of this heading.

Many of the journals of this period showed their hankering after illustrations by occasionally indulging in an initial letter, if they could do nothing more. The animosities of party often caused them to forget their original purpose of spreading true intelligence, and they were quite as ready to apply the lash to each other as to chastise public wrongdoers or 'correct false reports.' At this time first appeared the familiar newspaper heading of the man on horseback blowing a horn. It was on the front page of the *Flying Post*, the first number of which was published on May 10, 1644. The full title was ' *The Flying Post, conveying Weekly Packets to all Forraigne Nations, of the Proceedings of both Houses of Parliament and the Armies in Great Brittain,*' and it was ' published for the cleere satisfaction of all Forraigners and others who desire Certain, and Weekly Information.' The introduction is as follows :—

' Gentlemen,—The too many errours committed of late time, by the irregularitie of the Presse (which since by the wisdome of the Parliament, is in a great measure suppressed), which did run Weekly in severall channels to the greatest part of Europe in great dishonour to our English Nation ; Have enforced this my Flying Post never to make stay, till it had intimated the same unto you, and fully vindicated this my Native Kingdome, by publishing a certain Weekly Intelligence of all Proceedings of our honourable Parliament and unhappy wars of this Kingdome; wherein (though a well wisher to his Excellencie the Earle of Essex, and the Proceedings of Parliament) I shall write with the greatest indifference, truth, and modestie, as shall satisfie the impartiallest that reades me; attributing to the Enemy no otherwise than Truth will warrant it, be it to their honour or shame according to their demerit. Therefore give me leave to beg your credence beyond Sea and elsewhere, as you find me.'

The *Flying Post* gives intelligence from York, then besieged by the Scots; from Hull, Newark, and Mansfield; some notes of the proceedings in Parliament, respecting which the journalist says cautiously :—'As for our proceedings in Parliament, I shall be very cautious and tender in divulging them.' It was 'Published according to order,' and printed at London for Bernard Alsop, 1644.

HEADING TO THE 'KINGDOMES WEEKLY POST,' 1644.

The *Kingdomes Weekly Post* had the same heading, which is here copied.

In a tract entitled '*Strange true and lamentable news from Exeter and other parts of the Western Countreys*' there is a woodcut of a woman on her knees praying for mercy. The pamphlet relates the cruelties inflicted by the Cavaliers on the inhabitants of Exeter, Bristol, and other towns. Prince Maurice is charged with breaking the articles of agreement made with the city of Exeter, and both he and Prince Rupert are likened to 'Tigers or Savage Beares.' It is stated that in the city of Exeter 'the rude Souldiers would not forbeare upon the least discontent given to them to

draw their Rapiers upon the Citizens, and wound them,
but especially when they are in their cups, they swagger,
roare, sweare, and domineere, plundering, pillaging, or
doing any other kind of wrong ; to break shops and
houses they count as nothing, taking away Boots, Shoes,
Stockings, Hats, or any other commodities they can lay
their hands on, and no Justice dares to resist them, and by
this means the City is in such a miserable condition that
they are even terrified to the death.' At Cirencester,

STRANGE NEWS FROM EXETER, 1643.

having entered the town by force, they slew all the men
who opposed them, took the unresisting inhabitants prisoners, and pillaged the town. At Bristol ' They went into
some Cellars, where was plenty of wine and beere, drank
what their gormandising guts would hold, and let the rest
run about the house, with many other antique tricks that
they used, which I cannot omit to speak of; moreover, they
breake the Covenant which was made in every respect the
very first hour that they entered the city, and fell to plundering, pillaging, robbing, stealing, cutting and slashing, as
if they had never been brought up to any other practice.'

K

In an account of the defence of Plymouth against the Royalists there is a very elaborate map showing the fortifications of the town, ' with the workes and approaches of the enemy at the last siege.' The account of the siege is very long, but the following passage may be quoted :—' One remarkable passage of God's providence to us we must with all thankfulnesse remember and acknowledge, that after the Towne had been a long time strictly beseiged and no fresh victuall either flesh or fish could be had, whereby the poore people were grievously punished, there came in an infinite multitude of Pilchards into the Harbour, within the Barbican, which the people took up with great ease in baskets, which did not only refresh them for the present, but a great deal more were taken, preserved, and salted; whereby the poore got much money ; such a passage hath not happened before.

' We cannot forget the humanity of the good women of Plymouth, and their courage in bringing out strong waters, and all sorts of provisions in the midst of all our skirmishes for refreshing of our souldiers, though many shot through the cloathes.'

I have already made the remark that the military atrocities of recent times were equalled, if not exceeded, during the Civil War in England and Ireland. In a tract of 1644, containing various items of news, the following woodcut is given as an illustration of recent events. The same woodcut is found in another tract entitled ' *Terrible and bloody Newes from the disloyall Army in the North :*'—' The proceedings of the Scots and Irish appears more visible and inhumane than formerly ; their actions are tyrannical, their ways most insufferable, and executeth nothing but blood thirstinesse and cruelty tending only to utter ruin and desolation ; they have burned down divers stately buildings in these parts, executed some of my Lord Wharton's tenants, and threatens others, which causeth the Country to rise and joyn with Lieu. Gen. Cromwell, insomuch that there will be a sudden engagement.

The sect called the ' Levellers ' is thus alluded to in the same tract :—' Colonel Martin's approach with his Levellers in these parts hath alarmed the Country and put themselves into a posture to receive them, and for preservation of their ancient rights and liberties against their new design of levelling, who by their strange, politick, and subtill delusions have wrought into the hearts of divers people to ingage with them, especially among those who are of a desperate fortune, and mean condition, the basest and vilest of men resorting to them. They rob and plunder exceedingly wheresoever they come, saying they will levell all sorts of people, even from

CRUELTIES OF THE CAVALIERS, 1644.

the highest to the lowest, and that he that hath the most shall be equall with him that hath the least.'

In a pamphlet relating to the events of Charles I.'s reign there are some of the etchings previously noticed, together with nine others illustrating the history of the same period. They are:—1. The Court of High Commission and Star Chamber. 2. The Execution on Tower Hill of Sir Alexander Carew, Sir John Hotham, Captain Hotham, and the Archbishop of Canterbury. 3. The King's Escape from Oxford. 4. The Execution of the Duke of Hamilton, Earl of Cambridge, Earl of Holland, and Arthur Lord Capel. 5. The Coronation of Charles II. in Scotland, 1650. 6. A Meeting of Cavaliers. 7. A Seapiece illustrating Charles II.'s Escape from England after the Battle of Worcester. 8. Reading the Act of General Pardon and Oblivion, 1651. 9. The House of Commons in Session. The full title of the pamphlet is as follows :—'*A Brief Review of the most material Parliamentary Proceedings of this present Parliament, and their Armies, in their civil and Martial Affairs, which Parliament began the third of November, 1640, and the remarkable Transactions are con-*

ESCAPE OF CHARLES I. FROM OXFORD, 1646.

tinued untill the Act of Oblivion February 24, 1652. Published as a Breviary, leading all along successively, as they fell out in their several years. So that if any man will be informed of any remarkable passage, he may turne to the year and so see in some measure in what Moneth thereof it was accomplished. And for information of such as are altogether ignorant of the rise and progress of these times, which things are brought to pass that former ages have not heard of, and after ages will admire. A work worthy to be kept in Record, and communicated to Posterity. London : Printed for Tho. Jenner at the South Entrance of the Royal Exchange.' From the above I have copied the etching of the escape of Charles I. from Oxford.

It is stated by Hume that when the King escaped from Oxford he was accompanied by two persons only—Dr. Hudson and Mr. Ashburnham—and that he rode before a portmanteau and called himself Ashburnham's servant. The engraving scarcely corresponds with this account; but the scene represented is evidently outside the city of Oxford, and other persons may then have joined the King's party.

The city of Oxford surrendered to the Parliament on June 24, 1646, the King having signed a warrant for the surrender fourteen days previously. This event is recorded in a pamphlet entitled '*Good Newes from Oxford of the Treaty for the Surrender thereof, and how they are packing up to march away on Thursday next, June* 18, 1646.' The 'march away,' however, was not accomplished till the 24th. Amongst those who left the place were Prince Rupert and Prince Maurice, and the King's second son, James, the young Duke of York. The illustration to this pamphlet has no relation to the event, and was used on other occasions.

The funeral of the Earl of Essex, the Parliamentary General, who died in 1646, was made the occasion of a great display of pomp and ceremonial magnificence, which was duly chronicled and illustrated by the journalists of the time. '*The true manner and forme of the proceeding to the Funerall of Devereux, Earl of Essex,*' contains, besides a copperplate portrait of the Earl, numerous woodcuts of banners, and the funeral canopy. Several illustrated broadsides relating to this event were also published. In looking over the old newspapers we are frequently reminded of the truth of the saying that 'history repeats itself.' The Duke of Wellington's funeral in 1852 was a repetition, on a much more splendid scale, of the funeral of the Earl of Essex in 1646, with such differences as arose from the taste and circumstances of the time. Portraits of the Earl of Essex are of frequent occurrence in the pamphlets of this period.

In the pamphlet containing the escape of the King from Oxford there is an etching of the burning of the Book of Sports on the site of Cheapside Cross, which is thus de-

scribed:—' 10 of May the Booke of Sportes upon the Lords
Day was burned by the Hangman in the place where the
Crosse stoode and at Exchange.'   There is also in the same
pamphlet a representation of breaking the Great Seal:—
' The Great Seale broken before the Lords and Commons,
on Tuesday, the 11 of August, 1646.'   Some authorities say
the Great Seal was not broken till January, 1649, new style.

Sir Thomas Fairfax succeeded the Earl of Essex as commander of the Parliamentary army, and had Oliver Cromwell

THE GREAT SEAL BROKEN, 1646.

for his Lieutenant-General.   Though a Presbyterian, he suffered himself to become the tool of the Independent party,
and followed the councils of Cromwell until the Army had
become master both of the Parliament and of the kingdom.
All that related to a person of so much importance must
have had uncommon interest for the popular mind, and
accordingly we find Sir Thomas Fairfax and his military
council form the subject of an engraving in a pamphlet of
1647.   It is entitled ' *The manner of His Excellency Sir Thomas
Fairfax and the officers of his Army sitting in Council.*'   In this
engraving it will be seen that Fairfax, though farthest

removed from the spectator, is made the largest figure in the picture, apparently for the purpose of giving him proper importance. Note also the huge pens, and the mysterious way in which the foreground figures appear to grow *out* of the benches instead of sitting *on* them.

SIR THOMAS FAIRFAX AND HIS MILITARY COUNCIL, 1647.

Though Cromwell was at this time the real director of the army, and ere long became its acknowledged head, I have met with no representation of him in the illustrated news of the period. The art of 'interviewing' had not then been developed, and the 'Special Artist' did not exist. The most enterprising correspondent would probably have hesitated to intrude upon that stern and resolute leader of a revolutionary army, if he had no better excuse than to describe how he looked and what he said. Fancy the Special Artist of the *Mercurius Civicus*, for instance, sending in his card to Oliver Cromwell with a polite request that the General would give him five minutes of his valuable time for the purpose of making a sketch for the next number of his journal! And fancy how the uncomely countenance of the *ci-devant* brewer would redden at the request, and how, probably, the unlucky artist would be consigned to the custody of the sentinel at the door!

There is not much said about naval matters in the newspaper chronicles of the Civil War. The earliest account of a sea-fight that I have met with occurs in a pamphlet published in 1647. It is illustrated with a woodcut representing ships of war in action—which woodcut, by-the-by, afterwards appears in other pamphlets. The narrative is in the form of a letter, dated at sea, off Dover, May 4th, 1647; and, as the pamphlet is dated May 10th, we have another example of the extreme eagerness of the news-writers to supply the public with early intelligence. The combatants were not at war, and the fight appears to have arisen out of a mere question of naval etiquette. The following account is given of the transaction:—

'A full Relation of a late Sea-Fight, betwixt the Parliament Ships and the Queene of Sweathlands, upon the Coast of England, neere Portsmouth, May 1.

'Sir,

'On the 2 of this instant moneth, being the Lords day, our Commander in chiefe of the Sea Forces, received a packet from a small Frigat, that came from the Rear-Admirall who had been in Fight the day before with five of the Queen of Swethlands ships, which they conveyed, being all laden with salt from Tubey in Portingale.

'The reason of the fight was, the Swedish ships wore flags, viz., Admirall, Vice-Admirall, and Rear-Admirall, which they refused to take in, or to low their top-sales (although commanded by Cap. Owen, Capt. of the Parliaments Reare-

Admiral so to do) whereupon the said Capt. Owen gave them a broadside, insomuch that divers shots past betweene them, and great execution done upon the Switzers, scouring their upper decks with small shot severall times. Captain Owen lost not above 8 men, besides some few wounded, the fight continued sixe hours, til night began to aproach, where the Swedish Fleet tooke their opportunity, and got away. But so soon as Vice-Admirall Batten* heard of it, he set saile with the St. Andrew, Garland, Convertine, and Mary-Rose, and stood over for the coast of France in the night; and in the morning about 8 of the clock, being the 3 of May near Bulloign, he came up with the Admiral of the Swedes ship whose names was Martin Tysin, the ship was called the Leopard and had 32 guns; the Vice-Admiral Daniel John-son, a lusty stout ship, called the Angel Raphael, and had 24 guns; the Rear-Admiral the Neptune, Moris Cook Captain, with 18 guns; the other two ships of 22 guns apiece, one being called the Anne-Free, the other the Neptune.

'The Captaines of all these ships, hee commanded aboard, and asked them what they had done with his Rear-Admiral; they at first denied that they saw him, but he pressing it so hard upon them, at length confessed, that they had been in fight with him, and that the reason was, because they would not take in their flags, being so commanded by their Queen, and had instructions to that purpose, which he caused them to send for, and took copies of them, which appeared to be true in a high manner.

'And they further told our Commander Vice-Admiral Batten, that they would rather die in honour, than to go home and be hanged, for disobeying their commissions; a brave resolution, and I could wish it were imprinted in the hearts of all our commanders; they further told him, that if

---

* There is an Admiral Batten often mentioned by Pepys. If this is the same man who was an active commander under the Parliament he must have trimmed his sails well to hold a place in the Navy office under Charles II.

these flaggs were then abroad, they would die before they made one shot at him, though he shot never so many at them, yet would not take them in, and indeed were very respective to him. But they did much blame the Rear-Admiral, for that all the shot he made was at their Vice-Admiral and Rear-Admiral, and not at their Admiral, whom he ought first to have commanded, the others being subordinate to his commands; and although he was 4 or 5 hours by the Admirals side never shot gun at him, but sent his Boat 3 times aboard. Our Vice-Admiral demanded of them, where the Rear-Admiral left them, they told him off Beachey which to him did seem strange, that he should begin a quarrell and not follow them, till he came neer where the Vice-Admiral was, having sent a Frigot to him, to give him intelligence, and might undoubtedly expect his relief.

'All Munday was spent in taking of Examinations, and Copies of Commissions; the Swedish Commanders being detained aboard by our Vice-Admiral as prisoners, but used with great civilitie.

'At length a Councell of Warre was called by our Commander in chiefe with his Captaines, the result whereof was, that the Swedes Vice-Admiral, who had been the man which was most active was with his ship to be carried into the Downes, till the pleasure of the Parliament be further known which was done accordingly, and the next day we arrived in the Downes, being the 4. instant; the rest of the Swedes in regard of their shortness of Victuall, and having charge of the Convoy, were left to their own dispose, and this was performed without shooting so much as a Musket; but truly, if the Queene of Swethland leave not out that peremptory command in her instructions, not to strike to any of our Commanders, enjoyned to keep the Sovereignty of the Seas, and to expect homage from all, even to sinking, or burning, this must in time breed ill-bloud between the two Kingdomes, which might be wisht might be prevented, by a letter from our Parliament to the Queen of Swethland.   Thus

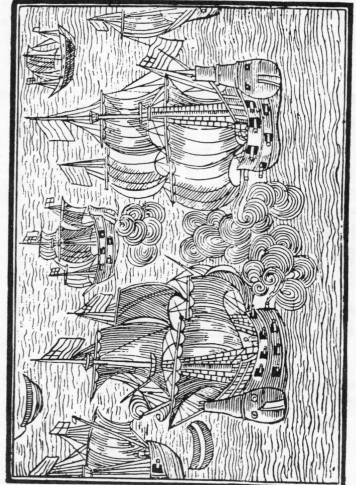

NAVAL BATTLE, 1647.

have I given you a perfect Relation of the whole proceedings.
Sir, I have not else at present, but to let you know, I am
your most humble servant and kinsman,   'R. B.

'Dated at Sea off Dover the 4. of May 1647.'

Another piece of illustrated news bearing upon naval
affairs is entitled, '*News from the Royall Navie, Colchester, and
Portsmouth, declaring the proceedings and intentions of the
Prince of Wales, &c.*'

THE PRINCE OF WALES'S SQUADRON, 1648.

'We have received intelligence from the *Brill* in Holland,
that his Highness the Prince of Wales since his arrival there
hath embarked himself in a great Vessell for England, the
Earl of Newcastle, the Lord Gerhard, the Lord Culpepper,
and divers others Lords and Gentlemen, being now floating
upon the Neptune Seas towards the North of England,
accompanying of his Royall person; we hear that they
intend to land about Berwick, or else on the South side of
the Holy-Island, and to march in the Van of the English
Army. It is likewise said that divers Scottish Lords hath
been with his Highnesse, and have treated with his Councell
declaring the grounds and reasons of their engagement with

England, and their resolution to redeem their dread Sovereign from imprisonment, to re-invest His Royall Person, and to make both him and His Posterity happy, and so Peace and Unity may flourish throughout all His Majesties Realms and Dominions. Severall urgent invitations were also presented to his Highness for his speedy and personal appearance in the North of England. The like to the Duke of York for his hastening with the Royal Navie towards the Downs, which unexpectedly is now come to pass; for we hear that the Prince with a great number of Royalists are sayled from the Brill in Holland towards the North of England, and that the Duke is come upon the Downs with a great and numerous Fleet, consisting of about 10 of the Kings great ships, and 30 Flemings, but they have not meddled on either side as yet; six of the Dukes ships, on Saturday last strook sayle before the town and Castle of Deal, and by their churlish tokens they sent us made it appear what they were, for they shot very neer 100 great Pieces at us, which killed 8 or nine of our men.'

This account is illustrated with the woodcut on the opposite page.

Some of the rough woodcuts to be found in many of the Civil War tracts would be unworthy of notice, did they not show the constant efforts that were made to illustrate the news of the hour. Such is the illustration to a tract entitled, *'A true Relation of the late Great Mutiny which was in the City of Norwich April* 24, 1648.' This gives an account of the explosion of ninety-eight barrels of gunpowder, whereby 200 mutineers were slain, and the woodcut is intended to show the effects of the explosion.

Bloody News from the Scottish Army contains a woodcut representing two men on horseback charging each other. The description gives an account of the advance of the Scottish army on the English near Penrith, intending to surprise the latter; 'but by the vigilance of our scouts they were discovered.' After a 'furious conflict gallantly maintained on both sides, we gained ground, and beat them out of the field. This action happened upon Sunday morning last about 2 of the clock in the morning.'

During the last struggles between the Parliamentarians and the Royalists, the latter, under Lord Goring, were driven into Colchester by Fairfax, and there besieged for

EXPLOSION AT NORWICH, 1648.

more than two months. There are several pamphlets detailing incidents of this siege, one or two of which are illustrated. One of them is in the form of a letter to the writer's brother, and it has a quaint woodcut of ' Colchester Leaguer.'

Another tract, dated July 27, 1648, is entitled '*A great Fight at Colchester upon Tuesday night last, being the 25 of this instant July, and the advancing of General Lucas and his forces to the very Guards of the Parliamenteers, with the particulars of the Fight, and the number that were killed and taken prisoners on both sides, and the springing of a Mine to blow up part of the Leaguer. Likewise a letter from Colchester concerning the marching of an Army to London. And Message from Prince Charles to Gen. Lucas. And a bloudy Fight at Deal Castle in Kent. London. Printed for R. Woodus, and are to be sold at the Royall Exchange in Cornhill*, 1648. The letter describing this fight contains so much curious matter that it is worth transcribing entire :—

'Sir, we have received information from Yarmouth, Harwich, and other places, that there is great fear of the Prince of Wales landing in those parts with a very considerable Army, and that he is resolved to advance towards Colchester,

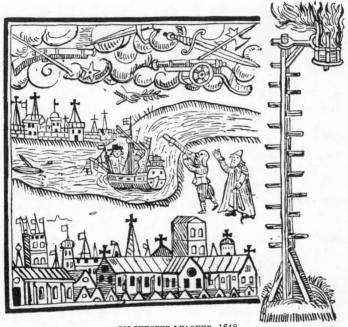

COLCHESTER LEAGUER, 1648.

to raise the siege, and to let those Birds at liberty, which he esteems to be the only instruments to advance his Father's Cause. We hear that the L. Gerrard is designed Lieutenant Generall of the new Eastern Army, and the Lord Culpepper Major Generall, and that his Highnesse will repose no trust in either of the Princes Rupert or Maurice, or any other Foreign Personage whatsoever. This morning a Corporall of a troop of horse deserted the Colchestrian service, and humbly submitted himself to the Lord Generall, who upon

examination touching their numbers and victualling said
that the last Muster Rolls made mention of above 6000
Horse and Foot, and for victualling, they had plenty of Rye
and bread-corn, but for flesh-meat they had none at all left,
being constrained to kill Horses to satisfie their hungry
appetites, which causeth many of the young Soldiers to
desert their hard commons.

'He further said, that at the last Muster upon Munday
last the E. of Norwich and Sir Charles Lucas rode to the
head of each Regiment, and read a paper to the Soldiery
(which they said was a Message from the Prince of Wales)
intimating that his Highnesse were resolved immediately to
land his Forces about Yarmouth, and from thence to march
downe to Colchester to raise the siege, and set them at
liberty, and that if they could but hold out till Satterday, he
doubted not of the day, and should take it as an acceptable
service from them.

'But I conceive the truth of this to be as palpable falsehood as the late report of the Royalists in these parts, who
would not stick to say, *that Colchester was relieved by the ship
called the Swallow, and that they shot in above 500 Holland
cheeses out of Mortar pieces &c.*

'Some who are come out of the Town reports that the
enemy within are springing a Mine, and doth intend to blow
up the Lord Lucas his house (in our possession) which doth
very much annoy them; their great Ordnance plaid very
hard this morning, and did some execution, ours answered
them again from the Great Mount, and plaid upon them for
the space of one hour.

'They are in very great streights for provision, and have
eaten horse-flesh these six or seven dayes, but as resolute as
formerly.

'A party came out to cut Barley which was repulsed
without losse, two only wounded of the party; some horse
grazing under the City walls were snapt by some of Col.
Whalleyes Forces, some shot, 38 taken, no way serviceable
at present, unless good keeping recover them.

'On Satterday last the Lord Generall gave Order that several Papers should be shot into the town out of Arrows, offering the private Souldiers quarter, and passes to go home, if they will deliver up Goring, Capel, Lucas, Loughborough, Farre, &c.

'This morning betwixt three and four of the clock, we received some tokens from the besieged, a party of them

GENERAL LUCAS AT THE SIEGE OF COLCHESTER, 1648.

sallied out, and advanced up a narrow Lane neer to one of our Guards, thinking to surprise them unawares; but an Eagle ey'd Centinel discovering them, presented her bill, and fired; whereupon the rest of the Guardians received an allarm and immediately man'd the Line, the Colchestrians advanced and charged with great fury, this action was disputed by both parties with great courage and resolution, the enemy fell on without mercy, and fought it with much violence, but our Forces bodying, they retreat, our men pursues with great execution, killed about 20. and took as

L

many prisoners, with the losse of 12. men; the like dispute
hapned the last night; we expect every hour when we shall
have Orders to fall on, the work will be difficult, and the
storming dangerous, the town being disadvantageous for
such a Military action.

'*Colchester Leaguer July* 26. *at* 8. *in the morning.*'

This tract is illustrated with a portrait of General Lucas
on horseback, which is copied on the previous page.

Colchester surrendered to the Parliament on Aug. 27,
1648, when Fairfax determined to make an example of Sir
Charles Lucas. This unexpected severity was attributed to
Ireton, who had been set by Cromwell to watch Fairfax.
There was a strong protest made against the intended
execution, but it nevertheless took place. Lucas was shot,
together with Sir George Lisle. The former suffered first,
and he himself gave the order to the soldiers to fire, with as
much coolness as if he had been a mere spectator. It is said
that Lisle ran and kissed the dead body of his friend, and
then presented himself to a like fate. Thinking that the
firing party was too far off, he called to them to come
nearer; one of the soldiers replied, 'I'll warrant you, Sir,
we'll hit you.' 'Friends,' said the gallant Royalist, smiling,
'I have been nearer you when you have missed me.'

Other tracts describe the proceedings of the Prince of
Wales in his attempts to retrieve his father's fortunes. One
of them has a portrait of the Prince, and contains a message
sent by him to the Mayor of Yarmouth concerning the
landing of his forces there for the relief of Colchester.
Another is adorned with a very elaborate title-page, and
describes 'The Resolution of the Prince of Wales, concerning the landing of his Army in the Isle of Loving-
Land, within the County of Suffolk, and his Propositions to
all Englishmen concerning his Engagement for King, City,
and Kingdom, against the Army, and to fight for their
Liberties, Freedom, and Privileges. Likewise, the further
proceedings of the Royal Navie, under his Highness the
D. of York, and the Declaration of the Seamen in the Isle of

Wight and Portsmouth, concerning the Kings Majesty and the Fleet Royall, 1648.'

The contest between the Royalists and the Parliament was now drawing to a close. The King was a prisoner in Carisbrooke Castle, and while he lay there he continued to occupy the pens of the pamphleteers and journalists. One writer addressed an exhortation to the nobility, clergy, and civil magistrates, in favour of the imprisoned Monarch;

CHARLES I. IN CARISBROOKE CASTLE, 1648.

and he adorned his work with the above representation of the King in prison, which afterwards appeared in other pamphlets.

It is remarkable that such important events as the trial and execution of Charles I. should not have tempted the newspapers of the day to illustrate subjects of so much interest. It may have been that such a terrible termination of the Civil War in some degree paralysed men's energies, and drove all thoughts of trading on such an event from their minds. I have met with two very rough woodcuts professing to represent the execution. One is contained in the Confession of Richard Brandon, the Hangman, and the other forms half of a woodcut frontispiece to a broadside describing the execution of the Regicides, which I shall refer to in its proper place. The Confession of Richard Brandon was published in 1649, the same year in which the King was executed, and purports to be a death-bed statement concerning that event. There were two Brandons, Gregory and Richard, father and son. The former beheaded Lord Strafford, and was believed by Charles II. to have been the executioner of his father. According to Sir Nathaniel Wraxall, George Selwyn, ' that insatiable amateur of executions,' told the story of King Charles's execution from information which he professed to have obtained from the Duchess of Portsmouth, who, he said, always asserted, on the authority of Charles II., that the King, his father, was not beheaded by either Colonel Joyce or Colonel Pride, as was then commonly believed, but that the real name of the executioner was *Gregory* Brandon ; that this man had worn a black crape stretched over his face, and had no sooner taken off the King's head than he was put into a boat at Whitehall Stairs, together with the block, the black cloth that covered it, the axe, and every other article that had been stained with the Royal blood. Being conveyed to the Tower, all the implements used in the decapitation had been immediately reduced to ashes. A purse containing one hundred broad pieces of gold was then delivered to Brandon, and he was dismissed. He survived the transaction many years, but divulged it a short time before he died. ' This account,' Wraxall adds, ' as coming from the Duchess of Portsmouth, challenges great respect.' * Popular belief, however, at the time pointed to Richard Brandon, son of the above-named Gregory Brandon, whose confession, published immediately after his death, I here quote :—

' The Confession of Richard Brandon the Hangman (upon his Death bed).

* *Old and New London.* By Edward Walford.

'The Confession of the Hangman concerning his beheading his late Majesty the King of Great Brittaine (upon his Death bed) who was buried on Thursday night last, in White Chappell Church-yard, with the manner thereof.

'Upon Wednesday last (being the 20 of this instant June, 1649) Richard Brandon, the late Executioner and Hangman, who beheaded his late Majesty, King of Great Brittaine, departed this life. But during the time of his sicknesse his conscience was much troubled, and exceedingly perplexed in mind, yet little shew of repentance, for remission of his sins, and by past transgressions, which had so much power and influence upon him, that he seemed to live in them and they in him. And upon Sunday last, a young man of his acquaintance going in to visit him, fell into discourse, asked him how he did, and whether he was not troubled in conscience, for cutting off of the King's head?

'He replied by reason that (upon the time of his tryal, and at the denouncing of Sentence against him) he had taken a vow and protestation, *wishing God to perish him body and soul, if ever he appeared on the scaffold to do the act or lift up his hand against him.*

'Further acknowledging, *That he was no sooner entered upon the scaffold, but immediately he fell a trembling, and hath ever since continued in the like agony.*

'He likewise confessed that he had 30 pounds for his pains, all paid him in half-crowns, within an hour after the blow was given, and that he had an orange stuck full of cloves, and a handkircher out of the King's pocket, so soon as he was carried off from the scaffold; for which orange he was proffered 20 shillings by a gentleman in Whitehall, but refused the same, and afterwards sold it for ten S. in Rosemary-lane.

'About 6 of the clock at night he returned home to his wife living in Rosemary Lane, and gave her the money, saying, *That it was the deerest money that ever he earned in his life, for it would cost him his life.* Which prophetical words were soon made manifest; for it appeared that ever since he hath been in a most sad condition, and upon the Almightie's first scourging of him with the Rod of meeknesse, and the friendly admonition of divers friends, for the calling of him to repentance, yet he persisted on in his vicious Vices, and would not hearken thereunto, but lay raging and swearing, and still pointing at one thing or another, which he conceived to appear visible before him.

'About three dayes before he died he lay speechlesse, uttering many a sigh and heavy groan and so in a most desperate manner departed from his bed of sorrow. For the buriall whereof great store of wines were sent in by the sheriff of the City of London, and a great multitude of people stood wayting to see the Corps carried to the Church-yard, some crying out *Hang him Rogue, bury him in the Dung-hill;* others pressing upon him saying, *They would quarter him, for executing of the King;* insomuch, that the Church Wardens and Masters of the Parish were fain to come for the suppressing of them, and (with great difficulty) he was at last carried to White-Chappell Church-yard, having (as it is said) a bunch of Rosemary at each end of the coffin, on the top thereof, with a Rope tyed crosse from one end to the other.

'And a merry conceited Cook, living at the sign of the Crown, having a black Fan (worth the value of 30 shillings) took a resolution to rent the same in pieces, and to every feather tied a piece of packthread dy'd in black ink, and gave them to divers persons, who (in derision) for a while, wore them in their hats.

'Thus have I given thee an exact account and perfect relation of the life and death of Richard Brandon, to the end, that the World may be convinced of those calumnious speeches and erroneous suggestions which are dayly spit from the mouth of envy, against divers persons of great worth and eminency, by casting an *odium* upon them for the executing of the King; it being now made manifest that the aforesaid Executioner was the only man that gave the fatal blows, and his man that wayted upon him was a Ragman, living in Rosemary Lane.'

Subjoined is a copy of the cut on the title-page of this tract.

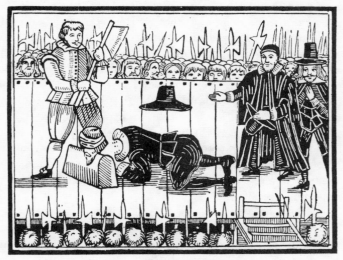

EXECUTION OF CHARLES I., 1649.

The death of Richard Brandon is entered in the register of St. Mary's, Whitechapel, under date June 21, 1649. To the entry is appended a note, evidently of about the same date, to the effect that ' this R. Brandon is supposed to have. cut off the head of Charles the First.' The 'calumnious speeches and erroneous suggestions' had indicated several persons as having struck the fatal blow on that dismal morning in January. Amongst them, besides those already named, were 'Squire Dun,' William Walker, Hugh Peters, Lord Stair, and William Hewlett. The last-named person was actually tried for the crime at the Restoration. The evidence against him went to show that ' his voice was heard upon the scaffold, and his Breeches were seen under his Frock, that he confest he was to have £100 and preferment in Ireland to doe it ; that being asked whether he cut off the

King's head or no, he said what he had done he would not be ashamed of ; and if it were to doe again he would doe it ; more to the same purpose was witnessed by several witnesses, and by one, who being sworn, said that the Common-Hang-man profest he did not doe it.' This sort of evidence was not fit to hang a dog ; and, though Hewlett was found guilty and sentenced to death, the sentence was never carried into effect—a proof that public opinion must have been too strong even for the hardihood of those who had foredoomed Hewlett to the gallows. The Government had evidently determined to fix the treason on this man with the sanguinary idea that some person ought to be made to expiate the deed, even though that person might be innocent. The prevalent belief, however, was that it was the common executioner who had been employed ; and it is highly improbable that a mere amateur would have been permitted to officiate on such an important occasion.

Although I have met with no native contemporary pro-duction representing the execution, other than the rude woodcuts before mentioned, there is in the British Museum a collection of broadsides relating to the period of the Civil War, one of which has a large and well-executed copperplate engraving representing the execution of Charles I. It was published at Frankfort, and the descriptive text is in German. The view of Whitehall is correctly given, and the engraving looks like a genuine representation of the event.

CHAPTER V.

Decrease of Newspapers after the Civil War—*Mercurius Democritus*—*The Faithful Post*—*The Politique Post*—Broadsides for the People—The Hollow Tree at Hampstead—Prodigious Monster taken in Spain—The Restoration—Trial of the Regicides—Execution of the Regicides—Licenser of the Press appointed—Popular Taste for the Supernatural—Apparition in the Air in Holland—Revival of *Mercurius Civicus*—Murder of Archbishop Sharpe—*The Loyal Protestant*—Frost Fair on the Thames—Monmouth's Rebellion—The Bloody Assizes—Funeral of Queen Mary, Consort of William III.—Increase of Newspapers after the Revolution.

WHEN the Civil War was over the newspapers it had called into existence disappeared. The printing-press was, of course, not idle during the rule of Cromwell, but its productions were narrowly watched, and there is reason to suppose the newspapers were to a great extent under the influence of the party in power. Examples of illustrated journalism during this period are rare. We have '*A terrible and bloudy Fight at Sea*' between Blake and Van Tromp, and '*A great and wonderful Victory*' obtained by the English in the West Indies, each illustrated with a woodcut that had done duty in the pamphlets of the Civil War. A rough representation of an owl seated at a table writing in a book heads a tract ridiculing Lilly, the astrologer; while '*Black Monday, or a full and exact description of the great and terrible Eclipse of the Sun*,' is adorned with a representation of 'the true Figure of the Eclipse.' The grim and unsocial character of the times is set forth in '*The Vindication of Christmas*,' a pamphlet illustrated with a woodcut representing Old Christmas welcomed on one hand and forbidden on the other. After a pitiful lament for the misery of the times, Christmas sets out on a pilgrimage to London, where he enters a fair house that had

once been an Alderman's, but is now inhabited by a sour-
tempered miser.   Here he meets with such a cold reception
that he is fain to take himself off, 'and wandering into the
country up and down from house to house, found small
comfort in any.'

    I have spoken of *Mercurius Democritus* as being the
Punch of the seventeenth century.   It is singular that such

THE VINDICATION OF CHRISTMAS, 1653.

a publication as this should have existed under a Puritanical
Government.   The humour is so exceedingly broad that it is
difficult to understand how it could be circulated at a time
when the rulers of the land professed a stern and rigid
morality.   Unlike the modern *Punch*, who is refined and
courteous even when he is most severe, *Mercurius Democritus*
could seldom be facetious without being coarse and even
indecent.   In the same number that contains the cut of the
Smithfield ghost, referred to in Chapter III., occur the following jests, which are comparatively mild specimens of the

humour of *Mercurius Democritus:*—' The last Monday a Herd of Swine being driven through Long Lane 600 Jews were suddenly converted by them; some think it was for fear those Rumford Cattell should serve them as they served the Devill in the country of the *Gergesens* when they carried him headlong into the sea.'

' A Mad Country Parson coming riding up to London between Islington and the Red Bull met with a small-coale man, very black, with his sack of small coale at his back. The pitiful Parson minding to put a jeer on the small-coale man, made a sudden stop with his Horse, saying with a loud voyce, that those that rid after him might partake of the jest, Fellow, fellow (quoth he) I prithee tell 's some news from Hell, I see thou hast a whole sack full at thy back. Truly quoth the small-coal man, I can tell you but very little news from Hell, only the Devill wants a Chaplaine, and you ride but a little faster you may perchance have the place.'

Much of the news printed continued to be circulated by means of pamphlets and broadsides, but some regular newspapers were also published. An illustrated example of the latter occurs in the *Faithful Post* of 1653. The full title of the number for April 8, 1653, is ' *The Faithful Post Impartially communicating the Proceedings of the Parliaments forces in England, Scotland, and Ireland, comprising the sum of Intelligence from the English and Dutch Fleets; with the Affairs and Designs now on foot in France, Denmark, Sweden, Holland, and all other parts of Europe.*' It has a woodcut portrait of Admiral Van Gallen, and contains the following news from Amsterdam relating thereto :—

' Wednesday, April 6.

' From Amsterdam thus; Van Gallen Admiral of the Dutch Fleet in the Streights, has a golden chair sent him for his little great gallantry in the last service. And the Commons forsooth adore him extremely; insomuch that many of the Bores have erected his Statue and Portraiture, and hung it up as a memorial in the most eminent places of their Low country Fabrics, according to the figure following; with two silver keys in his hands; which, say they, are to unlock the Treasury of their enemy. *Pure Youths.'* (Here follows the portrait.)

PORTRAIT OF ADMIRAL VAN GALLEN.   FROM THE 'FAITHFUL POST,' 1653.

'And as we are informed, hath a golden Leg delicately set forth by Mr. Painter, in lieu of that shot off in the fight.'

In the foregoing *Faithful Post* there is a good deal of news about the English and Dutch fleets; and in the news from Lubeck it is reported that the English have printed a 'picture of Admiral Van Tromp represented with a man opening his breast to find his heart; but, searching, it was found in the Calf of his Leg, whereas, saith the Dutch Print, they know very well that Tromp behaved himself most gallantly, and like a man of courage.' In another number of the *Faithful Post* is an illustration of a comet or 'Blazing Star' seen in Germany. The foregoing portrait of Admiral Van Gallen, and the blazing star, together with a map show-

FLAG OF COL. CHARLES JAMES. FROM THE 'POLITIQUE POST,' 1653.

ing the effects of a great storm and flood in Holland, are printed in the *Politique Post* for January 4, 1653; but there is no reference made to the engraving of Van Gallen; and the blazing star is described as having been seen at Pembroke, in Wales. In the same number of the *Politique Post* is a woodcut of the flag of Colonel Charles James, which is thus alluded to :—' By the last Post and intelligence from the Navie, we have received very certain and credible intelligence, that Colonel Charles James having received a commission from the King of Scots, is launched forth into the deep with the Brest men of war who has now struck sail

upon the Coast of Brittain, and there set up his Flag on the
Poop of the Patrick, called the Vice-Ambral as here represented in the ensueing Figure.'

In 1654 there was a remarkable tree at Hampstead, which
was visited as a curiosity.   It was called 'The Hollow Tree,'

THE HOLLOW TREE AT HAMPSTEAD, 1654.

and was probably the central attraction of a place of entertainment.   In a broadside of 1654 there is an etching of it
by Hollar, with descriptive and other verses.   There was a
door in the trunk of the tree, and a turret on the top, the
ascent to which was in the hollow of the tree.   The turret
was large enough to seat six, 'and round about roome for
fourteene more.'   The following is a specimen of the verses
accompanying Hollar's etching :—

'THE SALUTATION.

'Welcome, before! welcome all you that follow!
Our heart is sound although our Tree be hollow,

Yet know nor age, nor weaknesse did distresse
Its willing bulk into this hollownesse:
But a desire markt out for noble ends,
To finde more room to entertain fast friends,
And in the compasse of itself to try
Laws of true Mirth and Hospitality.
In such a Hollow, Musick dwells; thus love
Laies forth itself, yet ne'er doth bankrupt prove.
And having read the riddle doth impart
Things sometimes hollow have the soundest heart.'

PRODIGIOUS MONSTER TAKEN IN THE MOUNTAINS OF ZARDANA IN SPAIN, 1655.

This broadside was an agreeable change from the prodigies and monstrosities with which the public were so liberally supplied. A specimen of the latter was published in 1655, which must have tried the faith of even the most credulous. It is described as ' *The True Portraiture of a prodigious Monster, taken in the Mountains of Zardana* ; the following Description whereof was sent to Madrid October 20, 1654, and from thence to Don Olonza de Cardines, Ambassador for the King of Spain now resident in London. Its stature was like that of a strong well set man, with 7 heads, the chief of them looking forward, with one eye in its front; the other heads have each two eyes in their natural situation, the ears of an Ass; with its principal head it eates, drinks, and cryes with an extraordinary and terrible voice; the other heads are also moved to and fro ; it hath seven Arms and Hands of a Man, very strong in each of them ; from the middle downward it is like a Satyr, with Goats feet, and cloven,' &c. This broadside has a very well-executed copperplate engraving of the monster; and another sheet of the same date has a woodcut copy of the same engraving, together with a long account in verse 'to the tune of Summer Time,' and and the following additional particulars: ' The News of this Satyrical Monster being noysed abroad throughout all Spain, France, and Italy, made a desperate fear, and general distemper amongst all the Popish Prelates, Cardinals, Jesuites, Monks, and Fryers ; yea, the very Pope himself trembled to hear this strange Report. There is a Prophesie in the 13 of the Revelation, of a great Red-Dragon and a Beast with seven heads that should arise out of the Sea, that should continue 42 moneths, which was to come to pass before the great and terrible day of judgement; which by the appearing of these strange Monsters is neer at hand now.'

At the Restoration several broadsides of news were published containing engravings. There is one giving an account of the coronation of Charles II., which is illustrated with a copperplate engraving of the King seated on his throne, robed and crowned, with the following complimentary lines :—

' The Second Charles, Heire of the Royal Martyr
Who for Religion and his Subjects Charter

Spent the best Blood, that unjust Sword ere dy'de
Since the rude Souldier pierced our Saviours side.
Who such a Father had'st, and such a Son ;
Redeem thy people and assume thy own,
Ascend thy Ancestors Imperial seat
Of Charles the Good, thou second Charles the Great,
That adds the worth ; this lustre to the Crown,
Whose solid Glorious weighed Usurpers down.
Such Majesty as never was profan'd
While Tyrants rul'd 'twas only Charles that reigned.

Another broadside of the same date (1660) is entitled ' *A Looking-Glass for Traytors, being the manner of the Tryall of those Barbarous Wretches at Justice-Hall in the Old-Baily, who contrived and compassed the Death of his late Sacred Majesty King Charles the First, of ever blessed memory; with an Account of their Severall Araignments, Conviction, Condemnation, and Execution.'* This sheet is also illustrated with a copper-plate engraving, representing the Old Bailey Court at the trial of the Regicides, which is interesting if it truly represents the appearance of the court at that time. Numerous letters of reference are given under the engraving to explain its different parts, and a short summary is given of the trial : ' His Majesty (in pursuance of an Act of Parliament which had left the persons following to be tried according to Law, for being the principal Actors in the said Tragedy of his Father's death) issued out a special Commission of *Oyer* and *terminer* to the Judges and other Commissioners for that purpose ; and accordingly *Wednesday* the 10th of *October* they met at the Sessions house in the *Old-Baily*, and the same morning the following persons were ordered to be brought from the *Tower* to *Newgate*, and a way was made from the Press-yard backwards to the Sessions house, privately to convey them to and again, to keep them from the pressing of the people.' Then follows a list of twenty-eight persons, including Major-General Harrison and Hugh Peters, ' all which being brought to the Bar, were indicted and arraigned to the following effect :—

M

'*That they not having the fear of God before their eyes, but being led by the instigation of the Divel had maliciously, traiterously, and advisedly imagined, consulted, contrived, and compassed the death of his late Majesty Charles the first of ever blessed memory, and that they had aided, procured, abetted, assisted, and comforted a certain person with a vizard upon his face, and a frock upon his body for that purpose.*

'Major-General *Harrison* in his Pleadings carried himself so confidently to the Court as if he thought himself Careless and Unconcerned in the businesse, and seemed to justify not only the Power under which he Acted but also the Act itself, saying that Kings had formerly been privately Assassinated and Murthered, but what they had done was in the face of the Sun and in the fear of the Lord; whereat the Court was much troubled to see that he should make God the Author of that Horrid Murther.'

Harrison was found guilty at once, and sentenced to be hanged, drawn, and quartered. The like fate awaited Hugh Peters. The sort of evidence that was brought against the prisoners is exemplified in this broadside, where it is stated that '*Mr. Hugh Peters* stood strangely amazed and could say nothing for himselfe against that Jury of witnesses that appeared against him; as that he said, *England* could not be settled till 150 were taken away which he said were L L L viz. the Lords, the Levites, and the Lawyers; that he was often conspiring privately with Oliver Cromwell the King's death, that he could even reverence the High Court of Justice, it lookt so like the judgement of the world which should be at the last day by the Saints; with many other blasphemies too large to enumerate.'

Amongst the prisoners arraigned on this occasion was the William Hewlett already referred to. In the other cases the jury promptly found the prisoners guilty without leaving the court; but it was a proof of the weakness of the evidence in Hewlett's case that 'they did withdraw themselves, and after a little consultation they found him guilty, and accordingly sentence was pronounced against him.' This sentence, however, as before stated, was never carried into effect.

The engraving of this historical trial at the Old Bailey is too crowded to admit of reproduction here. Other broadsides relating to the trial of the regicides were published at the time, but they are more of the nature of caricatures than illustrations of news.

It is well known that General Harrison, Hugh Peters, and others were executed with all the barbarous circumstances indicated in the words of their sentence. Peters was made to sit upon the scaffold, exposed to the jibes and jeers of the mob, and compelled to witness the mutilation of his fellow-victims. The executions were continued day after day both at Charing-cross and at Tyburn, and were stopped at last, not for lack of victims, or disinclination for more slaughter on the part of the authorities, but from a dread of the effect such bloodthirsty proceedings might have on the minds of the people. The horrors of such a scene, of course, attracted the sensational news-writer of the day ; and a broadside of the time gives us a picture and description of the executions, coupled with a representation of the execution of Charles I. This broadside was evidently intended to exhibit at one view the commission of a great crime and its just punishment. The engraving shows on one side the execution of the King and on the other the punishment of the regicides. The description of the latter is preceded by an account of the trial and death of Charles. The title runs thus : ' *A true and perfect Relation of the Grand Traytors Execution, as at severall times they were Drawn, Hanged, and Quartered at Charing-Crosse, and at Tiburne. Together with their severall Speeches and Confessions which every one of them made at the time of their Execution. London, printed for William Gilbertson,* 1660.'

The following account is given of the execution of Major-General Harrison : ' The next day being *Saturday* Major-Gen. *Harrison* was drawn upon a Hurdle from Newgate to the Round, or railed Place near Charing-Crosse, where a

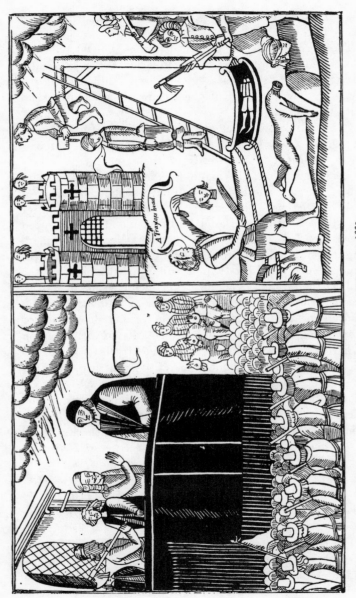

EXECUTION OF THE REGICIDES, 1660.

Gibbet was set upon which he was Hanged. Many of his acquaintance did seem to triumph to see him die so Confidently; whiles numbers of true Christians did grieve in earnest to see him die so impenitently. We have been told that when he took his leave of his wife, he comforted her, and told her that he would come again in three days; but we hear nothing as yet of his Resurrection.' In describing the execution of Hugh Peters, it is said, 'He came to the Ladder unwillingly, and by degrees was drawn up higher and higher. Certainly he had many Executioners within him; he leaned upon the Ladder being unwilling to part from it, but being turned off, the spectators gave a great shout, as they did when his Head was cut off, and held up aloft on the point of a Spear. The very souldiers themselves whom heretofore he did animate to slaughter, and a thorough execution of their Enemies were now ashamed of him, and upon the point of their Spears showed that guilty head which made them guilty of so much blood.'

Pepys, in his Diary, says, under date October 13, 1660 :— ' I went out to Charing Cross, to see Major-General Harrison hanged, drawn, and quartered ; which was done there, he looking as cheerful as any man could do in that condition. He was presently cut down, and his head and heart shown to the people, at which there were great shouts of joy. It is said, that he said that he was sure to come shortly at the right hand of Christ to judge them that now had judged him ; and that his wife do expect his coming again. Thus it was my chance to see the King beheaded at White Hall, and to see the first blood shed in revenge for the King at Charing Cross.'

It will be seen by the copy made from this woodcut that the design is of the rudest possible description, and must have been the work of a common ballad illustrator, whose fee was probably on a par with his ability. He evidently thought that, in such a scene as the execution of Charles I., the Church should be paramount, for he has made Bishop Juxon a much more prominent figure than the King.

The reign of the 'Merry Monarch,' though not the most creditable period in English History, would have supplied abundant materials for the journalist if there had been any newspapers. The Great Plague, the Fire of London, the sea-fights with the Dutch, were splendid opportunities for the pencil of the 'special artist' or the pen of 'our own correspondent.' A law had been passed prohibiting the publication of newspapers without being duly licensed. Sir John Birkenhead was appointed Licenser of the Press, and he was succeeded by Sir Roger L'Estrange. There was scarcely anything that could be called a newspaper except the *London Gazette*, and it only contained such news as the Government thought proper to make public, and it was never illustrated. The little that was done in the way of pictorial journalism was of a satirical or humorous character, or had reference to foreign affairs, and was either published in the form of broadsides or was put before the public in such a questionable shape that it was difficult to tell whether it was truth or fiction. As soon as the people were released from the domination of Puritanism a reaction set in, and the humours of *Mercurius Democritus* were supplemented by the still broader fancies of *Mercurius Fumigolus.* Occasional entertainment of a more serious character was supplied, such as '*A True and Perfect Relation of the Happy Successe and Victory obtained against the Turks of Argiers at Bugia.*' The popular taste for the mysterious and supernatural was touched by '*A true and perfect Relation, of a strange and wonderful Apparition in the Air, the Fourteenth of August, near Goeree in Holland.*' This was an illustrated broadside containing the following account:—'On the fourteenth of August this year 1664, towards the evening near Goeree in Holland, there was seen by many Spectators an Apparition upon the Ocean of two several Fleets of Ships engaged in a Fight, which lasted for the space of about half an hour, and then vanished. Afterwards there appeared two Lyons, who with great fury and violence, assaulted each other three several times, neither of them prevailing against the other, till at length both of

APPARITION IN THE AIR AT GOEREE IN HOLLAND, 1664.

them wearied with their continual striving, did, as it were, give over for breath, when on a sudden a third Lyon of a very great and huge stature appeared and falling first upon the one, and then on the other, destroyed them both. They being vanished, there appeared a King, with a Crown upon his head, and he so plainly and visibly discerned as that the spectators did discover the very Buttons on his Coat. After all was vanished, the said Spectators continueing there, and walking too and fro upon the sands, the Ocean, so far as they could see, seemed to be Blood. On the next morning, the same Apparition, in all its Circumstances, was seen again, and the truth thereof attested upon Oath, before the Magistrates of Goeree, by the said Spectators; so that there is no doubt made of the truth thereof. And this happening in this juncture of time, begets some strange apprehensions; for that about six Months before Van Trump was slain in the former Wars with England, there was seen near the same place, an Apparition of several Ships in the Air, as it were fighting with each other.'

This broadside was printed at London, 'by Thomas Leach in Shooe Lane in the Year 1664. *With Allowance* October 13, 1664. Roger L'Estrange.' The illustration is an etching, very well and freely executed.

Amongst other things which appear to have been revived at the Restoration was the *Mercurius Civicus.* In Dr. Burney's collections in the British Museum there is preserved a copy of Number 4 of *Mercurius Civicus*, dated May 1, 1660. On the title-page it is stated to be 'published by order of the Lord Mayor and Court of Aldermen;' but it is not illustrated, as was its predecessor of the time of the Civil War.

One of the most atrocious deeds of the time, and one that had a powerful effect upon public feeling, was the murder of Archbishop Sharp in 1679. This prelate was held to have betrayed the Presbyterians at the time of the Restoration, and was hated accordingly. This hatred had been manifested by an attempt on his life in the streets of Edinburgh in the year 1668; but on that occasion the Archbishop escaped, and

THE MURDER OF ARCHBISHOP SHARP, 1679.

another person was wounded. On May 3, 1679, Archbishop Sharp was returning in his coach to St. Andrews from Kennaway, where he had passed the night, when, at a place called Magus Moor, he was set upon by nine men, who murdered him with pitiless barbarity in the presence of his daughter, who accompanied him. This dreadful event was commemorated in a broadside entitled ' *The Manner of the Barbarous Murther of James, late Lord Archbishop of St. Andrews, Primate and Metropolitan of all Scotland and one of his Majesties most Honourable Privy Council of that kingdom, May* 3, 1679.' A copperplate engraving represents the murder, and some verses are printed underneath. I have copied the engraving on this broadside, which forms part of the Luttrell collection in the British Museum.

In 1681 there existed a newspaper entitled *The Loyal Protestant and True Domestic Intelligencer.* In the number for April 2, 1681, there is printed the following curious news from Rome :—

'Rome, March 6. There did appear here about the middle of Dec. last, a strange and wonderful Comet near the Ecliptick in the sign of Libra, and in the body of the Virgin. At the same time a Prodigious Egge was laid by a Young Pullet (which had never laid before) with a perfect Comet in it, and as many stars, and in the same form as the enclosed figure shows. All the great ones of Rome have seen it, even the Queen and the Pope. What you see in the enclosed Paper is within the Egge most clearly exprest, and not upon the Shell. The Roman Wits are now very busy in guessing at what this Comet and Egge may portend.'

This account of the egg is printed on the front page of *The Loyal Protestant,* in the midst of Court news from Oxford, municipal news from Leicester, news from Edinburgh, &c., and is illustrated with a woodcut, which I have copied. A further description is appended to the representation of the egg :—'The true form of a Prodigious Egg brought forth at Rome the 11th of Dec. last in the year 1680 in which the Commet here printed does continue to appear.'

'The aforesaid 11th of Dec. about 8 of the Clock in the morning, a Hen Chicken, with a great Noise, crying extraordinarily, that never had laid an Egge before this day, brought forth an Egge of an extraordinary greatness, with all these several Forms as you see here exprest, to the great amazement of all those that have seen it. This is an exact draught of the Egge as it was printed in Italy. But all persons are left to their own choice whether they will believe either this or any of our own late home-bred Miracles or visions.'

EXTRAORDINARY EGG LAID AT ROME. FROM THE ' LOYAL PROTESTANT AND TRUE DOMESTIC INTELLIGENCER,' 1681.

Supernatural occurrences and uncommon events, even when traceable to natural causes, have always had great attractions for both the ignorant and the educated. We therefore find the talents of the old newsmen were most frequently exercised on mysterious appearances in the air, floods, fires, and frosts, earthquakes and upheavings of the sea. Having already quoted examples dealing with some of these subjects, I now come to two broadsides which describe and illustrate the great frost of 1683-4, when the river Thames was covered with ice eleven inches thick, the forest trees, and even the oaks, in England were split by the frost, most of the hollies were killed, and nearly all the birds perished. According to the testimony of an eye-witness, 'The people kept trades on the Thames as in a fair, till February 4, 1684. About forty coaches daily plied on the Thames as on drye land.' The broadsides under notice give representations of the fair held on the Thames, and describe it in doggerel verse. The one containing the engraving I have copied is entitled ' *Great Britain's Wonder ; London's Admiration,, Being a True Representation of a Prodigious Frost, which began about the beginning of December,* 1683, *and continued till the Fourth Day of February following. And held on with such violence, that Men and Beasts, Coaches and Carts, went as frequently thereon as Boats were wont to pass before. There was also a street of Booths built from the Temple to Southwark, where were sold all sorts of Goods imaginable— namely Cloaths, Plate, Earthen Ware ; Meat, Drink, Brandy, Tobacco, and a Hundred sorts of other Commodities not here inserted. It being the wonder of this present Age, and a great consternation to all the Spectators.'* The description opens thus :—

> ' Behold the Wonder of this present Age
> A Famous River now become a stage.
> Question not what I now declare to you,
> The Thames is now both Fair and Market too.
> And many Thousands dayley do resort,
> There to behold the Pastime and the Sport
> Early and late, used by young and old,
> And valued not the fierceness of the Cold.'

The illustration is a roughly executed woodcut, and represents a street of booths opposite the Temple, looking towards the Middlesex shore. On one side are men skating, sliding, riding on sledges, and playing at football ; whilst bull-baiting, skittle-playing, &c., go on on the other side. Coaches are driven across the ice, boats are dragged as sledges, and an ox is roasted whole in one corner.

The other broadside has a woodcut of the same scene, but taken from a different point, and looking *down* the river,

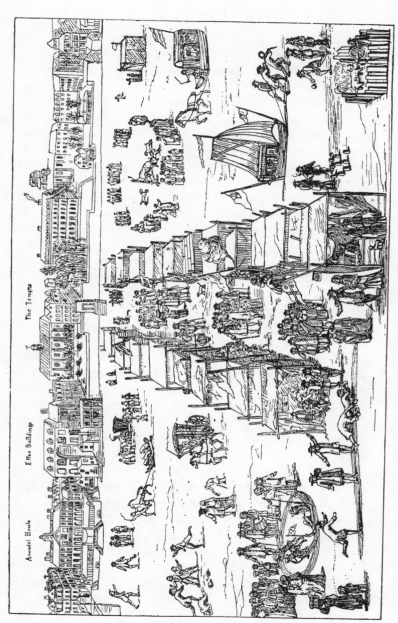

Arundel House   Effex Buildings   The Temple

FROST FAIR ON THE THAMES, 1683.

with London Bridge, the Tower, Monument, &c., in the distance. In addition to a description of Frost Fair, there is an account of all the great frosts from the time of William the Conqueror.

Some curious particulars of this great frost are recorded by contemporary writers. Evelyn describes the whole scene, and says that he crossed the river on the ice on foot upon the 9th, in order to dine with the Archbishop of Canterbury at Lambeth; and again in his coach, from Lambeth to the horse-ferry at Millbank, upon Feb. 5th, when 'it began to thaw, but froze again.' Hackney-coaches plied between Somerset House and the Temple to Southwark. There was a printing-press set up in one of the booths, 'where the people and ladys tooke a fancy to having their names printed, and the day and year set down, when printed on the Thames. This humour took so universally that 'twas estimated the printer gained about £5 a day for printing a line onely at sixpence a name, besides what he got by ballads, &c.' A specimen of this printing has been preserved. It was executed for Charles II., who visited Frost Fair accompanied by several members of his family. It contains, besides the names of the King and Queen, those of the Duke of York, Mary his Duchess, Princess Anne (afterwards Queen Anne), and Prince George of Denmark, her husband. The last name on the list is 'Hans in Kelder,' which literally means 'Jack in the Cellar,' and is supposed to have been suggested by the humour of the King in allusion to the interesting situation of the Princess Anne; and we can fancy the swarthy face of the 'Merry Monarch' smiling in the frosty air as this congenial joke was perpetrated.

In the Luttrell collection of broadsides there is one with a large woodcut representing the battle of Sedgemoor and other incidents of Monmouth's rebellion. The letterpress is in wretched verse, and is entitled, '*A Description of the late Rebellion in the West. A Heroic Poem.*' The unfortunate issue of Monmouth's rising excited the sympathy of the common people, to whom he was endeared by his many amiable qualities and his handsome person. Though this broadside was evidently written in the interest of the Government it was likely to have a ready sale, and it was sought to increase the interest by pictorial representation. The engraving, which is on an unusually large scale, is very rough, like all the woodcuts of the period.

The slaughter at Sedgemoor and the execution of the Duke of Monmouth were partly forgotten in the greater horror excited by the unsparing severity of Judge Jefferies in condemning to death hundreds of persons who were charged with being concerned in the rebellion. I have met with one illustrated tract relating to the ' Bloody Assize.' It is inserted at the end of the volume of the *London Gazette* for 1685, and has apparently been added by Dr. Burney, the collector, as bearing upon the events of the time. It forms no part of the *London Gazette*, though bound up with it. There is a rough woodcut on the title-page containing eleven portraits, and the title is as follows :—

' *The Protestant Martyrs; or the Bloody Assizes, giving an account of the Lives, Tryals, and Dying Speeches, of all those eminent Protestants that suffered in the West of England by the sentence of that bloody and cruel Judge Jefferies; being in all* 251 *persons, besides what were hanged and destroyed in cold blood. Containing also the Life and Death of James Duke of Monmouth; His Birth and Education; His Actions both at Home and Abroad; His Unfortunate Adventure in the West; His Letter to King James; His Sentence, Execution and Dying-words upon the Scaffold; with a true Copy of the Paper he left behind him. And many other curious Remarks worth the Readers Observation. London, Printed by F. Bradford; at the Bible in Fetter Lane.*'

At the end of the pamphlet is printed this curious sentence :—' This Bloody Tragedy in the West being over our Protestant Judge returns for London; soon after which Alderman Cornish felt the Anger of Somebody behind the Curtain.'

Alderman Cornish was afterwards executed at the corner

of King Street, Cheapside, for alleged participation in the
Rye House Plot.

This fragment of contemporary history shows that if there
were no regular newspapers to supply the people with illustrated news they obtained it in the shape of cheap fly-sheets

MARTYRS OF THE BLOODY ASSIZES, 1685.

and broadsides—the form in which it was supplied to them
before newspapers began.

Macaulay describes the unlicensed press at this period as
being worked in holes and corners, and producing large
quantities of pamphlets which were a direct infraction of the
law subjecting the press to a censorship. 'There had long
lurked in the garrets of London a class of printers who
worked steadily at their calling with precautions resembling
those employed by coiners and forgers. Women were on

the watch to give the alarm by their screams if an officer appeared near the workshop. The press was immediately pushed into a closet behind the bed; the types were flung into the coal-hole, and covered with cinders; the compositor disappeared through a trap-door in the roof, and made off over the tiles of the neighbouring houses. In these dens were manufactured treasonable works of all classes and sizes, from halfpenny broadsides of doggerel verse up to massy quartos filled with Hebrew quotations.'* The pamphlet I have just quoted probably issued from a press of this kind; but he must have been a bold printer who dared to put his name and address to a work wherein Jefferies was openly referred to as ' that bloody and cruel Judge Jefferies.'

Large broadsides continued to be the favourite form of illustrated journalism for some time after this. One gives a ' true and perfect relation ' of a great earthquake which happened at Port Royal, in Jamaica, on Tuesday, June 7th, 1692, and is illustrated with a large woodcut. On the death of Queen Mary, the consort of William III., an illustrated broadside was published, plentifully garnished with skulls and cross-bones, entitled, *'Great Britain's Lamentation; or the Funeral Obsequies of that most incomparable Protestant Princess, Mary, of ever Blessed Memory, Queen of England, Scotland, France, and Ireland, who departed this life the 28th of December, at Kensington, 1694, in the Thirty-second Year of her Age. She Reigned Five Years, Eight Months, and Seventeen Days. And was conducted from Whitehall to Westminster Abbey, in an open Chariot of State, on black cloath, by the Nobility, Judges, and Gentry of the Land, on Tuesday, the 5th of March, 1694-5.'* The large woodcut shows the funeral procession, and I have copied that part of it containing the funeral car, with the body of the deceased queen resting under a canopy.

In a few years after the Revolution newspapers began to increase rapidly. The censorship of the press ceased in 1695, and was immediately followed by the appearance of

* *History of England.*

N

FUNERAL OF QUEEN MARY, 1695.

great numbers of periodical papers. At first they were small in size, were wretchedly printed on the commonest paper, and each number contained only a small quantity of matter. The art of wood-engraving, the readiest and least expensive method of illustration, was now in the lowest possible condition; and the newspapers at the end of the seventeenth century contain scarcely any illustrations, except, perhaps, a heading of a rudely executed figure of a man blowing a horn, flanked by a ship or a castle, and numerous small woodcuts to advertisements.

CHAPTER VI.

Constant Attempts at Illustrated News—Increase of Caricatures—The
Postman, 1704—Fiery Apparition in the Air, seen in London—
Caricature against the Jacobites—The South-Sea Bubble—Eclipse
of the Sun, 1724—The *Grub Street Journal* an Illustrated Paper—
The *Daily Post*—Admiral Vernon's Attack on Porto Bello—The
Penny London Post—Henry Fielding and the *Jacobite's Journal*—
Owen's Weekly Chronicle—*Lloyd's Evening Post,* and the Trial of
Lord Byron for the Murder of Mr. Chaworth—The *St. James's
Chronicle*—Illustrated Account of a Strange Wild Beast seen in
France—The *Gentleman's Journal* of Anthony Motteux—The *Gentle-
man's Magazine* of Edward Cave—The *London Magazine*—The *Scot's
Magazine.*

Iɴ glancing at the early newspapers it is apparent that the
idea, in some shape, of illustrating the news of the day was
never quite absent from the minds of newspaper conductors.
Sometimes it took the form of a rude map of the country
where some war was going on, or the plan of some city
which was being besieged. In the *London Post* for July
25, 1701, is a map of the seat of war in Italy, which is
reprinted in other numbers, and the *Daily Courant,* for Sept.
8, 1709, contains a large plan of Mons. In the absence of
other means, even printers' lines were used to represent a
plan of some place, or an event of unusual interest. Such an
attempt at illustrated news was made in the *Dublin Journal*
for May 14, 1746, where there is a plan, set up in type and
printers' lines, of the battle of Culloden ; and in the number
for March 28, 1747, there is a similar plan of the trial of
Lord Lovat. This is doubly interesting as being *Irish.*
Engraving on copper, though it involved the expense of a
double printing, was sometimes resorted to for the purpose of
enlivening the pages of the early newspapers, and we have
seen that it was also employed in broadsides. There was

so much enterprise that even penny papers sometimes introduced engravings into their pages.

About the beginning of the eighteenth century caricatures began to increase in England. Religious animosities and political intrigues, always keen incentives to satire, had opened a wide field to the caricaturist in the years which followed the Revolution. But religious bigotry and party spirit, strong as they were at this period, were exceeded by the social follies which came afterwards. The trial of Dr. Sacheverell occasioned the publication of numerous songs, squibs, and caricatures ; but the South-Sea Bubble surpassed it as a fruitful source of lampoons and pictorial satire. The spirit of ridicule was fed by the political intrigues, the follies and the vices of the Georgian era, and reached its highest development in the days of George III. Amongst other early channels for circulation we find caricatures making their appearance in newspapers, and as we proceed I shall give one or two examples from the illustrated journalism of this period.

On March 14, 1704, *The Postman*, one of the papers that was started on the expiration of the censorship (and which Macaulay says was one of the best conducted and most prosperous), published what was called a Postscript for the purpose of making its readers acquainted with a prodigy seen in Spain in the air so far back as the year 1536. It is illustrated with a woodcut representing two men fighting in the air ; and the following account is given of it :—' The success of the expedition of K. Charles III. being now the subject of all Publick Discourses, the Reader, we hope, will excuse the following Postscript, which must be confest to be of an extraordinary nature, as containing some things hardly to be parallelled. All the states of Christendom being concerned some way or other in this great quarrell, it is not to be wondered at if the discovery of a Prodigy, which seems to foretell the decision of it, has made so much noise at Rome, and that we insert it in this place. The French Faction grew intolerably insolent upon account of the storms which have so long retarded the Portuguese expedition, and represented these cross accidents as a manifest declaration that God did not approve the same; and this way of arguing, though never so rash and impertinent in itself, prevailed over the generality of the people, in a City which is the Centre of superstition. The Partizans of the House of Austria were very much dejected and had little to say, when they happily discovered in the Library of the Vatican a Book printed at Bazil in the year 1557 written by Conradus Lycosthenes, wherein they found an argument to confute all the reasons alledged by their adversaries, and a sure Presage in their opinion of the success of K. Charles III. This made a great noise at Rome, and his Grace the Duke of Shrewsbury sent an account thereof. The Book perhaps is not so scarce as they thought at Rome; and the learned Doctor Hans Sloane having one in his Library, and having been so obliging as to give me leave to transcribe that passage, I present it here to the reader, leaving it to everyone to make his own observations. The Book is thus Intituled: "*Prodigiorum Ostentorum Chronicon, &c., per Conradum Lycosthenem, Rubeaquensem. Printed in Folio at Bazil per Henricum Petri* 1557," and amongst the infinite number of Prodigies he relates in his collection, which extends from the beginning of the world to his time, he has the following, page 558 (here follows the description on each side of the woodcut in Latin and English). 'In a certain place of Spain on the 7th of Feby, 1536, 2 hours after the setting of the sun as Fincelius relates it after others, were seen in the Air, which was rainy and cloudy, two Young Men in Armour, fighting with Swords, one of them having in his left hand a Shield or round Buckler, adorned with an Eagle, with this inscription, I SHALL REIGN, and the other having on a long Target with these words, I HAVE REIGNED. They fought a Duel, and he who had the Eagle on his Buckler beat down his enemy and was conqueror.' The whole affair refers to the war of the Spanish Succession between the partisans of Louis XIV. and the

House of Bourbon, and the House of Austria, and is made to foretell the downfall of the former. As the Bourbons did eventually obtain the Crown of Spain, this interpretation of the supposed prodigy may be referred to the same class as the prophecies of *Old Moore's Almanack.* I have copied the engraving, which is the only illustration I have found in *The Postman.*

We have already noticed that no class of marvels were so

PRODIGY SEEN IN SPAIN.   FROM THE 'POSTMAN,' 1704.

attractive to the early news-writers as apparitions in the air. Another example of this is found in a pamphlet, published in 1710, entitled ' *The Age of Wonders: or, A further and particular Description of the remarkable, and Fiery Apparition that was seen in the Air, on Thursday in the Morning, being May the 11th, 1710.*' It is illustrated with a rough woodcut, and has the following description :—

. . . . ' As for the strange Appearances which were seen on the 11th of May in the Morning, I suppose there is by this time few that do not give Credit to the same, since so many creditable People in several parts of the Town have apparently testified the same, and are ready still to do it upon enquirey, as in Clare Market, Cheapside, Tower-hill, and other places ; it was likewise seen by several Market Folks then upon the Water, who have since agreed in Truth thereof, most of which relate in the following manner :—

'On Wednesday Night, or rather Thursday Morning last, much about the Hour of two a Clock, several People,

FIERY APPARITION IN THE AIR, SEEN IN LONDON, 1710.

who were then abroad, especially the Watchman about Tower Street, Clare Market, Cheapside, and Westminster, plainly and visibly saw this strange Comet, it seem'd a very great Star, at the end of which was a long tail, or streak of Fire, very wonderful and surprizing to behold. It did not continue fix'd, but pass'd along with the Scud, or two black Clouds, being carried by a brisk wind that then blew.

'After which follow'd the likeness of a Man in a Cloud of Fire, with a Sword in his hand, which mov'd with the Clouds as the other did, but they saw it for near a quarter of an Hour together, to their very great surprize, and related the same the next Morning, which they are ready now to affirm if any are so curious to go and Enquire, particularly John Smith, near Tower-street, Abraham Wilsley, on Tower-hill, John Miller, near Clare Market, John Williams, in Cheapside, George Mules and Rebeccah Sampson upon the Water, and Mr. Lomax, Watchman of St. Anns, with many others too tedious to insert.'

Amongst the many newspapers that had sprung into existence the following so far improved upon their small and dingy predecessors as to be adorned with pictorial headings :—The *Post Boy*, 1720 ; the *Weekly Journal*, 1720 ; the *London Journal*, 1720 ; the *Weekly Journal, or Saturday's Post*, 1721 ; *Applebee's Weekly Journal*, 1721 ; *Read's Journal, or British Gazetteer*, 1718–31. The last named appeared for many years as the *Weekly Journal, or British Gazetteer ;* but the *Weekly Journal* was a favourite title, and was borne by so many other papers that after a time the publisher altered the title of his paper to *Read's Journal ; or British Gazetteer*, and gave it an engraved heading. Read was a man of enterprise, and surpassed his contemporaries in endeavouring to make his journal attractive by means of illustrations. In his paper for Nov. 1, 1718, there is a caricature engraved on wood. It is levelled against the Jacobites, and is called ' An Hieroglyphick,' and is introduced to the reader with the following rhymes :—

' Will *Fools* and *Knaves* their own Misfortune see
And ponder on the *Tories* villany
Behold this *Hieroglyphick*, and admire
What *Loyalty* do's in true Souls inspire !
Whate'er the *Figures* mean we shan't declare,
Because the *Jacobites* will curse and swear ;
But if our *Readers* will this piece explain,
Their Explanation we shall not disdain.'

Nobody appears to have responded to the invitation conveyed in the verses, for in the succeeding numbers of the

CARICATURE AGAINST THE JACOBITES. FROM 'READ'S WEEKLY JOURNAL,' 1718

paper there is no attempt to explain the 'hieroglyphick.' A copy of this early newspaper caricature is given on the opposite page.

In the same journal for May 20, 1721, there is a large woodcut entitled 'Lucifers Row-Barge,' which I have also copied. It is a caricature on the South-Sea Bubble, and appears, from what follows, to have been first published in the previous week : ' The Call for this Journal (last week) being very extraordinary, upon account of the delineation of Lucifer's Row-Barge in it, we are desired by several of our Correspondents both in City and Country, to present them with it in this week's paper, with an Explanation of every Representation in the aforesaid Cut, adapted to Figures ; with which Request we have comply'd, as supposing it will be acceptable not only to them with such a Design, but likewise pleasing to all our Readers in General.' The different parts of the engraving are described under the illustration on the following page.

Each of these divisions of the subject is further described in verse. In concocting this satire the author has allowed some symptoms of journalistic jealousy to appear by dragging in the correspondent of the *London Journal* (which was a rival paper), and describing him as the common hangman. The feeling about the South-Sea Bubble must have been very strong to have made this caricature acceptable. It was intended to satirise Mr. Knight, the cashier of the South-Sea Company, who fled the country when it became too hot for him. The verses which accompany the engraving, though by no means models of poetic elegance, might be commended to the attention of some directors of our own day :—

> ' Then what must such vile Plunderers expect
> When they upon their Actions do reflect ;
> Who barely have three Kingdoms quite undone
> From aged Father to the Infant Son ?
> From many Eyes they've drawn a briny Flood,
> But Tears to ruined People do no Good.'

SOUTH SEA BUBBLE CARICATURE. FROM THE 'WEEKLY JOURNAL AND BRITISH GAZETTEER,' 1721.

1. The Cashire of the South Sea Company
2. The Horse of an Accomptant to the South Sea Company
3. The Correspondent of the Author of the *London Journal*
4. A Stock Jobber, or Exchange Broker, whipt by the Common Hangman
5. Belzebub prompting a Director of the South Sea
6. Satan prompting the same Director in t'other Ear
7. The Worm of Conscience fastens on the above said Director
8. The Cup of Indignation
9. A Director's Sacrifice, which is a Villanous Heart
10. A Director in the Pillory
11. The Superscription over the pillory'd Director

paraphras'd from the prophet Ezekiel. Chap. XXII. Ver. 12, 13, and Chap. XXIII. Ver. 25, 26, 27
12. A Director decypher'd by the Knave of Diamonds Hanged
13. A Director wafting to Hell with the tide
14. Lucifers Row-Barge for first rate passengers
15. Moloch sounds his trumpet for Joy of meeting with a good Fare
16. Belial playing on the Violin to the Director
17. Mammon takes a trip at Helm for him
18. The South Sea
19. Lucifer rowing his own Barge
20. The Entrance into Hell, represented by the Mouth of the Leviathan, or great Whale, belching flames of sulphurous fire.'

There was a total eclipse of the sun in 1724, which appears to have excited much attention, and several notices of it occur in the newspapers. Parker's *London News* gives a long account, with a woodcut, which I have copied. This paper was published three times a-week — on Mondays, Wednesdays, and Fridays. In the number for Monday, May 4th, 1724, is the woodcut referred to, together with the following explanation :—

' Of the Eclipse of the Sun which will happen in the Afternoon on Monday, the 11th of this inst. May 1724.

' The Sun, the glorious Lamp of the Universe, being a large round Body of Light, is fixt in the Centre of the *Creation ;* so that all parts thereof might be partakers of his vivifying Rays, which otherwise would be shut up in perpetual Darkness.

' The Earth is a dark round Ball, which turneth round on its own Axis, from West to East, once in twenty-four Hours Time, causing thereby Day and Night, also at the same Time, the Earth with the Moon, going round in its Orbit in 365 Days and some Hours, constituting thereby the true Length of our Year.

' The Moon is likewise a round dark Ball, void of Light, and circumvolveth the Earth once a Month ; so that whenever she passeth in her Orbit, in a direct line between the Sun and Earth, she Eclipses the Earth not the Sun, by depriving us of a Sight thereof; And whenever the Earth happens to be between the Sun and Moon, at such times the Earth obstructs the Light of the Sun from the Moon, and then the Moon is Eclipsed by the dark Body of the Earth.

'Now to prevent any Consternation, which People, through Ignorance may fall under, by means of that great Eclipse which is now approaching ; at which time it will be so dark, that the stars, (if the Air be clear) will be seen ; and the Planets Mars, Venus, and the seldom to be seen Mercury, will appear a little above the Sun, towards the South ; also Venus a little higher to the Left of Mercury, and Mars in the S.S.W. Parts of the Heavens; The several Appearances of this Eclipse will be according to the Types before inserted.

'The beginning of this Eclipse, according to the nicest Computation of the most Judicious, will happen at 39 Minutes past 5 in the Afternoon when the Limb of the Moon will just touch the Sun's Limb, as it is represented by the Uppermost Figure to the Right Hand. At 44 Minutes after 5 it will be enter'd the disk, and so much darkened as the 2d Scheme on the Right Hand shews. At 48 Minutes past 5 as the 3d denotes. At 53 Minutes past 5 as the 4th shews. At 58 Minutes after 5, as the 5th represents. At 3 Minutes past 6, as in the 6th Scheme. At 7 Minutes after 6, as in the 7th. At 12 Minutes past 6, as is shewn by the 8th Figure. At 17 Minutes past 6, as the 10th Figure shews. At 26 Minutes past 6, as the next succeeding Scheme denotes, beginning always to number from the Right Hand. At 31 Minutes after 6, so much of the Sun's Body will be darkened, as the 12th represents: and at 36 past 6, will be the greatest darkness, when only a small thread of Light will be seen at *London*, on the upper part of the *Sun* as the 13th Scheme informs; but to all the Southern parts of the Kingdom, it will be totally darkened.

'After this the *Sun* will begin to shew its Light, which will appear first on the lower part of that Glorious Body, towards the Right Hand; and the darkness will gradually lessen, as the several Figures represent, till the Sun's Body be perfectly clear of the Shadow, which will be at 27 Minutes past 7 a-clock that Afternoon.'

This description is reprinted, together with the woodcut, in the same paper for May 8th, and to it is added the following:—'Directions for the better viewing the Eclipse that will happen on Monday next'——'Take a Piece of Common window Glass and hold it over a Candle, so that the Flame of the Candle may make it black, through which look upon the Sun, and you will behold the *Eclipse* without Danger to the Eyes.'

Or thus

Take a Piece of thick writing Paper, and prick a hole in it with a fine Needle, through which the *Eclipse* may be seen.'

The same paper (May 8th, 1724) contains some advertisements about the eclipse, which seems to have been for the moment the absorbing topic, and was apparently made the vehicle for advertising the shops of different tradesmen.

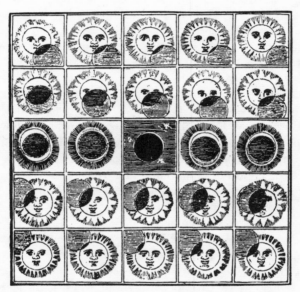

ECLIPSE OF THE SUN. FROM 'PARKER'S LONDON NEWS,' 1724.

The notices were published ostensibly ' to lessen the consternation of ignorant people,' but it is evident the advertisers had an eye to business. 'An exact curious Draft' was to be ' given *gratis* at Mr. Garway's original shop, the Sign of the Practical Scheme at the Royal Exchange Gate, on Cornhill Side. Up one pair of Stairs at the Sign of the celebrated Anodyne Necklace for Childrens Teeth, next the Rose Tavern without Temple Bar. At Mr. Gregg's Bookseller, next to Northumberland House, at Charing Cross; and at R. Brad-

shaw's the author's Servant, at his House, next to the King's
Head, in Crown Street, right against Sutton Street End, just
by Soho Square. Note, it will not be given to any Boy or
Girl.'

The cut and description are again reprinted in the
number for May 11th, where, amongst other items of news,
is the following:—' His Royal Highness went last Monday
to Richmond, as did also the Right Hon. the Lord *Chancellor*,
Judge Fortescue, and other persons of note; some of the
Judges went to Hampton Court, and other gentlemen of
Learning and Curiosity to more distant places, to make their
Observations, as 'tis said, upon the great Eclipse of the Sun
that happen'd in the Evening, and exactly answered the
Calculations made of it by our Astronomers.'   In the number
for May 18th are accounts of how the eclipse was observed in
the country. It is stated :—' We are advised from the Isle
of Wight that the Eclipse on the 11th instant, which was
Total, and caused very great Consternation there lasted about
a Minute and a half; but that the chief sufferers thereby
were the gentry of that Island, who by the great concourse of
Strangers to their Houses, had but very little French Claret
left upon their hands; But the comfort is, they have frequent
opportunities of running some more.'

Parker's London News blended amusement with instruction. The following items of news occur in the same number
that contains the account of the eclipse, and show how our
forefathers were entertained by the newspapers 160 years
ago :—' The Papers of the week, from the highest to the
lowest rank have killed one Sir Nicholas Raymond in the
Isle of Wight; but as no such knight ever inhabited therein,
we can impute it to nothing but want of home news.'

' Last Saturday Night, two Servant Maids at a Snuff
Warehouse, at Mile End took *so much Snuff*, that they
quarrell'd, and one of them stabbed the other in so many
places with an Iron Scuer, that 'twas thought she could not
live. The other therefore, was instantly apprehended and
committed.'

' Last week an Apothecary was attacked by two High-waymen, between Winchester and Southampton, who robbed him of his money, and finding two Vials of Purging Potions in his Pocket, that he was carrying to a *Patient*, they were so inhuman as to force him to swallow 'em himself.'

' Last Sunday Night, Sir Basil Firebrass, noted for his humanity to young Vintners, whom he first set up, and afterwards upon Default of payment took execution against 'em, departed this life.'

The *Weekly Journal or British Gazetteer* for May 9th, 1724, contains an account and illustration of the same eclipse that is described in *Parker's London News*. The illustration is a diagram, and is called, 'A Representation of a Solar Eclipse. The Time of the Beginning, Middle, and End of the Eclipse and the continuance of Darkness, together with its Appearance at London and Bristol.'

The celebrated *Grub Street Journal* now comes upon the scene ; and we find it not only surpassing its contemporaries in wit and satire, but it also comes out as an illustrated paper. In No. 43, for Oct. 29th, 1730, a whole page is occupied with woodcuts of the arms of the City Companies, which are reprinted about the time of Lord Mayor's Day in succeeding years. In No. 48 there is a very well-executed copperplate portrait, presumably of the Lord Mayor of London. As it is printed on the same page with type (involving two printings), and the journal was sold for twopence, it shows some enterprise for the year 1730. On the front page of No. 95, for Oct. 28th, 1731, there are very rude woodcuts of the Lord Mayor's procession, surrounded by the arms of the City Companies before referred to. No. 147 has a curious copperplate at the head of an article entitled, ' *The Art and Mystery of Printing Emblematically Displayed.*' The engraving represents human figures with animals' heads at work in a printing-office. An ass is setting up the types, a pig is using the inking-balls, a horse is acting as pressman, a sheep is arranging the printed sheets, while a two-faced man and a many-horned

o

devil are watching them all. This, like the portrait of the
Lord Mayor, is printed on the same page with the type, with
no printing at the back of the engraving. The article is a
satirical conversation between certain printers' devils, and is
continued in the next number, where the engraving is also
reproduced. The *Grub Street Journal* is the first example I
have met with of a newspaper employing the expensive process of copperplate engraving for illustrations, and printing
the plate in the body of its pages. It was probably thought
to be too costly, for we find the conductors recurring to the
almost extinct art of wood-engraving. In the number for
Oct. 25th, 1733, there is a coarsely executed woodcut heading
a satirical allegory, entitled, *The Art of Trimming Emblematically Displayed.*

The *Daily Post* of March 29th, 1740, is interesting as
being an early example of a daily paper attempting to illustrate current events. The *Daily Post* consisted of a single
leaf, with the page divided into three columns. In the
number referred to there is a long account of Admiral
Vernon's attack on Porto Bello, illustrated with a woodcut,
which the writer says will give the reader a clearer idea of
the position of the town, castle, and ships engaged. The
narrative is introduced by the editor in these words :—
' The following is a letter from a gentleman on board
the Burford at Porto Bello to his friend at Newcastle,
which, as it contains a more particular account of Admiral
Vernon's glorious achievement at that place than any yet
published here, we thought we could not in justice to the
Bravery of our English Officers and Sailors, refuse it a Place
in our Paper.'

' On the afternoon of the 21st about two o'clock we came
up with Porto Bello Harbour, where the Spaniards had
hoisted upon the Iron Castle the Flag of Defiance ; and, as
we were told by themselves afterwards, they wished earnestly
for our attempting to come in, as believing they could sink
us all immediately, but said they feared we were only making
a second Bastimento Expedition, and would not give them

the pleasure of engaging us.' Then follows a long and circumstantial account of the conflict. 'Notwithstanding they had discharged very few Guns for some Minutes before we came up; yet as if they had resolved to summon up all their Courage against the Flag, they welcomed us with a terrible Volley, which being at so short a Distance, took

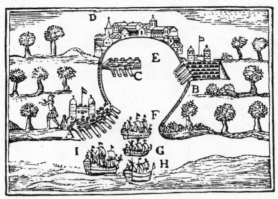

ADMIRAL VERNON'S ATTACK ON PORTO BELLO.   FROM THE ' DAILY POST,' 1740.

A. The Iron Castle on the North side of the Mouth of the Harbour with 100 Guns.
B. The Castle Gloria, with 120 Guns, on the South side of the Harbour, and a Mile from the Iron Castle.
C. The Fort of Hieronymo, with 20 Guns.
D. The Town of Porto Bello lying along the Extremity of the Harbour.
E. The station of the Spanish Ships.
F. The Hampton-Courts place of Action, Commodore Brown.
G. The Norwich's ditto, Cap. Herbert.
H. The Worcester's ditto, Cap. Main.
I. The Admiral's Ship, the Burford.

Place with almost every Shot. One struck away the Stern of our Barge; another broke a large Gun upon our upper Deck; a third went thro' our Foretop-Mast; and a fourth, passing thro' the Arning within two Inches of our Main-Mast, broke down the barricado of our Quarter-Deck, very near the Admiral, and killed three Men in a Moment, wounding five others which stood by them. This look'd as if we should have bloody work, but was far from discouraging our brave Fellows.' The Spaniards being driven from their guns, the English landed:—'One man set himself close under an Embossier, whilst another climbed upon his

Shoulders and enter'd under the Mouth of a great Gun. This so dismay'd the Spaniards that they threw down their Arms and fled to the Top of the Castle; from whence scaling backwards we could see them run into the woods by hundreds and fly for their lives.' The place being taken, the writer gives a minute account of the damage done and the booty taken. He says:—' We have also had the good luck to find about 10,000 Dollars belonging to the King of Spain, which I had the Pleasure of being present at the searching for, when we found it in the Customhouse,' &c.

The writer of the above account signs himself Wm. Richardson, and gives the explanations to the letters on the woodcut, a facsimile of which is engraved.

To account for the enthusiasm with which Admiral Vernon's victory at Porto Bello was received we must remember that the nation had previously been wrought up to a high state of fever about Spain, and the declaration of war had been received in the most jubilant manner. We can therefore understand that the conductors of the *Daily Post*, infected by the popular fervour, would gladly seize the opportunity of producing in their pages the drawing and description by an eye-witness of this naval victory. This early example of illustrated news, though it has nothing pictorial about it, is extremely interesting, showing as it does the tendency of newspapers, in times of excitement, to call on the artist's pencil to aid the writer's pen. It was in reference to this war that Walpole said, when the bells were ringing joyfully, ' They may ring the bells now, but they will soon be wringing their hands.'

To the preceding example of a *daily* paper attempting to illustrate current events I will add an· instance of a *penny* paper doing a similar thing at about the same period. *The Penny London Post, or, The Morning Advertiser*, was a paper published three times a-week, and in the number for Jan. 9th, 1748–9, there is given 'A view of the Public Fireworks to be exhibited on occasion of the General Peace concluded at Aix La Chapelle the 7th Day of October 1748.' The engraving is little more than a diagram, and accompanies a description of the arrangements made for the occasion, amongst which there was to be a band of a hundred musicians to play before the fireworks began, ' the Musick for which,' says the *Penny London Post,* ' is to be composed by Mr. Handel.'

We are accustomed to think of the immortal author of *Tom Jones* as a novelist only. Henry Fielding was, however, also a journalist, a pamphleteer, and a justice of the peace for Middlesex and Westminster. Amidst his other labours he found time to edit the *Jacobite's Journal,* a paper started to support the House of Hanover after the Rebellion of 1745. It was a sheet of four pages, published every Saturday, and the first twelve numbers were adorned with a woodcut heading which has been attributed to Hogarth. This heading was discontinued after the twelfth number, and in number 13 there is an elaborate article, replete with sarcastic humour, explaining the reasons for its discontinuance. The *Jacobite's Journal* purported to be edited by ' John Trott-Plaid, Esq.,' and was essentially satirical in its tone. In the second number there is the following reference to the engraved heading :—

'As my Wife appears in her Plaid on *Ass-back* behind me at the Head of this Paper, it will not I hope be imagined that I have brought her abroad only to take the Air, without assigning to her any share in this undertaking.

' The *Mystery of Jacobitism* doth not, like that of *Free Masonry,* exclude the Female World; for tho' all Jacobites are not, as some wicked Whigs have represented us, *old women,* yet women we have in great Numbers among us, who are as learned in the knowledge of our Mysteries, and as active in the celebration of our Rites, as any of the Male Species; and many of these are so far from deserving the name of *old,* that their age scarce yet entitles them to the name of *women.'*

As I before stated, the heading is left out after the twelfth number. Whether it had sufficiently served its purpose as a caricature of the Jacobite party, and was no longer needed, or whether it really took up too much room, as stated by the editor, its discontinuance was made the occasion of publishing a leading article, part of which I am tempted to transcribe as an excellent specimen of Fielding's satire.

'There is scarcely anything more provoking than to be totally misunderstood, and by that means to have our compliments received as Affronts, and our Panegyrick converted into Satire.

'It cannot therefore be wondered at, if I am not well pleased with that gross misunderstanding of the Emblematical Frontispiece so long prefixed to my Paper, which hath generally prevailed, and which, among other good Reasons, hath at length induced me to displace it for the future. By this Error of the Public, a Contrivance of mine (the expense of much laborious thinking) to do Honour to the Jacobite Party, hath been represented as the Means of vilifying and degrading it.

'But, seriously, could the Art of Man have carried the Glory of Jacobitism higher than it was carried in this print, where a Jacobite of either Sex was seen cloathed in Mystery, and riding on one of the most honourable Beasts in the Universe, while Popery servilely attends, leading it by the Halter, and *France* and the Republican Party are dragged after Heels. Is not here depictured that notable and mysterious Union of *French* Interest, Popery, Jacobitism, and Republicanism; by a Coalition of all which Parties this Nation is to be redeemed from the deplorable State of Slavery, under which it at present labours?

'It would be endless to enumerate all the Mistakes and ridiculous Conceits entertained on this occasion. Some have imagined we intended to insinuate that the Protestant Jacobites were led by the Nose by Popery, and spurr'd on by *France* and the Republicans; whereas nothing can be more certain in Fact, than that Popery and *France*, and the Republicans, have ever been the mere Dupes and Fools of the said Jacobites.

'Many have endeavoured to discover Resemblances to real Persons in the figures there exhibited. By the Popish Priest, it hath been said we design to represent the old Chevalier; and by the Figures on the Ass, the young Chevalier his Son and the famous *Jenny Cameron.*

'Others have found out Likenesses of less Importance, and several Squires and Country Gentlewomen of *Stafford-shire* and other Counties, who never travel beyond the limits of a Fox chace, have been supposed to ride, once a week, Post all over the Kingdom in this Paper.

'But the most egregious Errors have been committed in Misconstructions concerning the Ass. Several ingenious and witty Printers of News Papers have very facetiously taken occasion to call the Author himself an Ass; supposing probably, that as Scripture informs us an Ass once spoke, so certain Descendants of the same Family might write, which Faith, perhaps something within their own Experience, might sufficiently encourage them to receive.

'To mention no more of these absurd Conjectures, I must here inform my Reader, that by the Body of the Ass we intend to figure the whole Body of Jacobitical doctrine.

'Now as there was no Symbol among the Antients, of which the Emblematical Meaning was so plain and easy to be discovered, our Party could never have so universally mistaken it, had it not been for that want of Learning among us, which I lamented in my last Paper. Hence being misled by those erroneous opinions, which the Moderns have propagated to the great disadvantage of Asses, the Jacobites have been unwilling to discover any Resemblance between themselves and an Animal which the wise Antients saw in so respectable a Light, and which the ignorance of latter Ages hath highly dishonoured by odious Comparisons with certain Individuals of the Human Species.

'Thus *Homer* is well known to have liken'd one of his principal Heroes to this noble Animal; which was in such Esteem among the antient *Jews,* that he was not only an

object of their Devotion, but they are said to have preserved
his Figure in massy Gold in the Temple of *Jerusalem.*

'If the Transfiguration of *Midas* in the *Metamorphosis*
doth but little Honour to the Ears of our Symbol, the Story
of *Lotis* which the same Poet tells in his Fastorum, is greatly
in praise of his Braying, by which the Chastity of that
Nymph was rescued from the wicked Designs of her insidious Lover.

'In such esteem hath this noble Beast been held among
the Learned, that I have seen a Book composed in his Favour
and entitled *Laus Asini :* not to mention the celebrated performance of *Apuleius* to which he hath given the Name of
the *Golden Ass.*

'Instead therefore of being displeased with the Emblem,
our Party have great Reason to be vain on this Occasion,
nor do I think there can be a greater Comparison than of a
Protestant Jacobite to an Ass, or one more to the Honour of
the former.

'First, what can so well answer to that noble and in-
vincible obstinacy, which I have more than once celebrated
in our Party, as the intractable and unalterable Nature of
this Animal, which gave rise to an antient Proverb alluded
to by *Horace* in his Satires :—

<blockquote>
' " ———— Your Art
As well may teach an Ass to scour the Plain
And bend obedient to the forming Rein."
</blockquote>

'And again in his Epistles :—

<blockquote>
" ' Democritus would think the writers told
To a deaf Ass their story ———— "
</blockquote>

'Which may most strictly be applied to all those writers,
who have endeavoured to convince the Jacobites by argument.

'Again what can give us a more adequate Idea of that
Firmness, with which we have supported all the ill-usage
of the worst of Sovereigns without Resentment, than the

laudable Indifference which an Ass hath for the same; whom you may beat, whip, kick, and spur as long as you are pleased, he still trudges on without altering his Pace.

'To omit many other obvious Resemblances, such as Braying, &c., the famous story of the Countryman and the Ass, briefly touched upon by *Horace* in the Epistle addressed to his own Book, is so perfect a Picture of Jacobitism, that I have been inclined to think as the Antients are known to have inveloped all their Mysteries in Fable and Allegory, that no less than Jacobitism itself was intended to be couched under this story: "A certain Countryman observing an Ass making towards a Precipice, ran to him, and catching hold of his Tail, endeavoured with all his Might to withhold him from Destruction; but the more the Countryman attempted to preserve him, the more obstinately the Ass contended against his kind Preserver, and the more eagerly was bent upon accomplishing his fatal Purpose. The Countryman at last, wearied out with his Endeavours to save an obstinate Beast against his own will, and having probably received some Thanks from his Heels for his intended kindness, instead of pulling any longer, gave the Ass a Push, and tumbled him headlong down the Precipice which he had been so industriously pursuing."

'I make no doubt but many of our good Enemies the Whigs, who have well imitated this Countryman in the former part of his Behaviour, would imitate him likewise in the latter, was it not that they cannot precipitate us without tumbling down themselves at the same time.

'These are the Mysteries, then, which have been couched under my Frontispiece, and which, tho' their meaning must now appear to have been so plain, have nevertheless stood exposed so long at the Head of this Journal, without having been, as I can find, understood by any.

'Perhaps I shall be asked, why I have now displaced them, since, after so large and full an Explanation, they cannot fail of being highly agreeable to that Party for whose use chiefly this Paper is calculated; and who would,

for the future, worship my Ass with the same Veneration
with which the *Jews* of old did theirs.

'Now, tho' the Indignation which I have exprest in the
Beginning of this Essay at the many gross and absurd
Misconceptions which have been vented by the Public,
would alone very well justify the. Discontinuance of my
Emblem so much abused, there are, to say the Truth, two
other Reasons which have had a stronger Weight with me
in producing this Determination. The former of these is,
that the Ass and his Retinue do indeed take up too much
room, and must oblige us either to suppress Part of our
Lucubrations, or some of those material articles of News
which we weekly transcribe from others; or lastly those
pieces of Intelligence called Advertisements, which tho' not
always most entertaining to our Reader, do afford very
agreeable Entertainment to ourselves.

'A second and a very strong Motive with us, is to lend
all the Assistance in our Power to a very worthy and willing,
tho' weak Brother, the learned and facetious Novelist, Mr.
Carte; whose great Romance, tho' in our Court of Criticism,
where we shall always act impartially, we have been obliged
like other Judges, to condemn, contrary to our own Inclina-
tions, to be grubb'd, we shall always privately esteem as a
work calculated solely for the use of our Party. As we have
therefore, to our great Concern, received very credible Information that the said work begins already to be considered
only as a Heap of Waste Paper, we have thought proper to
lend our Frontispiece to our good Brother, in order that it
may be prefixed to the future Volumes of that great Work
advising him to omit the words *London Evening Post*, and to
insert *English History* in their stead. This will not fail of
greatly recommending his Performance to our Party, who
never willingly read anything but what an Ass may at least
be supposed to have bray'd.

'I could wish, moreover, that the learned Novelist would
take our Advice in another Instance, and for the future deal
forth his excellent work in weekly Portions or Numbers; I

do not mean in such a Form as the real History of *England* is now publishing by Mr. Waller ; but in the same manner with those true and delectable Histories of *Argalus* and *Parthenia, Guy,* Earl of *Warwick,* the *Seven Champions,* &c., in which Form, at the price of 1d. each, when embellished by our Frontispiece, I make no doubt of assuring him as universal a Sale as the inimitable Adventures of *Robinson Crusoe* formerly had throughout this Kingdom.'

The 'Mr. Carte' to whom Fielding proposed to lend his ' Frontispiece' was Thomas Carte, the historian, who had just brought out the first volume of his *History of England,* in which he showed such decided Jacobite predilections that his work was ruined in consequence. He professed to be acquainted with the case of a person who had been cured of the King's Evil by the Pretender, then an exile in France, and this so disgusted many of the subscribers to his book that they withdrew their names and abandoned the author and his work together. He, however, brought out two more volumes, and a fourth was published after his death. It was probably in allusion to this story of the Pretender curing the King's Evil that Fielding speaks of Carte as ' the learned and facetious novelist ;' and doubtless the ' great Romance' referred to was intended for his history of England. Fielding and Carte both died in the same year, 1754.

During the next ten years I have found no illustrations in the newspapers of that period. In 1758 there was a newspaper published entitled *Owen's Weekly Chronicle, or Universal Journal,* a sheet of eight pages, size of the *Athenæum,* price two-pence halfpenny. About this time the English Government, in carrying on the war against France, despatched several expeditions to the French coast, none of which redounded much to the credit of the British arms. One of these expeditions was against Rochfort, and it turned out a failure, which caused much dissatisfaction. *Owen's Weekly Chronicle* for June 3, 1758, published a long article on the subject, illustrated with a woodcut view of Fort Fouras. The writer concludes, with true newspaper

vehemence, in the following words :—' Where is the glory of
the British name ? Where are the terrors that used to
accompany our fleets and armies ? Let it not be said the
treasures of the country are poured forth in vain by an
united and willing people ; that our enemies are become
invulnerable ; and every blow our Ministers meditate im-
practicable. The Duke of Marlborough and Lord George
Sackville are gone with Lord Anson and Sir Edward Hawke
upon the present grand expedition ; and we hope their

PERSPECTIVE VIEW OF FORT FOURAS, AS IT APPEARED IN THE SHIPS FROM THE
CHARENTE, FROM ' OWEN'S WEEKLY CHRONICLE,' 1758.

courage and experience will revive the sinking honour of
their country ; and show that France is both vulnerable and
impotent when the power of Britain is properly exerted.'
Unfortunately, the sinking honour of the country was not
much revived by the ' grand expedition ' here referred to ;
for, after an ineffectual attempt on St. Maloes, the Duke of
Marlborough embarked in such haste that he left his tea-
spoons behind him : and these were afterwards sent home in
a cartel-ship by the Duke d'Aiguillon in polite contempt. I
have copied the woodcut above referred to, which is entitled,
' A Perspective view of Fort Fouras as it appeared in the
ships from the Charente,' and the following description is

given of it :—'Fouras was the tower of an old parish church, which, soon after the foundation of Rochefort, in 1688, Louis XIV. purchased of the proprietors to make a Tour de Garde, for repeating signals from the Isles of Oleron and Aix up to Rochefort, which is one of its present uses. A fort and garrison being established in the isle of Aix, Fouras was found to be the nearest and most secure communication in all weathers with that island; so that in process of time barracks and lodgments were built therein, and it was fortified to the sea by a strait curtain.'

For the view of Fort Fouras *Owen's Weekly Chronicle* must have been indebted to some one on board one of the British ships. Naval and military officers in all parts of the world are among the most valued correspondents of the modern illustrated newspaper; and it is interesting to notice that so long ago as the taking of Porto Bello and the attack on Rochefort there were men engaged in those expeditions whose spirit and intelligence prompted them to supply the newspapers of the day with sketches and information. The view of Fort Fouras is the earliest attempt I have seen in a newspaper to give a pictorial representation of a place in connexion with news.

Wood-engraving was the only cheap method of illustration within the reach of newspapers, but the art barely existed at this time. The few woodcuts published in newspapers were not only coarsely and rudely executed, but sometimes the efforts of the illustrator did not get beyond a rough plan or map, and even this, as I have before remarked, was not always engraved. In further confirmation of this statement I may refer to *Lloyd's Evening Post* of April 17, 1765, where one of the pages is taken up with a plan representing the trial of a Peer in Westminster Hall. This is done entirely with lines, type, and printer's ornaments. Although there is no account given of this trial in *Lloyd's Evening Post*, the plan must have referred to the case of Lord Byron, who was tried in Westminster Hall for the murder of Mr. Chaworth, April 16 and 17, 1765.

In the winter of 1764–5 a strange wild beast was said to have appeared in France, devouring women and children, and spreading dismay and terror through the whole of Languedoc. What this ferocious creature was, or whence it came, no one knew; but the fear inspired by its presence was universal. The district which it specially haunted procured for it the name of the Wild Beast of the Gévaudan, by which designation it became famous not only in the South of France but throughout the country, and even in foreign lands. The earliest account of this ferocious monster appeared in the official journal of Paris in the following words :—

'A very strange wild beast has lately appeared in the neighbourhood of Langagne and the forest of Mercoire which has occasioned great commotion. It has already devoured twenty persons, chiefly children, and particularly young girls, and scarcely a day passes without some accident. The terror he occasions prevents the woodcutters from working in the forests; so that wood has become dear. Those who have seen him say he is much higher than a wolf, low before, and his feet are armed with talons. His hair is reddish, his head large, and the muzzle of it is shaped like that of a greyhound; his ears are small and straight; his breast is wide, and of a grey colour; his back streaked with black; and his mouth, which is large, is provided with a set of teeth so very sharp that they have taken off several heads as clean as a razor could have done. He is of amazing swiftness; but, when he aims at his prey, he crouches so close to the ground, that he hardly appears to be bigger than a large fox; and at the distance of some one or two toises, he rises upon his hind legs and springs upon his prey, seizing it by the neck or throat. He is afraid of oxen, which he runs away from. The consternation is dreadful throughout the district where he commits his ravages, and public prayers are offered up on the occasion. The Marquis de Marangis has sent out four hundred peasants to destroy this fierce beast; but they have not been able to do it.'

In spite of the efforts made to capture or destroy it the wild beast of the Gévaudan continued its ravages. In a letter from Meude, dated December 21, 1764, it is stated, 'The wild beast, which hath ravaged several provinces, has been for some time in ours. He was seen a few days ago near St. Flour, ten leagues from hence, and he is now in our neighbourhood. The day before yesterday he devoured a little girl who looked after cattle. A detachment of dragoons has been out six weeks after him. The province has offered a thousand crowns to any person who will kill him.' On the 8th of February, 1765, the following statement was sent from Montpellier :—' On the 12th ultimo the wild beast attacked seven children, five boys and two girls, none of whom exceeded eleven years of age. The beast flew at one of the boys; but the three eldest of them by beating him with stakes, the ends of which were iron, obliged him to retire, after having bitten off a part of the boy's cheek, which he ate before them. He then seized another of the children; but they pursued him into a marsh which was close by, where he sunk in up to his belly. By continually beating him, they rescued their companion; who, though he was under his paw for some time, received only a wound in his arm, and a scratch in the face. A man at last coming up, the creature was put to flight. He afterwards devoured a boy at Mazel, and, on the 21st, flew on a girl, who, however, escaped with some dangerous wounds. The next day he attacked a woman, and bit off her head. Captain Duhamel, of the dragoons, is in pursuit of him, and has caused several of his men to dress themselves in women's apparel, and to accompany the children that keep cattle.'

The eyes of all France being fixed upon the doings of this wild beast, the attention of Louis the Fifteenth himself was called to the bravery of the boys in the preceding account. 'The King having been informed of the bravery with which the young Portefaix attacked the beast on the 12th of January last, at the head of his companions, and being willing to reward such gallant behaviour, has given him a recompense of four hundred livres, and has ordered three hundred to be distributed among his companions.'

The Government also offered a reward for the destruction of the wild beast. The following placard was fixed up in all the cities and towns of Languedoc :—' By the King and the Intendant of the province of Languedoc. Notice is given to all persons, that His Majesty, being justly affected by the situation of his subjects now exposed to the ravages of the wild beast which for four months past has infested Vivarais and Gévaudan, and being desirous to stop the progress of such a calamity, has determined to promise a reward of six thousand livres to any person or persons who shall kill this animal. Such as are willing to undertake the pursuit of him may previously apply to the Sieur de la Fout, sub-deputy to the Intendant of Meudes, who will give them the necessary instructions agreeably to what has been presented by the ministry on the part of his Majesty.'

A letter from Paris dated the 18th of February, 1765, gives the following circumstantial description of the wild beast :—

' You know how I acquainted you, some months ago, that Monsieur Bardelle, his son and I, designed going by the Diligence, and opening the New Year at our old friend Monsieur Dura's chateau, near Babres, in Languedoc. We spent the time very agreeably, our host and his family having done all in their power to make us welcome. The party broke up and took leave the first of this month, amongst whom was Monsieur Lefevre, a counsellor, and two young ladies, who were engaged to pass a week at Monsieur de Sante's, the curé of Vaistour, about three days' journey distant from the chateau of Monsieur Dura. The company went away in a berlingo and four, and the footman Michel, on a saddle-horse ; the carriage, after the manner here, being drawn by four post-horses, with two postilions, the berlingo having no coach box. The first night the party lay at Guimpe, and set out next morning at nine, to bait half way between that and Roteux, being four posts, and a mountainous barren country, as all the Gévaudan is. The parish of Guimpe had been greatly alarmed by the frequent appearance of, and the horrid destruction made by, the fiery animal that has so long been the terror of the Gévaudan, and is now so formidable that the inhabitants and travellers are in very great apprehension. The bailiff of Guimpe acquainted the party that this animal had been often lurking about the chaussée that week, and that it would be proper to take an escort of armed men, which would protect the carriage; but the gentlemen declined it, and took the ladies under their protection, and set out, on the 2nd of February, very cheerfully. When they had made about two leagues, they observed at a distance a post-chaise, and a man on horseback, coming down the hill of Credi, and whipping the horses very much; and at the descent unfortunately the wheel-horse fell down, and the postilion was thrown off; whereupon the horseman who followed the chaise, advanced to take up the boy, in which moment, when he had got down, we perceived the wild beast so often described make a jump towards the horses, and on the footman's raising his right hand to draw a cutlass and strike the creature, it pricked up its ears, stood on its hind feet, and, showing its teeth full of froth, turned round and gave the fellow a most violent blow with the swing of its tail. The man's face was all over blood; and then the monster, seeing the gentleman in the chaise present a blunderbuss at its neck, crept on its forehead to the chaise-step, keeping its head almost under its forelegs, and getting close to the door, reared upright, vaulted into the inside, broke through the other side-glass, and ran at a great rate to the adjoining wood. The blunderbuss missed fire, or it is possible this had been the last day this brute-disturber had moved. The stench left in the carriage was past description, and no cure of burning frankincense, nor any other method removed, but rather increased the stink, so that it was sold for two louis; and though burned to ashes, the cinders were obliged, by order of a commissary, to be buried without the town walls. We came

P

up very well in time; for the beast would doubtless have destroyed some one, had it not espied three of us advancing with guns. It certainly jumped through the chaise to get away from us.'

These accounts appear to have been received with some incredulity abroad. In the same number of *Lloyd's Evening Post* that contains the plan of Lord Byron's trial there occurs the following passage about this curious wild beast: ' One of the Dutch Gazetteers by Monday's mail says :—" The accounts of the wild beast seen in the Gévaudan are of such a nature that it is hardly possible to give any credit thereto, and yet most of them have appeared in the *Paris Gazette,* a paper whose authors, known to be men of letters, are too judicious to be suspected of credulity, too prudent, too well informed of what passes at the Court of the King their master, one should think, to attribute to his Most Christian Majesty a reward for an action which never had any existence—an action which was only a fable." ' This is, no doubt, an allusion to the reward of 400 livres bestowed upon the boys who beat off the ferocious monster.

While the interest and excitement about this terrible wild beast was at the highest, the *St. James's Chronicle* published an engraving and description of it. The *St. James's Chronicle; or the British Evening Post*, was a folio of four pages, published three times a-week, price twopence-half-penny. In the number for June 6, 1765, there is printed the following description and woodcut :—

' For the *St. James's Chronicle.*

' Of this beast, which has already devoured upwards of seventy Persons and spread Terrour and Desolation throughout the whole Gévaudan, the Sieur de la Chaumette, who lately wounded it, has given us the following Description. It is larger than a Calf of a year old, strongly made before, and turned like a Grayhound behind. His Nose is long and pointed, his Ears upright and smaller than a wolf's, his Mouth of a most enormous size, and always wide open; a

STRANGE WILD BEAST SEEN IN FRANCE.   FROM THE 'ST. JAMES'S CHRONICLE,' 1765.

Streak of Black runs from his Shoulders to the Beginning of his Tail. His Paws are very large and strong; the Hair on his Back and Mane thick, bristly, and erect; his Tail long and terminating in a Bush, like that of a Lion; his Eyes small, fierce, and fiery. From this description it appears that he is neither a Wolf, Tiger, nor Hyena, but probably a Mongrel, generated between the two last, and forming, as it were, a new Species. All the accounts lately received agree in assuring that there are several of them.'

The *St. James's Chronicle* does not state from whence the portrait was obtained. A representation of the wild beast of the Gévaudan was sent in April, 1765, to the Intendant of Alençon, and a description of that picture corresponds with the woodcut in the *St. James's Chronicle,* so that the latter was probably a copy of the former.

About three months after the publication of the woodcut and description in the *St. James's Chronicle*, the career of this much dreaded animal was brought to a close. On Sept. 20th, 1765, it was encountered in the wood of Pommières by a certain Monsieur Beauterme, a gentleman of a distant province and noted as a successful hunter. He had come into the district on purpose to seek out this notorious wild beast, and having found it, shot it in the eye at the distance of about fifty paces. The animal, however, though wounded, showed fight, and was rushing on Monsieur Beauterme with great fury, when he was finally dispatched by a gamekeeper named Reinhard.

Several inhabitants of the Gévaudan who had been attacked by the beast declared it to be the same which had caused such consternation in the country, and Monsieur Beauterme set out with the body to Versailles in order to present it to the King. The animal was found to be thirty-two inches high, and five feet seven and a half inches long including the tail. The surgeon who dissected the body said it was more of a hyena than a wolf, its teeth being forty in number, whereas wolves have but twenty-six. The muscles of the neck were very strong; its sides so formed that it could bend its head to its tail; its eyes sparkled so with fire that it was hardly possible to bear its look. Its tail was very large, broad, and thick, and bristled with black hair, and its feet armed with claws extremely strong and singular.

In Paris it was thought that this mysterious animal was a cross between a tiger and a lioness, and had been brought into France to be shown as a curiosity. It is not unlikely that it had escaped from some travelling show, and was probably a hyena. The imagination of the country people would easily transform it into any shape suggested by their terrors. That such fancies easily begin and rapidly grow was proved in the case of Captain Sir Allan Young's pet Esquimaux dog, which was either stolen or wandered from the Arctic ship *Pandora* as she lay in Southampton harbour after returning from the Polar regions. Quite a panic arose in that part of Hampshire where this most valuable and harmless animal was wandering about, and every sort of story was circulated of the ravages and dangers the country was exposed to. The people began to think that besides their sheep and pigs their children were in danger. Some said it was a gigantic black fox, others that it was a Canadian wolf. Expeditions were organized to attack it, and after being chased for some miles by people on horseback, it was ultimately shot and exhibited at sixpence a head in Winchester market-place. There could be no doubt about the dog's identity, for Sir Allan Young afterwards got back his skin.

Before concluding my sketch of illustrated journalism in the eighteenth century I must refer to a class of publication that possessed many of the characteristics of the newspaper, without exactly belonging to that category. This kind of journal is represented by the *Gentleman's Magazine;* but, although Edward Cave considered himself the inventor of the magazine form of publication, the *Gentleman's Magazine* was not the first journal of the kind. Nearly forty years before it came into existence a monthly publication was started in London with the following title :—' *The Gentleman's Journal; or, the Monthly Miscellany. By way of Letter to a*

*Gentleman in the country, consisting of News, History, Philosophy,
Poetry, Music, Translations, &c. January,* 169½.' Its projector
and editor was a refugee Frenchman, one Peter Anthony
Motteux, and the design appears to have met with considerable
success, but it did not last more than four years.

In the second number of the *Gentleman's Journal* appeared the following:—' The author desires to be excused
for not answering the many ingenious letters that have been
sent to him that he may have the more time to apply himself
to this journal ; he judges that he answers them enough
when he follows the advice they give him, or inserts what is
sent to him, which he will always be very careful to do.
But such things as any way reflect upon particular persons,
or are either against religion or good manners, he cannot
insert.   He will take care to settle correspondence both
abroad and at home, to inform his readers of all that may
be most worthy their knowledge ; and if anything offers
itself that deserves to be engraved, he will get it done.   But
it being impossible he should know by himself a thousand
things which the publick would gladly know, such persons
as have anything to communicate may be pleased to send it
to him, at the Black Boy Coffee House in Ave Maria Lane,
not forgetting to discharge the postage.'

It would appear by the above that Peter Anthony Motteux had a vague perception that engravings might increase
the attractions of his journal ; but it does not seem that
much came in his way that ' deserved to be engraved.'   I
have found only two small woodcuts in the *Gentleman's
Journal*.   They both occur in the volume for 1694.   One
is a representation of snow crystals, and the other is a
diagram of a mock sun.

Motteux tells us that his journal was patronised by the
Queen, and was much favoured by the ladies generally.   He
had amongst his contributors Dryden, Matthew Prior, Sedley,
and Tom Durfey.   Charles Wesley, brother of the famous
John, sent serious verses, as did also Tate, of ' Tate and
Brady' celebrity.   All these contributions were introduced

into a long letter, which, as the title indicates, was the shape in which the *Gentleman's Journal* was written, and in this respect it was modelled upon the early manuscript news-letters.

Peter Anthony Motteux, the editor of the first English magazine, was also the author of several songs, plays, and prologues, and he also published a translation of *Don Quixote*. He kept a large East India warehouse in Leadenhall Street, and afterwards obtained a situation in the Post Office. He was found dead on the morning of his fifty-eighth birthday, in a low drinking-house in Butchers' Row, near Temple Bar, and had either been murdered or had lost his life in a drunken frolic. The *London Gazette* of the succeeding week contained the offer of a reward of fifty pounds for the discovery of the murderer, and the King's pardon to any but the actual criminal; but the mystery was never cleared up, and the bones of the clever exiled Frenchman lie unavenged and forgotten in the vaults of St. Andrew Undershaft, Leadenhall Street, celebrated amongst City churches as the burial-place of John Stowe.*

Edward Cave, the early patron and friend of Dr. Johnson, projected and brought out the *Gentleman's Magazine* in 1731. It was printed at St. John's Gate, Clerkenwell, a view of which place embellished its title-page.

The full title was, '*The Gentleman's Magazine, or Monthly Intelligencer*, containing Essays, Controversial, Humorous, and Satirical; Religious, Moral, and Political; collected chiefly from the Publick Papers. Select Pieces of Poetry. A Succinct Account of the most remarkable Transactions and Events, Foreign and Domestick. Births, Marriages, Deaths, Promotions, and Bankrupts. The Prices of Goods and Stocks, and Bill of Mortality. A Register of Books. Observations on Gardening.' It will thus be seen that the Magazine possessed many of the characteristics of a newspaper. On the front page of the earlier numbers were printed the names of the various newspapers from which it derived its infor-

* *New Quarterly Magazine*, January, 1878.

mation. It was some time before illustrations began to appear. The most important subjects were engraved on copper, and rough woodcuts were sprinkled here and there among the type. Sometimes the most incongruous subjects were engraved on the same plate, such as the section of a man-of-war and the figure of a locust. There was occasionally an illustration of news, as in the volume for 1746, where there is a map of the country round Carlisle, showing the route of the Scottish rebels; and in the same volume there is a portrait of Lord Lovat. The frontispiece to this volume is a portrait of the Duke of Cumberland, with the motto *Ecce Homo.* Portraits, plans, and bird's-eye views are of frequent occurrence. In the volume for 1747 is a very elaborate bird's-eye view of the city of Genoa, illustrating an account of an insurrection there. The same volume contains a view of Mount Vesuvius, with a description of the last great eruption. In the volume for 1748 are views of Amsterdam, the Mansion House, London, Greenwich Hospital, the Foundling Hospital, &c. The volume for 1749 contains an engraving of the fireworks on the occasion of the Peace, and views of Blenheim House and Covent Garden. In the volume for 1750 there is a woodcut with ' J. Cave sc.' in the corner. This was probably a son or some other relative of the proprietor, who was either in training as an engraver, or was trying his hand merely as an amateur. His name does not appear again, and I have never met with it elsewhere in connexion with the art of wood-engraving.

In the number for November, 1750, there occurs the following amongst the list of deaths :—' Mr. Edward Bright, at Malden in Essex, aged 30; he was supposed to be the largest man living, or perhaps that ever lived in this island. He weighed 42 stone and a half, horseman's weight; and not being very tall, his body was of an astonishing bulk, and his legs were as big as a middling man's body. He was an active man till a year or two before his death, when his corpulency so overpowered his strength that his life was a burthen, and his death a deliverance. His coffin was three feet six inches over the shoulders, six feet seven inches long, and three feet deep ; a way was cut thro' the wall and stair-case, to let the corpse down into the shop; it was drawn upon a carriage to the church, and let down into the vault by the help of a slider and pulleys.'   In the number for the

EDWARD BRIGHT. WEIGHT 42½ STONE.   FROM THE ' GENTLEMAN'S MAGAZINE '
FOR FEBRUARY, 1751.

following February there is a woodcut of Mr. Bright, and the reader is referred back to the November number for the above description.   This seems to show that the *Gentleman's Magazine* did not consider it of vital importance, in illus-trating news, to follow very close upon the heels of events. I have copied this engraving as a specimen of the woodcut illustrations of the *Magazine.*

The *Gentleman's Magazine* attracted the notice and admiration of Dr. Johnson before he came to London as a literary adventurer. He afterwards became a regular contributor to its pages, and for many years it was his principal source of income. His first contribution was a complimentary Latin poem addressed to Sylvanus Urban, and when Cave died Johnson wrote an account of him in the magazine. Dr. Johnson told Boswell ' that when he first saw St. John's Gate, the place where that deservedly popular miscellany was originally printed, he "beheld it with reverence."'

Edward Cave was born at Newton, in Warwickshire, Feb. 29th, 1691; he died Jan. 10th, 1754. 'He was peculiarly fortunate,' says Boswell, 'in being recorded by Johnson; who of the narrow life of a printer and publisher, without any digressions or adventitious circumstances, has made an interesting and agreeable narrative.'

The *Gentleman's Magazine* still exists, but retains nothing of its original character beyond the name.

Within a year the success of the *Gentleman's Magazine* brought into being the *London Magazine*, and, in 1739, the *Scots Magazine*, published in Edinburgh. In the second volume of the latter, under date March, 1740, there is a larger version of the woodcut of the taking of Porto Bello, already described. The account also is given, quoted, however, from the *London Evening Post*, and not from the *Daily Post*, where the woodcut appeared. Maps, plans, and views of places occasionally occur in other volumes of the *Scots Magazine*. In vol. iii. there is a plan of the harbour, city, and forts of Cartagena, and the number for July, 1743, contains a plan of the battle of Dettingen.

CHAPTER VII.

Revival of Wood-engraving by Thomas Bewick — The *Observer* started, 1791 — The *Times* an Illustrated Paper — Illustrations of News in the *Observer* — St. Helena and Napoleon Bonaparte — Abraham Thornton and the 'Assize of Battle' — Mr. William Clement and Illustrated Journalism — The Cato Street Conspiracy — Trial of Queen Caroline — The House of Commons in 1821 — Coronation of George IV. — Royal Visits to Ireland and Scotland — Murder of Mr. Weare — Illustrations of the Murder in the *Morning Chronicle*, the *Observer*, and the *Englishman* — *Bell's Life in London* — Prize-Fight at Warwick — Liston as 'Paul Pry' — 'Gallery of Comicalities,' &c. — *Pierce Egan's Life in London* — Death of the Duke of York — Death of Mr. Canning — Opening of Hammersmith Bridge, 1827 — Mr. Gurney's Steam Coach — The Thames Tunnel — The Murder in the Red Barn — The Siamese Twins — Death of George IV. — Opening of New London Bridge, 1831 — Coronation of William IV. and Queen Adelaide — Fieschi's Infernal Machine — Funeral of William IV. — Queen Victoria's First Visit to the City — Coronation and Marriage of the Queen — Christening of the Prince of Wales — *The Weekly Chronicle* — The Greenacre Murder — Mr. Cocking and his Parachute — The Courtney Riots at Canterbury — Burning of the Tower of London, 1841 — *The Sunday Times* — Burning of the Houses of Parliament, 1834 — *The Champion* — *The Weekly Herald* — *The Magnet* — Removing the Body of Napoleon I. — *The Penny Magazine* — Charles Knight — Humorous Journalism of the Victorian Era.

THERE appears to have been little or nothing done in the way of illustrated journalism during the remaining years of the eighteenth century. It was during this period that Thomas Bewick revived the almost extinct art of wood-engraving, and about the time he brought out the first of his illustrated natural history books a weekly newspaper was started in London which afterwards became the pioneer of modern illustrated journalism. This was the *Observer*, the first number of which came out on Sunday, Dec. 4th, 1791. It is the oldest of our existing weekly newspapers, and is one of the rare instances of a Sunday paper becoming established.* Many years had to elapse before wood-engraving began to be used as a means of popular illustration; but when some of Bewick's numerous pupils began to diffuse the fruits of their master's teaching the *Observer* was the first newspaper that availed itself of the restored art. Before this, however, there were symptoms of the reawakening of a dormant idea. In looking back to the early years of the present century it is curious and interesting to notice that the *Times* was occasionally an illustrated paper. The battle of Trafalgar and the death of Nelson stirred the national heart to such a degree that the *Times* of that day was induced to introduce into its pages engravings of Nelson's coffin and funeral car, when the hero's remains were carried to St. Paul's. In the number for Jan. 10th, 1806, there is an account of the State funeral, which is illustrated with the above-named woodcuts. They are very rudely executed, and plainly show that the influence of Bewick's labours had not yet penetrated into the region of journalism. Annexed is a copy of what the *Times* of 1806 presented to the public in response to the intense interest felt by the whole of the British nation about Nelson's death and funeral. It is a noteworthy example of renewed effort in the direction of illustrated news at a time when insufficient means of production clogged the spirit of enterprise. Like the *Swedish Intelligencer* of 1632, the *Times* did not hesitate to point out its shortcomings in the following notice at the foot of the engraving :—' The only difference in the appearance of the Funeral Car from the engraving is, that, contrary to what was at first intended, neither the pall nor coronet appeared on the coffin. The first was thrown in the stern of the Car, in order to give the public a complete view

* There was another Sunday paper in existence about this time, the *Sunday Reformer and Universal Register*. In the number for Dec. 29th, 1793, there is a copperplate portrait of Robert Lowth, D.D., Lord Bishop of London, then recently deceased.

NELSON'S FUNERAL CAR. FROM THE 'TIMES,' JAN. 10, 1806.

of the coffin; and the coronet was carried in a mourning-coach. We had hot time to make the alteration.'

To the above engraving the following description was appended:—' The Car, modelled at the ends in imitation of the hull of the Victory. Its head towards the horses, was ornamented with a figure of Fame. The stern carved and painted in the naval style, with the word "Victory" in yellow raised letters on the lanthorn over the poop. The coffin placed on the quarterdeck with its head towards the stern, with the English Jack pendent over the poop lowered half-staff. There was an awning over the whole, consisting of an elegant canopy supported by four pillars, in the form of palm-trees, as we have already mentioned, and partly covered with black velvet. The corners and sides were decorated with black ostrich feathers, and festooned with black velvet, richly fringed, immediately above which, in the front, was inscribed in gold the word "Nile" at one end; on one side the following motto, "Hoste devicto, requievit;" behind was the word "Trafalgar;" and on the other side the motto "Palmam qui meruit ferat," as in the engraving. The carriage was drawn by six led horses, in elegant furniture.'

In 1817 the *Times* also illustrated the projects of Robert Owen, who laboured long and ardently to promote the doctrines of Socialism. In the number for Aug. 9th, 1817, there is a large woodcut called Robert Owen's agricultural and manufacturing villages of Unity and Mutual Co-operation. In those days a page of the *Times* was not so valuable as it is now, or probably the enthusiastic Socialist would not have found it so easy to enlist that journal in helping to propagate his doctrines. In 1834 Owen made in London another attempt to put in practice the principles he had so long advocated. He died in 1858, aged ninety.

I have mentioned that the *Observer* was the first newspaper that availed itself of the revived art of wood-engraving; but it had previously essayed the then difficult task of illustrating the news of the day by the more costly means of engraving on copper. The island of St. Helena having been selected as the place of residence of Napoleon Bonaparte, the *Observer* of Oct. 29th, 1815, published a large copperplate view of the island, with a descriptive account. The plate is printed on the same page with the letterpress, so that there must have been two printings to produce this specimen of illustrated news. Three years later the *Observer* produced another copperplate example of news illustration, also printed on the letterpress page. This was a portrait of Abraham Thornton, whose remarkable case attracted much public attention. He was tried for the murder of a young woman, Mary Ashford, with whom he was known to be acquainted, and in whose company he was seen shortly before her death. He was, however, acquitted, the jury probably believing it to be a case of suicide. The brother of the girl then appealed, and Thornton claimed his right to defend himself by wager of battle. This claim was allowed, after long arguments before the judges. It was found, much to the surprise of the general public, that by the law of England a man in an appeal of murder might demand the combat, thereby to make proof of his guilt or innocence. In the present case the girl's brother refused the challenge, and Thornton escaped. This was the last appeal to the 'Assize of Battle' in this country; and the attention of the Legislature being drawn to the obsolete statute, it was repealed by 59 Geo. III., 1819. It was during the progress of the arguments in this case, and while the public interest was very great, that the *Observer* published the portrait of the accused.

After this the *Observer* became remarkable for its illustrations of news. Mr. William Clement, the proprietor, was a man who early saw the attractiveness of illustrated journalism. I am not aware when he first became associated with the *Observer;* but under his management frequent illustrations of news were given in that paper. In 1820 *Bell's Life in London* was started, and very soon Mr. Clement became the proprietor of that paper also. In 1821 he purchased the *Morning Chronicle*, which, however, turned out a bad speculation. Having invested a very large sum of money in the latter paper, Mr. Clement spared no effort to make it profitable, and the *Observer* was neglected. It suffered in consequence, and fell in circulation. Frequently the illustrations of news that were printed in the *Observer* were published the day previously in the *Chronicle*. They were also occasionally printed in *Bell's Life* and the *Englishman*, a fourth paper belonging to Mr. Clement. All four papers were carried on together; but it is the *Observer* that stands out as the prominent representative of illustrated journalism at this period. Other journals came into existence which took up the idea of illustrating the news of the day; among them the *Sunday Times*, started by Daniel Whittle Harvey in 1822, when he was member for Colchester. Another paper which for a time rivalled, if it did not excel, the *Observer* in the frequency of its news illustrations was the *Weekly Chronicle*. It flourished a few years before the birth of the *Illustrated London News*, but has long been extinct. Mr. Clement sold the *Morning Chronicle* in 1834, and soon restored the *Observer* to its old position. The *Morning Chronicle* started in 1769 and expired in 1864. The *Englishman* has long been defunct, but I am not acquainted with the date of its disappearance. There was a paper called the *Englishman* in 1714, and the name was again revived by the late Dr. Kenealy.

The *Observer* and *Bell's Life* were both published at the same office for many years, but their companionship was terminated in 1877, when they left the office in the Strand where they had so long lived amicably together, the great sporting journal migrating to Catherine Street, and the *Observer* seeking a new home in the Strand further west.

One or two other newspapers occasionally published engravings during the few years immediately preceding the *Illustrated London News*, and of them I will speak in the proper place. The most prominent, however, were the *Observer*, *Bell's Life in London*, and the *Weekly Chronicle*, and to these three I propose first to direct attention as being the main supporters of the pictorial spirit until it culminated in the *Illustrated London News*. It was during the ten years preceding 1842 that the founder of that journal noticed the growing inclination of the people for illustrated news, and it was chiefly in the pages of the *Observer* and the *Weekly Chronicle* that he thought he saw the growth of a hitherto uncultivated germ.

In 1820 all England was startled by the discovery of a mysterious plot of some political desperadoes who planned the assassination of the Ministers of the Crown and the overthrow of the Government. This came to be known as the Cato Street Conspiracy, the place of meeting of the conspirators being in Cato Street, Marylebone. The extravagance of the Prince Regent, the high price of bread, and the heavy taxation, had brought about a feeling of discontent among the lower orders which, unhappily, was greatly increased by the Spa Fields riots, and the collision between the soldiers and the people in Lancashire, at what was called the massacre of Peterloo. Thistlewood, the leader of the conspirators, had already been tried for treasonable practices, but acquitted. He had also been in trouble for his connexion with the Spa Fields riots. The sanguinary plan of the conspirators was to murder the Cabinet Ministers while they were all assembled at dinner at Lord Harrowby's house in Grosvenor Square. They were to seize certain pieces of cannon, take the Bank of England, destroy the telegraph to Woolwich, set fire to different parts of London, and then establish a provisional government at the Mansion House, sending emissaries to the outports to prevent the escape of obnoxious persons. They reckoned on large numbers of the discontented joining them as soon as they had destroyed the tyrants and oppressors of the people, as they termed the Ministers. They had provided pikes, pistols, sabres, knives, blunderbusses, and hand-grenades;

Q

and one of the gang, a butcher, had furnished himself with a heavy butcher's knife, to cut off the heads of 'Castlereagh and the rest as he came at them.' Adams, one of their number, turned informer, and the conspirators were surprised by the police at their meeting-place in Cato Street. After a conflict in which one of the police-officers was killed, several of the gang were secured, and others were taken soon afterwards. Thistlewood, the leader, escaped in the first rush, but was captured next day.

The place where the seizure was made is described as a hayloft over a deserted stable with a step-ladder leading from the stable to the loft above, with two apertures in the floor of the loft, opening on the racks in the stable below; opening from the loft were two small inner rooms. On the evening of the 23rd of February, 1820, the conspirators were assembled in this stable, where they were arming themselves for the bloody work they had planned, when the police, aided by a party of the Coldstream Guards under Lieut. Fitzclarence, broke in upon them. Police-officers Ruthven, Ellice, and Smithers, were the first to mount the ladder, and enter the loft.

'There were about five-and-twenty men in the room, eating bread and cheese, and drinking porter, or selecting arms from a long carpenter's bench which stood close by the wall. Just at that juncture, Thistlewood, hearing a noise, and some one calling, "Hallo! Show a light!" took a candle, and looked down the stairs to see who was coming, and, on seeing that there was a surprise, he put the candle back on the bench, seized a sword, and with three or four others retreated stealthily to the further of the inner rooms —the one that had a window looking out into Cato Street. At that moment one of the men seized below called out to warn his comrades, "Look out there above!"

'At the same time, two of the constables, at first almost unnoticed, appeared at the top of the ladder, and presenting their pistols, said, "Hallo, is anybody in the room? Here's a pretty nest of you!"

'Then another of the patrol cried, "We are officers; seize their arms."

'And a third, "Gentlemen, we have got a warrant to apprehend you all, and as such we hope you will go peaceably."

'Just then Smithers, distrusting further parley, and believing, in his staunch way, in promptitude, before the conspirators could discover the scantiness of the assailing numbers, or could muster courage to use their arms, cried, "Let me come forward," and pushed towards the door of the inner room, where Thistlewood stood thrusting with a very long sword. The leader of the conspirators instantly rushed forward, and struck Smithers through his right side. The constable threw up his hands, his head fell back, he staggered against Ruthven, cried, "O my God, I am done!" and fell dead near the opening of the stairs. Ellice held up his staff at Thistlewood, and threatened to fire with the pistol in his right hand, unless he instantly surrendered. The lights were immediately dashed out, and a voice cried in the darkness, "Kill the —— at once! Throw them down-stairs! Kill them!"

'Then there were twenty or thirty pistol-shots fired, and a tremendous headlong rush was made at the stairs, driving the Bow Street men backwards; the conspirators leaping down into the manger through the holes in the floor, or by the window, others firing at the officers on the stairs, or up through the manger, all making for the archway in John Street.'*

It would appear the conspirators were closely watched for some time before they were arrested. Indeed, it was suspected that Government emissaries were employed to foment the conspiracy in order that a terrible example might be made for the benefit of the disaffected. However this may have been, the plot excited the most intense interest among all classes. Thistlewood and the other prisoners were tried at the Old Bailey, April 17th, 1820,

* 'Old Stories Retold,' in *All the Year Round.*

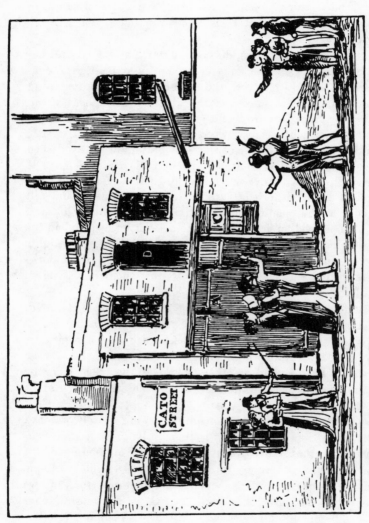

A. Door to the cart-house. B. Door by which the officers entered. C. Stable window. D. Loft-door.

STABLE WHERE THE CATO STREET CONSPIRATORS MET. FROM THE 'OBSERVER,' MARCH 5TH, 1820.

and found guilty of high treason. Six were transported for life, the other five, including Thistlewood, were hung on May 1st, and their heads severed from their bodies—the quartering, the usual doom of traitors, having been graciously forgiven.

The *Observer* for March 5th, 1820, published some illustrations of the Cato Street Conspiracy. One is an exterior view of the stable in Cato Street where the conspirators met, which is copied on the opposite page.

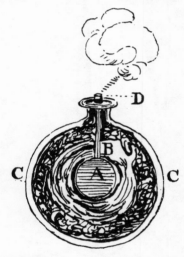

SECTION OF GRENADE PREPARED BY THE CATO STREET CONSPIRATORS.
FROM THE ' OBSERVER,' MARCH 5TH, 1820.

A. Cyclindrical tin Box containing gunpowder.
B. Pitched tow.
C. Bullets, old nails, Spikes, &c.
D. Tin Tube a Fuze filled with damp powder.

There was also an interior view of the hayloft, together with sections of some of the grenades, daggers, &c., large quantities of which were found in the loft.

These cuts, which are roughly done, were reprinted in the *Observer* for March 12th, and two new ones were added, ' Interior view of the Hayloft at the moment when Smithers received his Death Wound,' and a view of the interior of the stable. They are all interesting as examples of illustrated news at a time when the means of producing such things were extremely limited.

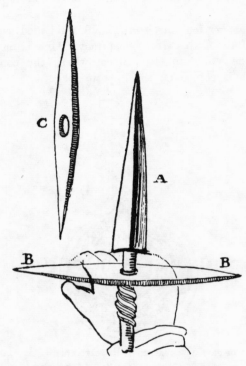

DAGGER PREPARED BY THE CATO STREET CONSPIRATORS.   FROM THE
' OBSERVER,' MARCH 5TH, 1820.

A. Dagger made out of a bayonet to use singly or on top of a pike handle.
B. Dagger with hole in the middle to receive dagger A. when screwed on, to be used
    right and left.
C. Section of the transverse dagger B.

Mr. Clement, the proprietor of the *Observer*, gave a remarkable proof of his enterprising spirit when the Cato Street conspirators were tried. At that time newspapers were prohibited under a penalty of 500*l.* from publishing reports of cases in the courts of law before they were concluded. Mr. Clement, seeing the universal interest excited by the trial, determined to publish a report without waiting for the verdict. He accordingly sent reporters to the court, and published the whole in the *Observer* before the verdict was given. This was a contempt of court for which he expected to have to pay, and, though the penalty was duly inflicted, it was never exacted. The *éclat* attending this proceeding was of immense value to the *Observer*, and the sale of that number was so great that the proprietor could easily have paid the penalty of 500*l.*, and he would still have been a gainer.*

The Prince of Wales (afterwards George IV.), whose unhappy marriage with Caroline of Brunswick produced so much scandal and excitement in this country, had long been separated from his wife, who was residing abroad at the time her husband became King. Her Majesty announced her intention of returning to England; and though the King's Ministers endeavoured to dissuade her from her purpose, she persisted in her resolution, and on June 6th, 1820, she landed at Dover. Her journey through London was one long triumph, thousands of people escorting her to her temporary residence, and giving her the warmest possible welcome, for they looked upon her as an ill-used and persecuted woman. The question of omitting her name from the Liturgy had been debated in Parliament, and afterwards a 'Bill of Pains and Penalties' was brought in, which was in effect placing the Queen upon her trial. Contemporary newspapers show what intense excitement filled the public mind upon this subject, and how the nation ranged itself on the side of the King or Queen—by far the greater number being for the latter. Nothing was talked of but the 'Queen's trial,' and the wrongs and indignities that had been heaped upon the head of an innocent woman.

On Aug. 16th, the married ladies of the metropolis presented Her Majesty with an address, and three days after the trial commenced, the defence being conducted by Mr. Brougham and Mr. Denman. When the Queen

* Grant's *Newspaper Press.*

attended the House of Lords large crowds accompanied her
through the streets, and manifested by their cries their
sympathy for her cause.   The Bill of Pains and Penalties
was carried on a second reading by a majority of twenty-
eight, but it sank on the third reading to a majority of nine,
and was finally abandoned owing to the threatening attitude
of the populace.   Great rejoicings ensued, London was illu-
minated for three nights, and on Nov. 29th the Queen went
in state to St. Paul's.   On this occasion William Hone, who
had distinguished himself as one of the Queen's champions,
displayed a transparency at his house on Ludgate Hill,
which was painted by George Cruikshank, and is engraved
in Hone's collected pamphlets.

The *Observer*, having to some extent laid itself out for
' illustrated news,' the occasion of so much interest and
excitement as the Queen's trial was not likely to pass unnoticed.   Accordingly, we find in the number for Sept. 17th,
1820, a large woodcut, entitled, 'A Faithful Representation
of the Interior of the House of Lords as prepared for the
Trial of Her Most Gracious Majesty Queen Caroline.'   This
was published at the time the excitement was at the highest,
and no doubt the eager public properly appreciated the
enterprise of the conductors of the paper.

In 1821 the House of Commons contained many notable
politicians and eminent men who afterwards became leaders
and champions among the ranks of Whig and Tory.
Amongst the most prominent were Canning, Brougham,
Peel, and Palmerston.   The question of Reform was becoming more and more pressing, and the House of Commons
as then constituted was tottering to its fall.   The conductors
of the *Observer*, ever on the look-out for what would interest
their readers, published on Jan. 21st, 1821, two views of the
interior of the House of Commons, one looking towards the
Speaker's Chair, the other looking from it.   In one the
House is empty, but in the other most of the leading
politicians of the day are introduced.   The figures, however,
are on too small a scale to be likenesses of the persons

intended, but the reader is assisted by references showing the places occupied by the most prominent members of the House.

The national excitement about Queen Caroline's trial was dying out when the first gentleman in Europe prepared for his coronation. On this occasion the *Observer* gave the lieges appropriate pictures of the august ceremony. The best draughtsmen and engravers on wood, then very few in number, were employed to prepare views of Westminster Abbey and Westminster Hall during the coronation ceremony and the banquet which followed. The *Observer* of July 22nd, 1821, contains four engravings, which, considering the limited artistic means at command, are by no means discreditable to the management of the paper. On this occasion a double number was published, the price of which was fourteen pence, and the publisher evidently thought it was very cheap. He announced that he would keep the number on sale for ten days after publication, so that no one might be disappointed in getting a copy. All these engravings of the coronation of George IV. were done on what was then considered a large scale, though none of them exceed a half-page of the present illustrated newspapers, and were finished as regards light and shade, according to the best ability of the artist.

The coronation number of the *Observer* produced a great sensation, and it had a very large sale. Nothing like it had ever been done before, and the public eagerly paid the double price for the sake of the engravings. Fourpence was paid for stamp duty on each sheet, amounting on the whole to 2000*l.* paid to Government for stamp duty, exclusive of paper duty. The number consisted of two sheets, each of which had a sale of 60,000 copies. This was a very good stroke of business, and Mr. Clement had fair reason to congratulate himself on his successful enterprise. It prompted him to further efforts; but, unfortunately, he had not the wisdom to confine his energies to one channel, and what he gained by one speculation he lost by another. It was at this time he purchased the *Morning Chronicle* for 42,000*l.*; but, as I have before stated, this turned out a disastrous investment, and also injured for a time the otherwise successful *Observer*.

Soon after his coronation George IV. visited Ireland, and while on his way received the melancholy intelligence of the death of his consort, the unfortunate Queen Caroline, which, however, did not prevent His Majesty from continuing his journey. The *Observer* of Sept. 2nd, 1821, published 'A correct View of his Majesty King George the Fourth landing from the *Lightening* Steam Packet, Capt. Skinner, on the Pier of the Harbour of Howth, on Sunday, the Twelvth of August, 1821.' In describing this event the *Observer* spoke of it as the opening of a new era for Ireland, and of the highest importance both in an historical and political point of view.

In the following year the King went to Scotland; but, though the *Observer* published long and elaborate descriptions of His Majesty's visit, the occasion was not deemed worthy of illustration. The opportunity, however, must have been far richer than the visit to Ireland in affording subjects for sketches. It would have been curious to see what a contemporary 'special artist' would have made of Sir Walter Scott; and posterity would have been glad to have had handed down to it the 'varra effigies' of George IV. and Alderman Curtis in the kilt!

In 1823 the city of Cadiz, in Spain, was invested by the French, who took possession of the place on Oct. 3rd in that year. The *Observer*, in its issue of Oct. 5th, printed a plan and view of Cadiz, the plan first appearing in the *Morning Chronicle* of the day before. The view of Cadiz is well engraved, in the manner of that day, by W. Hughes. The plan is also well done, and very complete.

Towards the end of 1823 a murder, unparalleled in the history of crime, excited immense public interest, and the *Observer* at once took up the case, and described and illustrated it with a particularity and minuteness of detail that must have satisfied the most ardent sensationalist. The incidents of this remarkable crime have been long forgotten; but I will give an outline of the story in connexion with the engravings published on the occasion by the *Observer*.

Mr. William Weare was an attorney in Lyon's Inn, who added to his legal practice the business of a bill-discounter, and enlivened the dulness of both pursuits by indulging occasionally in the excitement of gambling. He counted amongst his friends one Mr. John Thurtell, a notorious betting-man; and it was to keep an appointment with this friend that he left his chambers in Lyon's Inn on Friday, Oct. 24th, 1823. The two friends had agreed to go on a short shooting excursion to a lonely cottage on the St. Albans road, about fourteen miles from London. Thurtell was respectably connected, but had an evil reputation, he and his brother being then in hiding to avoid a charge of arson. Two other men were concerned in the murder, Hunt, a public singer, of doubtful character, and Probert, a spirit merchant, a fraudulent bankrupt, who lived at the cottage to which Thurtell and his friend were going. In the gambling transactions beween Thurtell and Weare the former conceived himself to have been cheated of 300*l*., and in revenge he determined to murder Weare, and by robbing him recoup himself as far as possible for his losses. The crime was coolly premeditated, and Hunt appears to have been an accessory before the fact, having arranged to meet Thurtell on the road, and to assist in despatching the victim. For this purpose the shooting excursion to Probert's cottage was planned, but, owing to a mistake of Hunt's, he did not join Thurtell as agreed, and the latter committed the murder alone.

Thurtell and Weare were seen driving in a gig towards Edgeware about five o'clock in the evening on Oct. 24th, and they afterwards called at the ' White Hart,' Edgeware, for refreshment. After they were gone Probert and Hunt, also driving in a gig, called at the same inn, where they had some brandy and water, and afterwards drove away.

Gill's Hill Cottage, the place where Probert lived, was about two miles from Elstree, and was approached by a narrow road called Gill's Hill Lane. Some country people passing in the neighbourhood of this lane about eight o'clock in the evening heard a shot fired and deep groans as if some one was injured. They also heard voices and the wheels of a cart or gig moving. Near nine o'clock Thurtell arrived at the cottage *alone*, and giving the horse and gig to the servant, went out to meet Probert and Hunt, with whom he soon afterwards returned.

Hunt being a stranger, was formally introduced to Mrs. Probert and a Miss Noyes who was staying at the house. The whole party supped together, and spent the evening in jollity. Hunt sang several songs, and Thurtell produced a gold hunting-watch which afterwards proved to be Weare's, and, taking off the chain, offered it to Probert for his wife, but he declining it, Thurtell put it round the lady's neck himself. It was after midnight before the ladies retired, and the sleeping accommodation being limited it was arranged that Thurtell should sleep on some chairs and Hunt was to occupy the sofa. A drawing of the sofa forms one of the illustrations in the *Observer*, and proves how thoroughly every circumstance of the horrid tale was followed up and exhibited to the public. All this time the body of the murdered Weare was lying behind a hedge in the lane.

Mrs. Probert's suspicions had been aroused by several strange circumstances. A vague and horrid alarm took possession of her, and when she retired to bed she stole to the head of the stairs and listened to the talk that was going on below in the parlour. She heard her husband and his two visitors apparently dividing money, burning papers, and making mysterious plans to conceal something dreadful that had been done. Then the parlour door was opened, and the frightened woman stole back to her room. She heard two of the men go to the stable and bring out the horse. Afterwards, hearing a noise in the garden, she looked out of the window, and it being a moonlight night, she saw a man dragging something large and heavy along the garden walk towards the fishpond. Then followed a hollow sound as if something had been thrown into the pond.

That night, when Probert went to bed, he found his wife sitting up and crying. She questioned him about the mysterious sounds she had heard, but he told her that he and his companions had only been out trying to net some game. In the morning she renewed her inquiries, but he only replied, 'Don't torment me; you make my life miserable.' He seemed in low spirits, and went moping round the

THE COUCH ON WHICH HUNT SLEPT AT GILL'S HILL COTTAGE. FROM THE 'OBSERVER,' NOV. 10, 1823.

garden and about the pond. Going into the kitchen Mrs. Probert observed the gig cushion drying at the kitchen fire, although there had been no rain the night before, and the cook was surprised to see in the stable a wet, ripped-up sack hanging on a nail.

Early on Saturday morning two labouring men were busy in Gill's Hill Lane repairing the road, when two gentlemen passed them on foot. At the bend of the lane they stooped down and appeared to be looking for something among the dead leaves and brambles. Coming back they had some conversation with the road-menders, and afterwards passed on up the lane towards the cottage. A

short time afterwards one of the labourers found at the spot
where the gentlemen had been looking an open penknife
covered with blood, and a little further on a pistol with hair
sticking to it, and also bloody.   These articles the man gave
to his master the same morning when he came round to
inspect their work.   About noon they saw the two gentlemen from Probert's drive-away in a gig.   They both looked
hard at the spot where the knife and pistol had been found,
but said nothing.

Mr. Nicholls, the road surveyor, to whom the knife and
pistol had been handed by the man who found them, went to
the magistrates at Watford and told how and where the
articles had been found.   The magistrates at once sent
information to Bow Street, and two of their number immediately went to Gill's Hill Lane, where they discovered
spots and gouts of blood on the bank and under the leaves,
and there was a gap in the hedge where a body seemed to
have been dragged through.   The field was also much
trampled.   They at once came to the conclusion that a
murder had been committed, and took instant measures to
trace the guilty parties.   The police seized Probert and
Thomas Thurtell at Gill's Hill, and searched the house and
premises.   John Thurtell was apprehended at the ' Coach
and Horses,' in Conduit Street.   Marks of blood were found
on different articles of clothing belonging to him.   At
Hunt's lodgings various articles belonging to Weare had
been found.   Weare being missing it was suspected he had
met with foul play at the hands of these men.   A billiard-
table keeper in Spring Gardens proved that Mr. Weare had
called upon him about three o'clock on Friday, October 24th,
and told him he was then on his way to join Thurtell in the
Edgeware Road, as they were going down to Hertfordshire
for a few day's shooting.   Thurtell, on being questioned,
admitted he knew Mr. Weare, but said he had not seen him
for eight days.

It appeared by the disclosures afterwards made by
Thurtell's two confederates that Thurtell had shot Weare

while they were riding in the gig down Gill's Hill Lane, leading to the cottage where Probert lived. Weare jumped out of the gig, crying he would pay Thurtell all he owed him if he would only spare his life. Thurtell jumped out of the gig and ran after him. He got Weare down and cut his throat with a penknife, and then struck him on the head with a pistol. He then dragged the body through the hedge and left it there. The same night Thurtell and Hunt went out from Probert's cottage to bring the body away, but they found it too heavy. Probert and Thurtell then went and brought the body on the horse, and put it in the fishpond with stones in the sack to keep it down. They afterwards removed the body from the fishpond and sunk it in a deep pond by the side of the Elstree road.

The cold-blooded indifference of the perpetrators of this atrocious crime was most extraordinary. The murder was committed on Friday night, and on Saturday Thurtell and Hunt returned to London and dined with Thomas Thurtell and Mr. Noyes, Probert's brother-in-law, at the 'Coach and Horses,' in Conduit Street. They were very jovial, and next day (Sunday) the whole party met again at Proberts' house in Gill's Hill Lane, when the afternoon was spent in playing at cards. On Sunday night Thurtell and Hunt went to dig a grave to bury the body, but the dogs were barking, and they were afraid some one was about. On Monday, while Hunt engaged Mrs. Probert in conversation, Thurtell and Probert got the body out of the fishpond, and cut off the clothes. Then they all three carried it to the garden-gate and put it into the gig. A grave half dug was found in Probert's garden, but the soil was hard, and it is supposed that Thurtell and Hunt were afraid of the noise pickaxes would make.

Hunt, to save his own neck from the halter, confessed that he knew where the body was, and went with four men in a hackney coach to a bridge on the Elstree Road, near which was a deep pond by the side of the road. In this pond the body of Weare was found tied in a sack, with stones to keep it down.

POND IN WHICH THE BODY OF MR. WEARE WAS FOUND. FROM THE 'OBSERVER,'
NOV. 10, 1823.

Thurtell, Probert, and Hunt were tried at Hertford on January 6, 1824. Probert was admitted King's evidence, and so escaped for that time, but he was afterwards hung at the Old Bailey for horse-stealing. Thurtell and Hunt were condemned to death, but only Thurtell was hung, Hunt being reprieved on the morning of execution, and transported for life. In those days prize-fighting was in much favour, and a great fight was coming off between Spring and Langham, two noted pugilists. To show the ruffianly and impenitent character of Thurtell, it is related that he said, a few hours before his execution, 'It is perhaps wrong in my situation; but I own I should like to read Pierce Egan's account of the great fight yesterday.'

Some of the incidents of the trial were appalling, others ludicrous. The production of the weapon with which the murder was committed, stained and rusted with blood, made every one shudder except the prisoners. The oft-quoted reason for a man being respectable ' because he kept a horse and shay' occurred during this trial; and when Probert's cook was asked whether the supper at Gill's Hill Cottage was postponed, she answered, 'No; it was pork.' *

The murder of Mr. Weare was committed on October 24, and discovered a few days afterwards. On November 10 the *Observer* published five illustrations of the murder :—1. Probert's cottage and garden. 2. The scene of the murder in Gill's Hill Lane. 3. The pond in which the body of Weare was found. 4. Front view (from the road) of Probert's cottage. 5. The parlour and the couch on which Hunt slept. On December 7 the *Observer* published a view of the interior of the Crown Court at Hertford at the moment the prisoners were brought up to plead ; and, having found that the public had eagerly purchased the illustrations already issued, the editor announced the publication of two sheets with additional engravings on the occasion of the trial :—
' The Trials of the prisoners at Hertford having been put off till Tuesday, Jan. 6, the publication of the intended Supple-

* 'Old Stories Retold,' in *All the Year Round.*

ment of this Journal, containing the plates illustrative of the
facts to be disclosed in the evidence, has been deferred till
Sunday, January 11, on which day Two Sheets instead of
one will be published. Booksellers, Postmasters, &c., are
requested to give their orders through their respective
Agents in London, as no papers whatever are on any
occasion forwarded through the Publisher.' Accordingly,
at the appointed time two sheets came out, containing the
cuts already enumerated together with three fresh ones, the
latter being the stable-yard of Probert's cottage with the
murderers conveying the body by the light of a lantern to
the stable; a front view of the cottage, showing the murderers dragging the body to the pond ; and a ground-plan of
the country round the scene of the murder.   The conductors
of the Journal appear to have had some misgivings as to the
good taste of their proceedings, but were unable to resist the
temptation of a large and profitable sale.   The engravings
are thus introduced to the reader :—' The unparalleled interest which has been created in the public mind by the
mysterious circumstances attending the death of Mr. Weare
has induced us, with a view to the gratification of our
readers, to use every exertion in our power, not only to give
a faithful and copious Report of the Trial of the persons
charged with this most foul and atrocious deed, but, with
the assistance of competent Artists, to obtain such Plates as
appear to us best calculated to illustrate the detail of circumstances disclosed in the evidence before the jury.   We are
aware that by some these illustrations will be condemned as
inconsistent with good taste ; and we are ready to acknowledge that on all occasions their adoption would be extremely
injudicious.   In a case, however, where the feelings and the
curiosity of the public have been so much excited, and where
so singular and ardent an avidity has been displayed to
obtain every possible light upon a subject so interesting, we
trust that those who may entertain, perhaps, a well-founded
objection to our plan, will, for a moment, grant us their
indulgence, and permit us to meet the wishes of persons who

may not be so fastidious as themselves. The strongest argument which we can adduce in favour of the continued pursuit of this plan—is the fact, that of three of the plates which we now feel it necessary to republish, many thousand impressions have been already sold, and yet the number, though high, has been insufficient to supply the continued demand. The necessity imposed on us, however, for breaking up our formes, forced us to refer the recent applicants to the present publication, which will be found to contain the most minute and correct particulars of everything connected with this extraordinary affair.'

Then follows a long and minute description of all the plates, when it is stated, 'For the sake of effect the artist has given all the views as they would appear in daylight; but, with the exception of Plate II. (finding the body of Weare in the pond), the scenes ought to have been represented as at night.' Some of the engravings illustrating the murder of Mr. Weare appeared in the *Morning Chronicle* the day before their publication in the *Observer*, and they were also published simultaneously in the *Englishman*, which appears to have been in substance another edition of the *Observer* without the advertisements. The name of W. Hughes is attached to them as the engraver.

The *Observer* was loudly condemned for publishing the Weare and Thurtell illustrations, and it did not for some time bring out any more engravings; but this was probably owing more to the commercial depression prevailing at the time than to the strictures that had been passed upon newspaper morality.

About this time *Bell's Life* came into Mr. Clement's hands, and henceforth it shared, with the *Morning Chronicle* and the *Englishman*, in the illustrations prepared for the *Observer*. It had, however, a distinct series of illustrations of its own, which was continued for several years. But before describing them I must refer to one or two characteristic engravings which appeared in *Bell's Life* in its early days. On November 28, 1824, the first large woodcut was published, representing a prize-fight on a raised stage, and entitled the 'Tip Top Milling at Warwick.' According to the account accompanying the engraving, this prize-fight was a most brutal exhibition, without any display of what boxers call 'science'—a mere exchange of hard blows, ending in one of the combatants being carried insensible from the stage. The coming fight was made known far and wide, so that when the day arrived vehicles from all parts of the country brought hundreds of spectators to the scene. The fight took place, openly and without fear of interruption, on the race-course at Warwick, the grand stand being crammed with spectators, and a ring of waggons, on which clustered crowds of eager gazers, surrounded the stage. This is all shown in the engraving in *Bell's Life;* and the different objects in the background, such as the church, the keep of Warwick Castle, the cemetery, &c., are pointed out by figures of reference with the most conscientious care. There is a very long account of the battle, couched in language only understood by members of the 'fancy.'

In 1825 the town was being amused by Liston, as 'Paul Pry,' then a recent creation of the stage. On November 8 in that year *Bell's Life* published a woodcut representing the comedian in that character, which I have copied as an early example of the illustrations of the great sporting journal.

In 1827 *Bell's Life* commenced a series of caricature sketches by Cruikshank, Seymour, and Kenny Meadows, entitled a 'Gallery of Comicalities.' This continued at intervals, along with other sketches entitled 'Phizogs of the Tradesmen of London' (half-lengths of Butchers, Cobblers, &c., commencing in 1832); 'Kitchen Stuff, or Cads of the Aristocracy' (heads of gentlemen's servants); 'Portraits down the Road' (heads of characters seen on a stage-coach journey, such as the Landlady, the Commercial Traveller, the Chambermaid, &c.); 'The Sporting Album' (sketches from life, commencing 1834). These caricature subjects were continued to the end of the year 1840. The

greater number are much too coarse, cynical, and vulgar for
the taste of the present day. Sometimes a series of sketches
extended through several consecutive weeks, such as 'The
Pugilist's Progress' and 'The Drunkard's Progress,' both
by Seymour. 'The Drunkard's Progress,' which appeared
in 1829, consisted of twelve scenes, and embodied the same

LISTON AS PAUL PRY. FROM 'BELL'S LIFE,' 1825.

idea that was many years afterwards more fully developed
by George Cruikshank in his series of large plates entitled
'The Bottle.' Now and then appeared a sporting subject
by Harvey, such as Coursing, Hunting, Bull-Baiting, &c.
In the number for February 8, 1829, appeared a curious
woodcut representing a view in the Isle of Anglesea, which
was said to have excited the attention and surprise of passing
travellers from its presenting an excellent profile of the

THE MAN WOT LOST THE FIGHT. THE MAN WOT WON THE FIGHT.

FROM 'BELL'S LIFE,' 1831.

Marquis of Anglesea, who was then very popular. In 1831 portraits of Young Dutch Sam and Ned Neal, the famous pugilists, were published; and in 1838 the initials of John Leech began to appear to some of the cuts. Portraits of prize-fighters, race-horses, representations of racing-cups, &c., were given at intervals until 1851, when the last illustration, a monument to Tom Cribb, appeared.

As further examples of the illustrations in *Bell's Life*, I copy two, which were published in 1831.

About 1825 there was another sporting paper in existence, conducted by the celebrated author of 'Tom and Jerry.' It was called *Pierce Egan's Life in London*, and, like *Bell's Life*, had its sporting and other columns decorated with little woodcut headings, and sometimes published an engraving of a racing-cup.

At the beginning of 1827 the *Observer* resumed its illustrations of news, and on the death of the Duke of York published a long memoir of his Royal Highness, accompanied by an equestrian portrait of the Duke, 'taken during his last visit to Newmarket.' In the number for January 21 are engravings of the remains of his Royal Highness lying in state in St. James's Palace, and a view of the interior of the Royal Mausoleum at Windsor. The above were engraved by Slader, and were published simultaneously in the *Englishman* and *Bell's Life*.

The number published on Aug. 13, 1827, contains a large portrait of Mr. Canning, then just deceased. This portrait has the names of Jackson and Smith attached to it as the engravers. In the number for Sept. 30 there is a 'correct view of the Suspension Bridge, Hammersmith, to be opened to the public on Saturday, Oct. 6, 1827.' This is engraved by Slader, and appears also in *Bell's Life* the same week. The following week the *Observer* published a large plan showing the alterations proposed in St. James's Park in connexion with the building of Buckingham Palace; and on Nov. 18 appeared a plan of the port of Navarino, accompanying an account of the naval battle at that place. In

HIS ROYAL HIGHNESS THE DUKE OF YORK, TAKEN DURING HIS LAST VISIT TO NEWMARKET.
FROM THE 'OBSERVER,' JAN. 8, 1827.

December was published a view of 'Mr. Gurney's new Steam-Carriage, as it appeared in the Regent's Park on Thursday, Dec. 6, 1827,' and later in the same month a representation of Mr. D. Gordon's new steam-coach. Both these engravings are curious and interesting, as showing the attempts that were made fifty years ago to apply steam to the propulsion of carriages on common roads.

Mr. Gurney was a medical man, but gave up his practice and devoted himself to scientific studies, and particularly to the construction of locomotive engines for turnpike travelling. He had seen Trevithick's engine, and when a youth had frequently met Trevithick himself. He had thus become imbued with a conviction of the practicability of making a steam-carriage that would travel on common roads. Other inventors succeeded in doing the same thing, but Mr. Gurney attained the greatest amount of success. With his steam-carriage he made a journey from London to Bath on July 28, 1829, performing the return journey at fourteen miles an hour, or the eighty-four miles in nine hours and twenty minutes, stoppages for fuel and water included. In 1831 he established a regular steam conveyance between Gloucester and Cheltenham, a distance of about nine miles. The steam-carriages commenced plying on Feb. 21, 1831, and continued running four times a-day for four months, with tolerable regularity and without accident. The project, however, received such determined opposition from coach proprietors and turnpike trusts that it was abandoned. The tolls exacted were so heavy that at one gate they amounted to eight guineas. Mr. Gurney is said to have expended 36,000*l.* on his enterprise, but without any permanent beneficial result. His inventive genius, however, contributed to develope the high speed of the locomotive and the subsequent success of railways. He died Feb. 28, 1875, aged eighty-two years.

Mr. Gordon took out a patent for a steam-coach in 1822, and constructed two different machines. One had its wheels surrounded by cogs, or projecting teeth. This engine was

MR. GURNEY'S NEW STEAM-CARRIAGE AS IT APPEARED IN THE REGENT'S PARK ON THURSDAY, DEC. 6, 1827. FROM THE 'OBSERVER,' DEC. 9, 1827.

to be placed within a large rolling drum, about nine feet in diameter and five feet wide, the inside of which should be fitted with circular rack-rails fitting the wheels of the steam-engine. Thus the motion of the engine would cause the drum to roll forward, on the same principle that a squirrel causes a cylindrical cage to revolve ; and the rolling of the drum was to move a carriage connected with it. The other machine had two long propellers or legs, intended to obviate the supposed tendency of wheels to slip when ascending a slope.

The Thames Tunnel, which was begun in 1825 by Mr. Brunel, was on more than one occasion threatened with destruction by irruptions of water. On Jan. 12, 1828, six workmen perished by a sudden rush of water into the workings, and on the 20th the *Observer* published an engraving representing the catastrophe. On the 9th of June appeared ' A correct view of Ascot Heath Race Course, taken by an eminent artist on Thursday last.' This ' eminent artist ' was William Harvey, and the cut bears the names of Jackson and Smith as the engravers. A sheet containing a selection of comic sketches from *Bell's Life* was issued with the *Observer* of July 20, 1828, accompanied by a statement that the sketches (twenty-seven in number) cost one hundred and forty-two pounds, drawing and engraving. This sounds very trivial when contrasted with the large sums now paid by illustrated newspapers.

In 1827 another exciting murder was committed, and the *Observer*, undeterred by former censures, published a portrait of the criminal and a view of the scene of his crime, but did not on this occasion deal with the case in the elaborate way in which the murder of Mr. Weare was treated. The story of the Red Barn is well known to provincial playgoers in the Eastern Counties, where it still sometimes figures in theatrical programmes on Saturday nights. William Corder was a farmer's son residing not far from Ipswich. He had for some time carried on an intrigue with a country girl named Maria Marten, whom he at last enticed into a barn

not far from her father's cottage, and there murdered her,
and buried her body under the floor of the barn. After this
he continued to visit her father's cottage, and by various
falsehoods accounted for the girl's continued absence.
Months went by, and Corder wrote several letters to the
girl's parents, in which he told plausible stories about her
being at the seaside with relatives of his own. The girl's
mother, however, had had her suspicions aroused by
several circumstances, and at length she dreamed three
times that her daughter had been murdered and her body
hid under the floor in the Red Barn. The woman's mind
was so worked upon by the recurrence of this dream that she
induced her husband to search under the floor of the barn,
and there, sure enough, the murdered body of the girl was
found. In the meantime Corder had advertised for a wife
in the *Morning Herald* in the following terms :—' A private
gentleman, aged twenty-four, entirely independent, whose
disposition is not to be exceeded, has lately lost chief of his
family by the hand of Providence, which has occasioned
discord among the remainder, under circumstances the most
disagreeable to relate. To any female of respectability, who
would study for domestic comfort, and is willing to confide
her future happiness to one in every way qualified to render
the marriage state desirable, as the advertiser is in affluence.
Many happy marriages have taken place through means
similar to this now resorted to. It is hoped no one will
answer this through impertinent curiosity ; but should this
meet the eye of any agreeable lady, who feels desirous of
meeting with a sociable, tender, kind, and sympathising
companion, they will find this advertisement worthy of
notice. Honour and secrecy may be relied on. As some
little security against idle application, it is requisite that
letters may be addressed, post-paid, A. Z., care of Mr.
Foster, stationer, 68 Leadenhall Street, with real name and
address, which will meet with most respectful attention.'

Through this advertisement Corder became acquainted
with a lady who kept the Grove House Academy at Ealing,

WILLIAM CORDER.   FROM THE 'OBSERVER,' AUG. 10, 1823.

near London. They were married, and he went to reside
with his wife at Grove House, where he was arrested one
morning in the spring of 1828. Various circumstances
pointed to him as the murderer of Maria Marten, and he
was tried for the crime at Bury St. Edmunds on Aug. 6,
1828. The crowd was so great that the counsel and officers
of the court had to fight their way to their places. Corder
appeared at the bar dressed in a new suit of black, and with
his hair combed over his forehead. He wore a pair of blue
French spectacles, through which he eyed the witnesses
smilingly. Being called on for his defence, he read a statement which amounted to charging Maria Marten with
having committed suicide. He said that in consequence of
a quarrel they had in the Red Barn she shot herself with
one of two pistols which he had with him :—' The instant
the mischief happened, I thought to have made it public ;
but this would have added to the suspicion, and I then
resolved to conceal her death. I then buried her in the best
way I could. I tried to conceal the fact as well as I could,
giving sometimes one reason for her absence, and sometimes
another.' He was found guilty and sentenced to death, and
the night before his execution he made the following confession :—' I acknowledge being guilty of the death of poor
Maria Marten, by shooting her with a pistol. The particulars are as follows : When we left her father's house, we
began quarrelling about the burial of the child, she appre-
hending that the place wherein it was deposited would be
found out. The quarrel continued for about three quarters
of an hour upon this and about other subjects. A scuffle
ensued, and during the scuffle, and at the time I think that
she had hold of me, I took the pistol from the side pocket
of my shooting-coat. . . . I have been guilty of great idle-
ness, and at times led a dissolute life, but I hope through the
mercy of God to be forgiven.—W. CORDER.'

This murder excited great and marked interest, not only
in Suffolk, but through the whole country. On Aug. 10,
1828, the day before the execution, the *Observer* published a

portrait of Corder and a view of the Red Barn, which are here copied. The excitement showed itself in the streets, where puppet shows represented the scene of the crime, and Methodist preachers held forth in the fields near the barn to thousands of attentive listeners. The Red Barn itself was nearly pulled to pieces by curiosity seekers.

On the Monday of the execution all the workmen in Bury struck work in order to see the murderer hanged, and persons came from long distances for the same purpose. One man

THE RED BARN. FROM THE 'OBSERVER,' AUG. 10, 1828.

was pestered by every one he met on his return by inquiries whether Corder had really been hung that morning. This was repeated so often that he became quite weary of the constantly recurring question, 'Is Corder executed?' In the evening, in order to get rid of the gloomy feelings created by what he had witnessed, he went to the theatre, where he arrived somewhat late. The play ('Macbeth') had advanced to the fourth scene of the first act as he seated himself in the pit. The newcomer, who was better acquainted with the details of the murder in the Red Barn than with 'the plays of Shakespeare, was not a little astonished when King Duncan entered, and, fixing his eye upon him, repeated what he thought was the same question that had been so often addressed to him that day, 'Is execution done on Cawdor?'

The *Observer* continued its illustration of events as they occurred, sharing the engravings with *Bell's Life* and the *Englishman.* St. Katharine's Docks were opened on Oct. 25th, 1828, and on the following day the *Observer* published a bird's eye view of the docks, showing the ceremonies attending the opening. In January, 1829, appeared two views of Buckingham Palace, then building for George IV.; and

THE SIAMESE TWINS.   FROM THE 'OBSERVER,' NOVEMBER 22, 1829.

in August a cut of the 'Post-Office Accelerator,' a carriage for conveying London postmen to their several districts. A portrait of Rowton, the winner of the Great St. Leger for 1829, was given in September. This year the lovers of wonderful shows were attracted to an exhibition in London of two Siamese youths who were united together by a short cartilaginous band at the pit of the stomach, but with no other connexion existing between them. They were perfectly straight and well made, and walked with a gait like other people; being perfect in all their parts, and having all their functions distinct. Their names were Chang and Eng; and they were first discovered on the banks of the Siam river, fishing, by Mr. Hunter, an American, by whom they were taken to New York, where they were exhibited, and were afterwards brought to England. They were supposed to be about eighteen years old when they were exhibited in London in 1829. The *Observer* of November 22, 1829, published a long account of the Siamese Twins, with a woodcut representing them as they were exhibited to the public.

After having been exhibited for several years in London and the provinces, the Siamese twins went to America, where they settled on a farm, and married sisters. In the year 1869 they returned to London, and were as elderly men again exhibited; but they soon went back to America, where in a few years they died, both together. A similar exhibition was made in London about 1868 of twin girls, named Millie-Christine, or the 'Two-headed Nightingale,' and it was probably the appearance of these two 'black birds' that suggested the idea of the Siamese twins appearing again in public.

In June, 1830, George the Fourth died, and the *Observer* published several engravings connected with the event. On June 24th appeared a portrait of 'His Majesty George the Fourth as he last appeared in his Pony Phaeton in Windsor Park;' and on July 18 three illustrations of the lying-in-state and the funeral were published.

'The King is dead! Long live the King!' So said the citizens of London when they invited William IV. and Queen Adelaide to a banquet at Guildhall on the following November 9; and on the 1st, eight days before the entertainment came off, the *Observer* duly supplied the public with 'A correct view of the grand civic entertainment,' as it was to be. On Aug. 1, 1831, new London Bridge was opened by the King and Queen, and two engravings illustrative of the event were published in the *Observer*, the *Morning Chronicle*, *Bell's Life*, and the *Englishman*. One of them is interesting, as it shows the relative positions of the

s

HIS MAJESTY GEORGE IV., AS HE LAST APPEARED IN HIS PONY PHAETON IN WINDSOR PARK,

FROM THE 'OBSERVER,' JUNE 29, 1830.

old and the new bridge. The view was taken from the tower of St. Saviour's Church, Southwark, looking towards Fish Street Hill.

The *Observer* of Sept. 11, 1831, contained four illustrations of the coronation of King William IV. and Queen Adelaide, together with long and elaborate descriptions. There was another paper in existence at this time called the *United Kingdom*, which also illustrated the coronation. This was the period of the great Reform agitation, when the newspapers were absorbed in political excitement; and after this the *Observer* for a time ceased to give any illustrations.

On July 28, 1835, a diabolical attempt was made in Paris to shoot Louis-Philippe, king of the French. The assassin, whose name was Fieschi, constructed an infernal machine, consisting of twenty-five barrels, charged with various kinds of missiles, and lighted simultaneously by a train of gunpowder. The machine was fired from a window as the King rode along the lines of the National Guard, on the Boulevard du Temple, accompanied by his three sons and suite. The King and his sons escaped, but Marshal Mortier was shot dead and many officers were dangerously wounded. Amongst the spectators upwards of forty persons were killed or injured. In its number for August 9, 1835, the *Observer* gave a sketch of the attempted assassination, a portrait of the criminal, and a representation of the infernal machine.

The actual infernal machine, with a waxen effigy of Fieschi, formed for many years a prominent attraction at Madame Tussaud's Exhibition.

The reign of William IV. was a short one, and soon the *Observer* had to illustrate his funeral, as it had done that of his predecessor. The number for July 3, 1837, contained three engravings of the royal obsequies, and ere long the brief rule of the Sailor King was forgotten in the dawning glories of the Victorian era. The epoch of railways was opening. The Greenwich Railway was the first railway out of London, and the next was the North-Western, or the London and Birmingham as it was then called. On

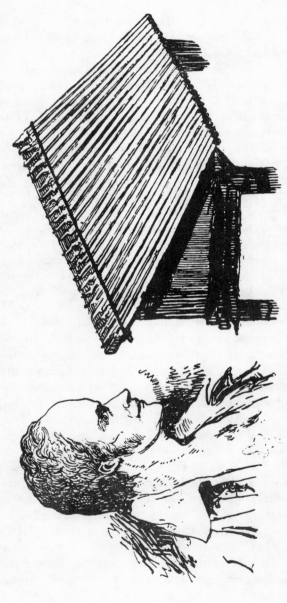

GERARD, ALIAS FIESCHI, AND THE INFERNAL MACHINE.   FROM THE 'OBSERVER,' AUGUST 9, 1835.

July 24, 1837, the *Observer* published a large woodcut of the 'Grand entrance to the London and Birmingham Railway at Euston Square.' Mr. Hardwick's massive structure was then in progress, and formed the entrance to the first of the great London railway stations—vast buildings, some of which have swallowed up whole streets, and contributed greatly to alter the appearance of London in their vicinity.

On July 24, 1837, a balloon ascended from Vauxhall with a parachute attached, in which was Mr. Cocking, who in descending was killed. The *Observer* published illustrations of this event, which excited great interest at the time. Other papers illustrated Mr. Cocking's death, which I will recount more at length when I come to treat of the *Weekly Chronicle*, which contained more illustrations of the event than any other paper. A large engraving appeared in the *Observer* for August 20, 1837, representing the Waterloo shield, given by Lord George Bentinck, and run for at Goodwood Races, 1837.

When Her Majesty Queen Victoria paid her first visit to the City of London after her accession, the *Observer* came out with larger engravings than it had ever before produced. Two large views of the interior of Guildhall were given, together with a panoramic sketch of the royal and civic procession, and a portrait of the youthful Queen, 'surrounded by a beautiful Emblematic Design, in which innocence and strength are happily portrayed by the playfulness of the Doves and the fearless defiance of the Lion.' Such was the flowery language of the *Observer* in those days.

The *Observer* of July 2, 1838, was a double number, price tenpence, and contained several illustrations of the coronation of Queen Victoria, which were also printed in *Bell's Life*. I have copied one of them, not because it is particularly good, but simply to mark an important historical event, which ought to have some record in an account of illustrated journalism.

THE CORONATION OF QUEEN VICTORIA.   FROM THE 'OBSERVER,' JULY 2, 1838.

On the occasion of Her Majesty's marriage, the *Observer* published a wedding number, containing several engravings, which were introduced to the reader thus:—' Little in the way of explanation is necessary to render the sketches in the opposite page, with which we have illustrated our account of the splendid ceremonials of Her Majesty's Nuptials on Monday last, intelligible. Our readers will no doubt make due allowance for any imperfections which may be discovered, when they reflect on the fact that the whole of the labours of the artists and the engravers have been accomplished in less than a week, and this under circumstances of difficulty, in obtaining admission to the scenes to be sketched, almost insurmountable. We should not be doing justice to our engraver were we not to state that it is to Mr. Orrin Smith we owe the consummation of our desire to gratify our patrons.'

On October 30, 1841, a fire occurred in the Tower of London, when the Armoury and 280,000 stand of arms were destroyed. On November 7 the *Observer* published three illustrations of this great fire. On November 14 it presented its subscribers with a large emblematic engraving on the occasion of the birth of the Prince of Wales. In the following January, when the Prince of Wales was christened, it published a large page engraving designed by W. B. Scott, and engraved by Smith and Linton, containing the ceremony of christening in St. George's Chapel, the banquet in St. George's Hall, illustrations of the history of the Princes of Wales from the presentation of the first Prince of Wales to the Welsh, to the religious instruction of Edward VI. by Archbishop Cranmer, including the battle of Cressy with the feats of the Black Prince, and the subsequent pageantry attending the introduction of the King of France as a prisoner into London over London Bridge; following this is the dismissal of Falstaff and his profligate companions by Henry V., with views of Windsor, &c. From this time until 1847 the *Observer* published no more engravings. In the interval the *Illustrated London News* commenced its career. On July 12, 1847, the *Observer* published the last of its illustrations. This was on the installation of Prince Albert as Chancellor of the University of Cambridge. The engravings have the name of W. J. Linton attached to them, and are on a larger scale, and are better done than anything hitherto appearing in the same paper.

The *Weekly Chronicle*, the first number of which was published September 18, 1836, started with the idea of illustrating the news of the day as one of its principal features. The price was threepence, and with it was incorporated the *Weekly Times*. In the first number the public were 'requested to be on their guard against the substitution of any other paper.' This probably had reference to some threatened rivalship, for exactly a year later appeared *Holt's Weekly Chronicle*, a paper which also gave illustrations of current events. It published engravings connected with the rebellion in Canada, and also illustrated the burning of the Royal Exchange in 1838. It appears to have had only a brief existence. The first number of the *Weekly Chronicle* contained an engraving of 'the new grand Balloon which ascended from Vauxhall Gardens with nine persons on Friday, September 9th, engraved by W. C. Walker, from a drawing made by a gentleman who ascended expressly for this paper.' Number 2 contained a page of comic sketches, apparently by Seymour, and with the number for October 30, 1836, was presented gratis an almanack containing a view of the new Houses of Parliament, not quite as the design was eventually carried out. Very early in its career the *Weekly Chronicle* selected the criminal records as favourite subjects for illustration. Perhaps some memory of the profits realised by the *Observer* on the occasion of the Weare murder induced the conductors to cultivate this class of news. Certainly nothing more repulsive ever figured in the pages of an illustrated newspaper than some of the woodcuts published by the *Weekly Chronicle*.

Towards the end of 1836 another attempt was made on the life of the King of the French, and on January 8, 1837, the *Weekly Chronicle* published a portrait of the criminal. A month or two later the public were enlightened as to the personal appearance of another murderer, one Pegsworth, who had his portrait taken in Newgate on the morning of his execution. The annals of crime were varied by the exploits of war, and a view of the heights of Amelzagame illustrated the career of the Spanish Legion under the command of General Evans. In the spring of 1837 occurred the Greenacre murder, and the *Weekly Chronicle* at once went into the case with an evident determination to do full justice to its sensational merits. From the first examination of the murderer before the magistrates to his final exit in the Old Bailey the artists of the paper were on the alert, pencil in hand. It is a painful fact that the numbers of the *Weekly Chronicle* containing the illustrations of the Greenacre murder had a very large sale. The details of the crime are too shocking to recapitulate, but I will give a list of the wood-cuts published in connexion with it.

April 2, 1837.—A sketch of Greenacre taken while under examination at the police-office. Head of the murdered woman as preserved in spirits at Paddington Workhouse.

April 9.—Greenacre taking notes at his examination before the magistrates at Marylebone Police Office. Exterior of Greenacre's house in Carpenter's Buildings, Windmill Lane, Camberwell. View of Pineapple Gate, Edgware Road, where the body was found. Matthew Hale, lock-keeper, who found the head. Rear of Greenacre's house. A back room looking into the garden. Portraits of Mrs. Gale and child taken while under examination at Marylebone Police Office. Room where the horrible mutilation was committed. Osier-bed in Cold Harbour Lane, where the legs were found.

April 16.—Trial of Greenacre.

April 23.—Chapel in Newgate, sketched during the preaching of the condemned sermon to Greenacre.

April 30.—Greenacre in condemned cell.

On May 7 the *Weekly Chronicle* wound up this series of illustrations by publishing a large cut, which it entitled, ' A

CHAPEL IN NEWGATE: THE CONDEMNED SERMON. FROM THE 'WEEKLY CHRONICLE,' APRIL 23, 1837.

1. Sheriffs' Pew.   2. Governor's Pew.   3. Condemned Pew.

scene in the Old Bailey, immediately before the execution, engraved expressly for the *Weekly Chronicle* by a distinguished artist.' According to an announcement in the paper itself, the sale of the *Weekly Chronicle* during the publication of these engravings was 130,000.

THE CONDEMNED CELL, NEWGATE. FROM THE 'WEEKLY CHRONICLE,'
APRIL 30, 1837.

On May 14, 1837, the *Weekly Chronicle* published portraits of Sir Francis Burdett and Mr. Leader, the former of a superhuman length, with a shocking bad hat. In the following number, as if the public had not been sufficiently supplied with horrors, there was printed 'a sketch of Eliza Davis as she lay on the mattress after the murder.' This was known as the Frederick Street murder, and was remarkable from the circumstances, and from the fact that the murderer was never discovered. This paper now commenced 'The Pictorial Gallery, illustrating every object of interest and curiosity in Art, Science, Literature, and Amusement. (To be continued weekly.)' In this series were published a view of the Euston Railway Station, a portrait of Madame Taglioni, a sketch of a novel mode of propelling balloons, representations of the Bedouin Arabs, the City of London School, the Adelaide Gallery, the Hippodrome at Bayswater, proclamation of Queen Victoria at Temple Bar, portraits of the Queen, the late King, the Earl of Durham, and the Duchess of Kent. Then followed a view of the Royal Mausoleum at Windsor, and several illustrations of Mr. Cocking's fatal descent in a parachute.

Mr. Cocking was an enthusiast in aerostation—he was, in fact, balloon mad, and had spent years in inventing a parachute which he believed to be perfectly safe, and in which he ascended from Vauxhall Gardens on July 24, 1837, attached to Mr. Green's Royal Nassau balloon. The experiment was widely advertised, and when the day and hour arrived the poor enthusiast faithfully appeared, and ascended in his fatal machine for more than a mile. He then himself liberated the parachute from the balloon. For a few seconds he descended steadily; the parachute then collapsed, broke, turned over, and shot straight down to the earth a hopeless ruin. Poor Cocking was still in the basket of the parachute when he reached the earth, but was quite insensible, and in ten minutes he was dead. The parachute fell at Lee; and it is recorded that not only was the machine itself carried away piecemeal, but the dead man's purse was stolen from his pocket, his watch, his snuff-box, his eye-glass were taken, even the cap was stolen from his head, the shoes were pulled from his feet, the buttons from his dress. Such statements seem incredible, and for the credit of human nature one could wish they were false; but they have been seriously made, and never contradicted.

The *Weekly Chronicle* published several illustrations of this event. They represent Mr. Cocking in the car of the

MR. COCKING IN HIS PARACHUTE AT THE MOMENT OF ASCENSION.   FROM THE
'WEEKLY CHRONICLE,' JULY 30, 1837.

parachute at the moment of ascension; the Nassau balloon
as it appeared from the Royal Gardens, Vauxhall; the parachute in its various stages in its descent; and Mr. Cocking
as he lay for the inspection of the jury in the room at the
Tiger's Head, at Lee. The first of these I have copied.

This rash adventure was wound up by the opening of a
subscription list for the benefit of Cocking's widow, which
was headed by the Queen with 50*l.* The Gas Company that
had supplied the gas for the disaster gave 30*l.*, and the proprietors of Vauxhall gave the gardens for a benefit. Thus
the friends who ought to have restrained the vanity of the
enthusiast and the speculators who led him on to his fate did
their best in the way of atonement; but it was clearly a case
where the civil power ought to have interposed to prevent
the fatal catastrophe.

The *Chronicle* varied its illustrations of events by an
occasional portrait of a public man, such as Mr. T. Wakley,
Mr. Roebuck, Lord John Russell, and Daniel Whittle Harvey. The Queen's first visit to the City, and her Majesty
delivering her speech to her first Parliament, furnished subjects for large woodcuts. Early in the year 1838 the Royal
Exchange was burnt, and this historical event was made
the subject of an engraving in the number for January 14,
1838.

This year the *Weekly Chronicle* also published several
engravings illustrative of the rebellion in Canada, including
a portrait of Papineau, the insurgent leader, and views of
Quebec and Montreal. The murder of Eliza Grimwood in
the Waterloo Road furnished another opportunity for sensational sketches, and in the same number that contained them
(June 10, 1838) appeared three illustrations of the Courtney
Riots at Canterbury.

In 1833 an eccentric person, calling himself Sir William
Courtney, appeared at Canterbury and attracted much attention by his half-crazed appearance and his frequent harangues
on the grievances of the poor. He presented himself as a
candidate to represent the city of Canterbury in Parliament,

but this ambition was frustrated by his being tried and found guilty of perjury, an offence he had committed on behalf of some smugglers on the Kentish coast. He was sentenced to imprisonment and transportation; but, being proved insane, the sentence was commuted, and he was confined in a lunatic asylum. Here he remained four years, and was then liberated under the belief that he was restored to a rational state. He was, however, madder than ever, having while in confinement brooded over his supposed wrongs and the sufferings of the oppressed poor until he fancied himself a prophet and a deliverer sent from heaven. With the cunning of madness he counterfeited sanity, and thus was able to resume what he considered his prophetic mission. He harangued about the new poor law, promised cheap bread to all who would follow him, and on May 29, 1838, he gathered together a band of about twenty men, with whom he marched from one place to another, proclaiming that he would make May 29 more memorable than it had ever been in connexion with the restoration of Charles II. This went on for a day or two, when a farmer, named Curtis, having his field-work stopped by the leading away of his men, went to a magistrate and obtained a warrant to apprehend them. In an attempt to execute this warrant a constable was killed by Courtney, who now broke into a rhapsody of exultation, declared that a second Gideon was come to slay the ungodly, and that all should perish who opposed the prophet. With outstretched sword he cried, 'I am the only Saviour of you all. You need not fear, for I will bring you through all.' The excitement had now become so general, and the menaces of Courtney and his armed party so alarming, that the magistrates resolved on the instant capture of this dangerous maniac and his ignorant followers. They came up with the rioters at a place called the Osier Bed, where Courtney's men threatened the magistrates and constables with bludgeons and fire-arms. After firing his pistol at one of the party who attempted to arrest him, Courtney and his men broke away to Bossenden Wood, and the magistrates, seeing no other resource, sent at

once for a detachment of the 45th Regiment from Canterbury Barracks. Courtney had now proclaimed to his followers that he was no other than Jesus Christ returned to
earth, and that they were safer with him than if they were
in their beds; therefore they must resist the soldiers, and
they were sure of victory. In the meantime a hundred men
of the 45th Regiment, headed by Lieutenant Bennett, surrounded Bossenden Wood. Accompanied by the civil magistrates, they advanced to close round the rioters, when Courtney fired at the young Lieutenant commanding the party,
and shot him dead. The next minute the prophet himself
was slain by a soldier, who covered him with his musket as
he fired at Lieutenant Bennett. Then ensued a hand-to-
hand fight, which resulted in the death of seven of the
rioters and one constable, besides several persons seriously
wounded.

The illustrations of these riots in the *Weekly Chronicle*
of June 10, 1838, consist of the following:—

1. 'Courtney with his troops leaving Bossenden Farm.'

2. 'The death of Lieutenant Bennett. Courtney in the
act of exhorting his men to advance.'

3. 'Interior of the Red Lion stables, with the bodies as
they were laid out after the conflict.'

Courtney, whose real name was John Thom, was undoubtedly mad. He never could have found followers,
except amongst the most degraded and ignorant; and it
is hoped he did better service to his countrymen than he
ever dreamt of by drawing attention to the dreadful evils
arising from the want of education among the rural population. Most of his followers could neither read nor write,
and were so totally unacquainted with the simplest truths of
Christianity that they believed him when he asserted that he
was Gideon, Samson, and Jesus Christ all in one, and that
he had descended from heaven to redress the wrongs of the
poor, but more especially to reduce the price of bread!

The *Weekly Chronicle* illustrated the coronation of Queen
Victoria by a view of 'The interior of the Abbey at the

THE DREADFUL RIOT AND LOSS OF LIFE AT BOSSENDEN WOOD, EAST KENT. FROM THE 'WEEKLY CHRONICLE,' JUNE 10, 1838.

1. Courtney.
2. Lieutenant Bennett.
3. Sergeant Langley making a thrust at Courtney with a bayonet, and was knocked down with a bludgeon.
4. Six Magistrates.
5. Soldier who stepped forward and shot Courtney.
6. Major Armstrong.
7. Detachment of the 45th Regiment loading.
8. Lieutenant Bennett's detachment.
9. The man Wills, who knocked down Sergeant Langley.
10. Courtney's flag.
11. J. N. Knatchbull firing at Courtney

T

moment of Her Majesty assuming the Crown,' and a full-page engraving of the Coronation Procession. Two pages of engravings were given on the occasion of the Queen's marriage; and on November 1, 1841, a large 'view of the Tower of London as it appeared on fire on the morning of

INTERIOR OF THE HOUSE OF LORDS, LOOKING FROM THE ENTRANCE TO THE SPOT LATELY OCCUPIED BY THE THRONE. FROM THE 'SUNDAY TIMES,' NOV. 2, 1834.

Sunday, the 31st ult., from a drawing by a distinguished artist.' On January 29, 1842, the same paper illustrated the christening of the Prince of Wales, with its attendant ceremonies and festivities; and later in the same year were published the last of its illustrations, relating to the employment of women and children in coal-mines.

The *Observer*, *Bell's Life*, and the *Weekly Chronicle*, which during more than twenty years had been the chief representatives of pictorial journalism, gradually abandoned the practice of giving illustrations after the *Illustrated London News* was established. Two or three other newspapers oc-

RUINS OF THE HOUSE OF COMMONS.   FROM THE ' SUNDAY TIMES,' NOV. 2, 1834.

casionally published engravings, but they were very few, and appeared at long intervals. The *Sunday Times* illustrated the trial of Thurtell for the murder of Mr. Weare, and on Nov. 2, 1834, it published several engravings of the destruction of the Houses of Parliament, two of which, representing the ruins, are of sufficient interest to introduce here.

The *Champion* of Nov. 13, 1836, has an engraving of the interior of a cotton-factory ; and the *Weekly Herald* in the same year issued two engravings illustrating the story of Wat Tyler:—' 1. Workshop scene ; Wat Tyler knocking the Tyrant Tax-gatherer's brains out ;' the principal characters equipped in boots, buckles, and belts, in true theatrical style   2. ' Smithfield scene ; the assassin Walworth treacherously murdering the brave but too-confiding Wat Tyler.' The same paper also issued this year a view of St. Peter's, Rome.   The *Magnet*, a paper started in 1837, illustrated the proclamation of Queen Victoria, William IV. lying in state, the Canadian rebellion, burning of the Royal Exchange, coronation of Queen Victoria, and on Jan. 4, 1841, the removal of the remains of Napoleon I. from St. Helena. There are two engravings of this interesting historical event. The first is entitled, ' A correct view, taken on the spot, of the interior of the tent at St. Helena, after the disinterment of the body of Napoleon, at the instant of the removal of the lid from the coffin ; the remains of the Emperor appearing (as one of the spectators remarked) as if he were asleep.'   I have copied the second cut, which represents the embarkation of the body, and is one of the last examples of pictorial journalism before the birth of the *Illustrated London News.*

Before concluding this part of my subject it is fitting that I should include the *Penny Magazine* amongst the pictorial journals which immediately preceded the establishment of a regular illustrated newspaper.   The *Penny Magazine,* though not a newspaper, was intended to supplant the cheap and pernicious contraband newspapers that then existed in large numbers.   It was the most successful experiment that England had then seen of the art of illustration in combination with the steam press, and was the best attempt that had been made in a cheap form to elevate the public taste.

Mr. Charles Knight, who thus, in the *Penny Magazine,* led the way in combining literature with art in a popular form, was a staunch advocate of education, and he never ceased in his endeavours to improve the condition of the

THE REMOVAL AND DELIVERY OF THE REMAINS OF THE EMPEROR NAPOLEON BY THE GOVERNOR OF ST. HELENA TO THE PRINCE DE JOINVILLE, ON THE 16TH DAY OF OCTOBER, 1840. FROM THE 'MAGNET', JAN. 11, 1841.

masses. He said, 'the poor man must be made a thinking man—a man capable of intellectual pleasures ; he must be purified in his tastes, and elevated in his understanding ; he must be taught to comprehend the real dignity of all useful employments ; he must learn to look upon the distinctions of society without envy or servility ; he must respect them, for they are open to him as well as to others ; but he must respect himself more. The best enjoyments of our nature might be common to him and the most favoured by fortune. Let him be taught how to appreciate them. Diminish the attractions of his sensual enjoyments by extending the range of his mental pleasures.'* With such convictions, Mr. Knight, in 1827, joined the Society for the Diffusion of Useful Knowledge, a new educational movement then just started by the Reform Party. He brought out, under its auspices, a great number of useful works, most of which were profusely illustrated. In 1832 Mr. Knight resided in the Vale of Health on Hampstead Heath. One of his neighbours was Mr. M. D. Hill, an active member of the Society for the Diffusion of Useful Knowledge. It was a time of great political excitement, and the town was flooded with unstamped weekly publications, which in some degree came under the character of contraband newspapers, and were nearly all dangerous in principle and coarse in language. Mr. Knight and Mr. Hill often walked to town together, and their conversation naturally turned to a subject in which they both felt a special interest—the means of improving the condition of the people by the diffusion of cheap literature, and so counteracting the dangerous and offensive publications which then abounded. One morning in early spring their talk was of this kind, when Mr. Hill exclaimed, ' Let us see what something cheap and good can accomplish ! Let us have a Penny Magazine !' Mr. Knight immediately adopted the suggestion, which was cordially approved by the Lord Chancellor Brougham ; and on March 31, 1832, appeared the first number of ' the *Penny*

* *Passages of a Working Life.*

Magazine of the Society for the Diffusion of Useful Knowledge.' It was necessary to avoid making the new periodical anything like a newspaper lest it should become liable to stamp duty, and at first very little expense was incurred for illustrations, most of the engravings in the early numbers being reprinted from other works of the Society. It was not till six months had elapsed that Mr. Knight ventured into the wide field of illustration, and made the public familiar with great works of art, such as the 'Laocoon,' the ' Apollo Belvedere,' the 'Dying Gladiator,' the 'Cartoons,' &c. The best pictures of the old masters were intermingled with scenes at home and abroad, with places of renown and illustrious men of all nations and of every age.

The success of the *Penny Magazine* was a surprise to the publisher and an astonishment to most persons. At the end of 1832 it had reached a sale of 200,000 in weekly numbers and monthly parts, and it soon produced a revolution in popular art throughout the world. Stereotype casts of its best cuts were supplied for the illustration of publications of a similar character which appeared in Germany, France, Holland, Livonia, Bohemia, Italy, Ionian Islands, Sweden, Norway, Spanish America, and the Brazils. The entire work was also reprinted in the United States from plates sent from this country.*

It continued its prosperous career for nine years, when a new series was commenced, with considerable improvements in engraving and printing. Five volumes of the new series were published, but the sale declined, owing to the commencement of illustrated newspapers, and the *Penny Magazine* in its old form came to an end in 1845, three years after the commencement of the *Illustrated London News*.† *Knight's Penny Magazine*, a smaller miscellany, commencing

* At this time there was another illustrated weekly magazine in existence—the *Mirror*, which began about 1822. The engravings it contained were chiefly of a topographical character.

† The *Saturday Magazine* was started in imitation of the *Penny Magazine*, and, like its prototype, had a considerable popularity for some years.

in January, 1846, kept up the old name for six months longer, and then it ceased to exist. In announcing its discontinuance, Mr. Knight thus closes this interesting chapter of literary history:—'The present series of the *Penny Magazine* is closed, after an experience of only six months. The editor has no reason to complain of the want of public encouragement, for the sale of this series has exceeded that of its predecessor in 1845. But the sale, such as it is, is scarcely remunerative; and there are indications that it may decline rather than increase. This is a hint which cannot be mistaken. It shall not be said of his humble efforts to continue, upon an equality with the best of his contemporaries, a publication which once had a decided pre-eminence, that

"Superfluous lags the veteran on the stage."

He leaves this portion of popular literature to be cultivated by those whose new energy may be worth more than his old experience. The *Penny Magazine* shall begin and end with him. It shall not pass into other hands.'

Mr. Knight attributed the falling off in the sale of the *Penny Magazine* to the extended sale of newspapers and the application of wood-engravings to their illustration; and in his *Passages of a Working Life* he relates how he first heard of the journal that was destined to succeed the *Penny Magazine* in the field of popular art:—'In 1842, having occasion to be in attendance at the Central Criminal Court, my curiosity was excited by an unusual spectacle—that of an artist, seated amongst the civic dignitaries on the bench, diligently employed in sketching two Lascars, on their trial for a capital offence. What was there so remarkable in the case, in the persons, or even in the costume of the accused, that they should be made the subject of a picture? The mystery was soon explained to me. The *Illustrated London News* had been announced for publication on the Saturday of the week in which I saw the wretched foreigners standing at the bar. I knew something about hurrying on wood-engravers for the *Penny Magazine*, but a newspaper was an essentially different affair. How, I thought, could artists and journalists so work concurrently that the news and the appropriate illustrations should both be fresh? How could such things be managed with any approach to fidelity of representation unless all the essential characteristics of a newspaper were sacrificed in the attempt to render it pictorial? I fancied that this rash experiment would be a failure. It proved to be such a success as could only be ensured by resolute and persevering struggles against natural difficulties.'

Charles Knight was born at Windsor in 1791. The son of a bookseller, he very early became connected with the press. At the age of twenty-one he conducted the *Windsor and Eton Express*, and a few years later he became the editor of the *Guardian*, a London weekly paper. He afterwards started a monthly magazine called the *Etonian*, and amongst his contributors were Macaulay, Praed, and other clever young men who had been educated at Eton, some of whom supported him in a later venture, *Knight's Quarterly Magazine*. In the midst of his varied duties as author and publisher he never lost sight of the great question of popular education, and heartily joined in the movement for repealing the taxes on knowledge. He gave expression to his views in *The Struggles of a Book against Excessive Taxation* and *The Case of the Authors as regards the Paper Duty*. He paid the enormous sum of 16,500*l.* for paper duty on the *Penny Cyclopedia* alone, and on the same work he expended 40,000*l.* for literature and engravings. When this great and useful work was completed Mr. Knight was entertained at a public dinner presided over by Lord Brougham, when the leading men in literature and art united to do him honour. The *Penny Cyclopedia* was not a commercial success, solely because of the paper duty.

Of the numerous illustrated works published by Mr. Knight, the *Pictorial Bible* was the most successful in a pecuniary sense, and he considered the *Arabian Nights* the most beautiful as regards illustrations. He was so ardent a promoter of illustrative art, that he invented a press for printing in colours, from which issued many coloured engravings for his various works, such as *Old England*, the *Farmer's Library*, &c.

Mr. Knight died at Addlestone, Surrey, March 9, 1873, and was buried in his native town of Windsor. A marble bust of him was placed by public subscription in the Council Chamber of that town, and two scholarships, bearing his name, were founded in the school of the Stationers' Company. It was well said of Charles Knight on the occasion of unveiling his bust at Windsor, that he set out in life with the desire to make knowledge a common possession instead of an exclusive privilege. He laboured for the good of his fellow-men rather than for the rewards of fame or fortune, and no man was more worthy of honour for his public services and his private virtues. The last time I saw him was at the grave of an old friend of his and mine; and as I recall the remembrance of his grey hair tossed in the wintry wind, I adopt in all seriousness what Douglas Jerrold said in jest, that two words would suffice for his epitaph—' good Knight.'

It is curious that the printing-press, which has worked such mighty changes, should have reproduced in another form the ancient jester who stood in cap and bells behind his master's chair, and the merry-andrew who made the rustics laugh upon the village green. The numerous satirical and humorous publications of the Victorian era represent a distinct kind of illustrated journalism, through which runs an amusing commentary on passing events, combined with a vein of satire always good-humoured and often instructive. At the head of this array of wit and wisdom stands *Punch*, who, however, was preceded by *Figaro in London*, conducted by Mr. Gilbert A'Beckett, afterwards one of *Punch's* strongest supporters. Mr. A'Beckett faithfully acted up to his motto:—

' Satire should, like a polished razor keen,
Wound with a touch that's hardly felt or seen ;'

but the constitution of *Figaro* was not strong, and he died young.

While the *Penny Magazine* was yet in vigorous life, and the *Illustrated London News* was as yet unborn, there used to be a weekly gathering of authors, actors, and artists, at a tavern in Wych Street, Strand, where the late Mr. Mark Lemon presided as the genial host. This company of merry men were mostly on the sunny side of life, and disposed to look upon the world and the world's cares with a laughing eye. They were ever ready to go out of their way for the sake of a joke, and a pun, good or bad, was pleasant to them. In this congenial atmosphere *Punch* germinated, and in July, 1841, that shrewd observer and good-humoured satirist appeared. Mr. *Punch*, like some other great men, had a hard struggle in his early days; but prosperous times came, and he now combines in his own person the dignity of age with the vivacity of youth. *Puck, Diogenes,* and numerous other imitators of *Punch,* attempted to obtain a share of public favour, but most of them died after a brief existence. The best of these that survive are *Fun* and *Judy,* which, with the *Hornet, Vanity Fair, Figaro* (a revival of the name), *Moonshine, Funny Folks,* and others, continue their weekly budgets with a smartness and vigour not unworthy of their great prototype.

CHAPTER VIII.

The *Illustrated London News*—The Early Numbers—The Burning of
Hamburgh—Facetious Advertisements—Bal Masque at Buckingham
Palace—Attempted Assassination of the Queen—The Queen's First
Trip by Railway—First Royal Visit to Scotland—Political Portraits—
R. Cobden—Lord John Russell—Benjamin Disraeli—The French
Revolution, 1848—The Great Exhibition, 1851—The Crimean War
—Coloured Pictures—Christmas Numbers—Herbert Ingram—The
Pictorial Times—Other Illustrated Journals.

HAVING traced the idea of illustrating the news of the day
from the early ' news-book ' through its various stages of
growth and development, we come to the first regular illustrated newspaper that was established. The projector had
long held the opinion, founded on his experience as a newsvendor at Nottingham, that such a publication would succeed.
He had noticed that when the *Observer* and the *Weekly
Chronicle* contained engravings, there was a much larger
demand for those papers than when they were without
illustrations, and he conceived the idea of starting a paper
whose chief attraction should be its *pictures*. He thought if
he could combine *art* and *news* together, he would be adding
greatly to the ordinary attractions of a newspaper, and
would probably secure a widely extended circle of readers.
His customers at Nottingham often asked for the ' London
news ' when anything of interest was astir in the Metropolis,
and his observant shrewdness led him to conclude that this
would be a good name for his paper. He accordingly called
it the *Illustrated London News*, and under that title the first
number appeared on May 14th, 1842. It contained sixteen
printed pages and thirty-two woodcuts, including all the
little headings to the columns, price sixpence, and it equalled
in size the *Atlas* which was then sold for a shilling, without

THE BURNING OF HAMBURGH. FROM THE FIRST NUMBER OF THE 'ILLUSTRATED LONDON NEWS,' MAY 14, 1842.

engravings. It was printed by R. Palmer (at the office of Palmer and Clayton), 10 Crane Court, Fleet Street, and published by J. Clayton, 320 Strand. The introductory address is written in a florid and inflated style; but it shows a correct perception of the wide and varied range that would have to be taken by an illustrated newspaper.

The well-known engraved heading represents a view of London from the Thames, as it was then,—St. Paul's towering in the centre, and the Lord Mayor's procession in State barges passing up the river. The first engraving is a 'View of the Conflagration of the City of Hamburgh,' which began

HEADING TO 'COURT AND HAUT TON,' COLUMN, 'ILLUSTRATED LONDON NEWS,' MAY 14, 1842.

on May 5th, and continued for several days. A great part of the city was destroyed, and more than one hundred lives were lost. As marking an epoch in the history of the Pictorial Press, I reprint this engraving and some others from the early numbers. The next cut is apparently a view of some town in Italy or France; but there is no name to the engraving or any reference to it in the surrounding text, which is all about the dreadful railway accident between Paris and Versailles which had then just occurred, whereby fifty persons were killed, and one hundred and fifty were more or less injured. On the next page are views of the city of Cabul and the fortress of Ghuznee, just then the seat of stirring events. The columns of 'Foreign Intelligence,' 'The Court and Haut Ton,' 'Births, Marriages, and Deaths,' were each headed by a small woodcut, an example of which is

given here. There is also an illustration of ladies' fashions,
accompanied by a gushing, descriptive letter from Paris,
beginning : 'Dear Mr. Editor, I feel an inexpressible delight in inditing my first communication to your lady
readers, upon the fashions of the *haut ton* of this *ville de*

FASHIONS FOR MAY, 1842.   FROM THE ' ILLUSTRATED LONDON NEWS,'
MAY 14, 1842.

gaitè. So suddenly and with such power has the sun lately
shot forth, that there is no end to invention in our spring
fashions.'

It would appear that illustrated police reports were to
have formed part of the attractions of the paper, and several
small cuts dealing with humorous subjects are scattered
through the early numbers. The cases were evidently
selected with a view to provoke merriment rather than to

indulge a morbid taste for criminal records, and seem to show that the paper in its early days possessed something of the frolicsomeness of youth, and did not consider a joke beneath its dignity. It had its wild oats to sow, and was not indisposed to emulate its contemporary *Punch*, then also a young joker. The first illustrations of the kind relate to a case at the Mansion House before Sir Peter Laurie, where the manager of a matrimonial institution sought to defend his establishment from the strictures of that celebrated 'putter-down.' A few pages further on we come upon two facetious advertisements, one of them professing to have been called forth by the report of the above case at the Mansion House :—

'MATRIMONY.—A *professional* gentleman, who has for some time past enrolled the category of his multitudinous graces, accomplishments, and *prospects*, in the portfolio of the "Matrimonial Alliance Establishment," fearing that. under the influence of Sir Peter Laurie's recent animadversion they will waste their sweetness unseen—unknown in the rose-tinted volume of the modern Hymen, avails himself of the glorious opportunity afforded to advertisers by the proprietors of the *Illustrated London News*, "and boldly and unhesitatingly submits his picture in little," to the approving smiles of the fair daughters (and *widows*) of Albion's Isle, conscious of his perfect sincerity in stating that he has no *insurmountable* objection to fortune being combined with beauty, taste, lively disposition, and cheerful temper ; he feels assured that the lovely creature whose eyes shall be fortunate enough, first to meet this advertisement (and then the advertiser), will secure to herself a perfect amenity, if truth be truth, and manners—not money—make the man. Address, with portrait (miniature set in gold, pearls, or other precious stones, not refused), A. Donis Slim, Esq., 320 Strand.'

The other advertisement referred to is of an entirely different character, being addressed to the commercial world :—

'CAPITAL SPEC ! Safe as the Bank !—Wanted a partner

A. DONIS SLIM, ESQ. FROM THE 'ILLUSTRATED LONDON NEWS,'
MAY 14, 1842.

in a snug, genteel little concern, with an airy and pleasant corner situation in one of the most densely crowded thoroughfares of the Metropolis, and doing a good, ready-money business, without much risk; which an increase of capital would considerably extend. The returns exceed the outlay, and the Sunday custom alone covers the rent. The taxes

PARTNERSHIP WANTED. FROM THE 'ILLUSTRATED LONDON NEWS,' MAY 14, 1842.

are redeemed, and there is a long unexpired term of the lease, which is held at a lolly-pop. The coming into a half-share, including plant and stock, very moderate—say a trifle above 0000*l*. Any person who can command the above sum will not only find this a decided bargain, but a very desirable opportunity of commencing business, and well worthy the attention of an industrious person of small means and less family. References exchanged. Address, prepaid, to B. B. (Brandy Ball), Pieman's Alley.'

The principal engravings in this first number illustrate the first Bal Masque given by Queen Victoria at Buckingham Palace. They were drawn by Sir John Gilbert, then at the beginning of his career, and it was most fortunate for the new enterprise that an artist of such great and varied abilities was found at the very outset to give his powerful aid to the undertaking. His wonderful facility and bold picturesqueness were exactly suited to the requirements of an illustrated newspaper. The first enabled him to do his work with marvellous quickness, and the second was an excellent counterpoise to the damaging effects of hurried engraving and rapid printing. The illustrations of the Queen's Bal Masque are eight in number, including character portraits of Her Majesty and the Prince Consort. There are two cuts from a book under review, and the last illustration in the number represents a long line of men carrying advertising boards ' to proclaim the advent of this important publication.'

The first number sold well, probably because the public was curious to see what the new paper was like. Twenty-six thousand copies were disposed of, but there was a great falling-off in the sale of the second number, which opened with a leading article explaining the principles that were to guide the paper in its future career. The cut on the front page represents the ceremony of taking the veil, and was evidently drawn by Gilbert. The next engravings illustrate Waghorn's Overland Route to India, then recently organized, followed by an illustrated account of the sale at Strawberry Hill, and a portrait of a then notorious criminal, Daniel Good, which is accompanied by an editorial apology disclaiming all intention of joining the ' raw-head and bloody-bones' school, but in the interests of science commending the portrait to the disciples of Lavater. This is the only instance of such an engraving being inserted in the paper (with the exception of the portrait of MacNaghten, who shot Mr. Drummond), and it is evident the editor's better feeling revolted against it, although he was only following the example of the *Observer* and the *Weekly Chronicle*.

HER MAJESTY AS QUEEN PHILIPPA. FROM THE 'ILLUSTRATED LONDON NEWS,'
MAY 14, 1842.

The first engraving in No. 3 is a portrait of Mehemet Ali, which is given in connexion with further illustrations of the Overland Route to India. But the most important picture in this number is a portrait of the Queen with the baby Prince of Wales in her lap, drawn by Gilbert. There is also the first example of a sporting illustration—a portrait of Attila, the winner of the Derby, which accompanies an account of Epsom Races, with several other engravings.

THE QUEEN'S FIRST RAILWAY JOURNEY. FROM THE 'ILLUSTRATED LONDON NEWS,' JUNE 19, 1842.

An event now occurred which afforded the first important opportunity of illustrating the news of the hour. This was the attempt on the life of the Queen, who was fired at as she was driving up Constitution Hill by a young man named Francis. The public excitement on this occasion was very great, and it is a little surprising that the *Illustrated London News* did not make more of it. In No. 4 there are two illustrations in connexion with this event, one representing the attempted assassination, the other the examination of the prisoner before the Privy Council. The engravings are not very imposing, but large blocks had not then

ATTEMPTED ASSASSINATION OF THE QUEEN.   FROM THE 'ILLUSTRATED LONDON NEWS,' JUNE 5, 1842.

come into use; and as the event occurred on a Monday there was not too much time, with the limited means then at command, to produce them on a large scale. In No. 6 there is a small cut entitled 'The Queen's first trip by Railway,' which illustrates an account of her Majesty's first journey by railway from Windsor to London. With the

MR. R. COBDEN, M.P. FROM THE 'ILLUSTRATED LONDON NEWS,' JULY 2, 1842.

exception of the drawings by Gilbert most of the illustrations in these first six numbers are of an inferior character, and show that the conductors of the paper had not yet obtained the best artistic help. Indeed it was a long time before the higher class of artists and engravers would believe that an illustrated newspaper was worthy of their professional attention. Illustrations of the Police Reports continued to be scattered through the early numbers, mingled with such subjects as a ballet at Her Majesty's Theatre, a public dinner, a launch, a horserace, and sketches of the Chartist riots at Preston. The Queen's first visit to Scotland was very copiously illustrated, and a series of 'Popular Portraits' was begun which included most of the prominent politicians of the day. In No. 11 the fatal accident to the Duke of Orleans is illustrated; and further on the hand of Gilbert is visible in the drawings representing the funeral of the Duke of Sussex, the Lord Mayor's Show, and the grand Polish Ball at Guildhall. With No. 19 the office was removed to 198 Strand, where it has remained ever since. The first Cattle Show illustrations occur in No. 31, and it is evident that the artists by whom they were executed had not made that kind of art their special study. The approach of Christmas is heralded by the introduction of various laughable sketches; the Pantomimes are illustrated by Alfred Crowquill, and Christmas himself is welcomed in a 'Song of the Wassail Bowl.' Kenny Meadows finishes the volume with a party of Cupids carrying the *Illustrated London News* through the air, while a literary and artistic Cupid, cap in hand, makes his bow to the reader.

The first volume ends with the year 1842, and it has for a frontispiece a large view of London, a title-page drawn by Gilbert, and headings to preface and index by Kenny Meadows. The preface is written in the florid style of the introductory address in the first number; but the following passage refers, not inappropriately, to the value and interest of the work to the future historian:—

'What would Sir Walter Scott or any of the great writers of modern times have given—whether for the purposes of fiction or history, or political example or disquisition —for any museum-preserved volume such as we have here enshrined. The life of the times—the signs of its taste and intelligence—its public monuments and public men—its festivals—institutions—amusements—discoveries—and the very reflection of its living manners and costumes—the variegated dresses of its mind and body—what are—what *must* be all these but treasures of truth that would have lain hid in Time's tomb, or perished amid the sand of his hour-glass but for the enduring and resuscitating powers of art—the eternal register of the pencil giving life and vigour and palpability to the confirming details of the pen. Could the days of Elizabeth or others as bright and earlier still be unfolded to us through such a mirror, what a mint of wisdom might we gather in from such dazzling periods of the past! Of just as much captivating value then is such a book to the future. It will pour the lore of the Antiquarian into the scholar's yearning soul, and teach him truth about those who have gone before him, as it were, with the Pictorial Alphabet of Art! It is in this sense that we regard the greatness of our design, and are proud of its envied and unexampled success; and it is for this end that we shall strain every nerve to perfect it into order and completeness that may accord with the beauty and brilliancy which many episodes of its execution have already been fortunate to display. Scott might carry Elizabeth to Kenilworth through the regions of his fine imagination, backed and supported by books, and we may take *cum grano salis* the Antiquarian's and the Poet's word, but the year two thousand will be ten times better assured of all the splendid realities of our own Victoria's visit to the native land of the Northern Magician who enshrined in fiction the glories of Queen Bess. This volume is a work that history *must* keep.'

At the end of the preface is printed the following ' Dedicatory Sonnet :'—

' To the great public,—that gigantic soul
   Which lends the nation's body life and light,
   And makes the blood within its veins grow bright
With gushing glory,—we this muster-roll
Of all the deeds that pass 'neath its controul
   Do dedicate,—the page of simple news
Is here adorned and filled with pictured life,
Coloured with thousand tints—the rainbow strife

Of all the world's emotions—all the hues
Of war—peace—commerce;—agriculture rife
With budding plenty that doth life infuse
And fair domestic joy—all—all are here
To gild the *new*, and from the bygone year
Present a gift to take—to cherish and to use.'

The second volume began with several improvements.
A 'Romance of Real Life,' by Henry Cockton, illustrated
by Kenny Meadows, was the first attempt to infuse a new
interest into newspaper literature by the introduction of
fiction.   Stories by Thomas Miller and others.followed.
This feature of the paper was continued for some time
until *fiction* was crowded out by *fact*.   The popular portraits
were done on a larger scale and were of a more ambitious
character.   In No. 40 there is one of Lord John Russell,
which is reprinted here as an example of the improved
portraiture of the period.

In the following year was commenced a series of
'Parliamentary Portraits,' one of which I have selected to
accompany the portrait of Lord John Russell.   It is that of
Mr. Disraeli, and it will perhaps interest the reader to com-
pare the present estimate of Lord Beaconsfield with what
was said of Mr. Disraeli in 1844.   The following is a portion
of the article which accompanies the portrait:—' The most
remarkable speeches in the recent debates have been those
of Mr. Disraeli, the Member for Shrewsbury.   He has lately
made himself more prominent in the sphere of literature and
politics as the expounder of the views and opinions of that
section of the Conservative party which has received the
name of "Young England."   His opinions however are too
peculiar, have too much individuality ever to become those
of a party.   We scarcely think "Young England" capable of
holding as points of belief the startling paradoxes to which
Mr. Disraeli occasionally gives utterance.   His speeches
abound with happily turned sentences, in which a clever
sarcasm is thrown into the antithetical form; they also

PORTRAIT OF LORD JOHN RUSSELL. FROM THE 'ILLUSTRATED LONDON NEWS,' 1843.

contain a large amount of historical information, on which he draws almost as often as Macaulay himself. He rarely announces a positively new principle, but he often places old ones in a strange and startling light, and states the most extraordinary inconsistencies with an air of such perfect earnestness and conviction that his auditors are sometimes puzzled whether to admire or laugh at him. But he is not one of those men who can be laughed at; we have seen him turn the laugh most sorely against those who thought themselves securely trenched behind form and precedent. He can hit hard, and none have suffered more from his sarcasm than the present Premier and the Home Secretary. He seems to mangle them with peculiar gusto, and deals with them as if he was annihilating the Tadpole or Taper of his own "Coningsby." His speeches have not much metaphor, nor does he indulge in rhetorical glitter and ornament; we cannot call him impassioned, nor say he is eloquent; but he interests, informs, and amuses. A speech from Disraeli is sure to command attention. His manner is not calculated to set off his matter to the best advantage. His delivery is heavy, and of action he has none whatever. He thrusts his hands deep into his side-pockets, leans forward a little, or turns from side to side according to whom he may be addressing. But that is all. Though he sets the House cheering or laughing for minutes together, his countenance remains impassive; he says a good thing as if perfectly unconscious of it.'

The paper rapidly advanced in public favour and soon reached a circulation of 66,000. It celebrated the completion of the first year of its existence by the publication of a double number, profusely illustrated by Gilbert, Harvey, and Kenny Meadows.

The *Illustrated London News* was not established without many misgivings as to its ultimate success. Its founder probably did not at first realise all the difficulties that lay in his way, but as fast as they appeared he met them with characteristic courage and energy, and overcame them by perseverance.

BENJAMIN DISRAELI, M.P.   FROM THE 'ILLUSTRATED LONDON NEWS,'
JUNE 22, 1844.

He seized on every opportunity to consolidate the strength of the paper, and paid a great amount of personal attention to its management, often denying himself sleep one or two nights a-week. As the profits increased he kept on increasing the scope and number of its attractive features. He made it a rule to spare no expense in every department of the journal; whatever money could command for its success he resolved to have. After a time he was able to act on this wise resolve to the fullest extent, and in the end he achieved a great success.

In describing the *Illustrated London News* during the first year of its existence, I have directed attention chiefly to the pictorial portion of its contents, that being the characteristic feature of the paper by which it was distinguished from its purely literary contemporaries. The engravings I have reprinted from it are given as curiosities and not as specimens of excellence. The succeeding volumes contain abundant evidence that the highest talent was afterwards employed in producing the best examples of art as well as in the illustration of news. In its sixth year the course of public events opened up new and stirring scenes for its pages. So great was the interest felt in the exciting events of the year 1848, that the sale of the *Illustrated London News* was more than doubled in three months. The vigorous sketches of the French Revolution published week after week were so eagerly bought that the publisher was not always able to meet the demand. On one occasion he was freely pelted with flour and other harmless missiles because the London 'trade' could not get their supply soon enough to satisfy their impatience. The noisy newsboys, in mocking imitation of the Paris mob which was then making the streets of that city ring with cries of 'à bas Guizot!' vented their indignation against the publisher of the *Illustrated London News* by shouting 'à bas Little! à bas Little!'

But though the year of revolutions was so rich in materials for pictorial journalism, the year of the Great Exhibition was yet more fruitful. The Great Exhibition of

1851 was a perfect novelty, and was hailed as the harbinger of peace on earth and good-will among men. Coming so soon after the convulsions of 1848, the peaceful display was more enchanting from the contrast. Such a golden opportunity was not lost upon the pictorial press, and every stage of the construction of the first Crystal Palace was represented. The very plan of the building was first made public in the pages of the *Illustrated London News*, the first design adopted by the Commissioners having been superseded by Sir Joseph Paxton's Palace of Glass. The building was shown in progress from the raising of the first column, and its removal was illustrated to the clearing away of the foundations. In this ' Festival of Labour ' the *Illustrated London News* took a prominent place. An edition was printed in the Exhibition building by one of Applegarth's vertical printing-machines, then the quickest method of printing in use. At this time the paper was distinguished by the number and excellence of its illustrations, and the ' *London News* ' printing-machine was one of the attractions of the ' World's Fair.'

In three years more the dreams of universal peace created by the Great Exhibition were rudely swept away by the declaration of war with Russia and subsequent invasion of the Crimea. The long and disastrous siege of Sebastopol, the assaults on the Redan and the Malakoff, the battles of Balaclava and Inkermann, supplied the most exciting subjects for illustration. It was the first great war since Waterloo, and the national excitement being intensified by the maladministration of the Government, the British public eagerly bought the war sketches. The sale of the paper at this time was very great, yet it is a curious fact that it never reached so high a figure as during the peaceful exhibition of 1851,—a proof that, after all, the arts of peace are more attractive than the excitement of war.

At Christmas, 1855, a novel feature was introduced into the *Illustrated London News*. For some years a Christmas number had been published, and it was now for the first time printed in *colours*. It is true the coloured pictures were little more than ordinary woodcuts with tints printed over them, but their imperfections were principally owing to the breakdown of machinery and the great hurry in which they were produced. In after years much better things were done, and the coloured Christmas pictures which have been for many years produced at the chromatic press of Leighton Bros. take rank among the best work of the kind. They have proved exceedingly popular, and always sold well. That of 'Little Red Riding Hood,' after J. Sant, R.A., published in 1863, was reprinted again and again, until the blocks were utterly worn out. They were then re-engraved, and again reprinted. The Christmas picture issued in 1882 (' Cinderella ') was specially painted by Mr. Millais, R.A., at the price of 3000 guineas. When it is noted that the large coloured reproduction of this picture, together with seventeen highly finished full-page engravings by some of the best artists of the day, were sold for a shilling, it will be seen that the pictorial press is no unimportant factor in diffusing the purifying and softening influence of art.

During the forty-two years that have elapsed since the first illustrated newspaper was founded, there has never been any long interval of peace. War of some kind, big or little, has broken out, like a volcano, on some part of the earth's surface, and kept the Argus-eyed newspaper editor on the alert. From Alma to Tel-el-Kebir and the desert warfare of the Soudan, there has been a succession of conflicts, with only a short interval of a few years between; so that the food on which picture newspapers thrive best has been abundantly supplied, and this remarkable offspring of the printing-press has consequently increased and multiplied, and is now found in every corner of the earth, ' from China to Peru.' The reader may form some idea of the magnitude of the operations in connexion with illustrated journalism when I state that at the marriage of the Prince of Wales the *Illustrated London News* of that week consisted of three sheets, and 930,000 sheets were printed of that issue in one week. These sheets, if placed side by side, would cover 660 miles, so that, as they were printed on both sides, they represent a printed surface of, after deductions for margin, more than 1115 miles in length. Nearly eighty tons of paper and twenty-three hundredweight of printing-ink were used in the production of that number. Larger quantities have been printed of some issues, but the production was spread over a longer period of time. 930,000 sheets is the largest quantity ever printed *in one week*. It will thus be seen what an amount of business this represents to the paper-maker, the ink-maker, the wood-draughtsman, the engravers, the electrotypers, the compositors, printers, machine-men, roller-makers, warehousemen, and the numerous other workers in a newspaper printing-office.

The first editor of the *Illustrated London News* was Mr. Bailey, who was nicknamed ' Alphabet Bailey ' on account of the great number of his Christian names, and the consequent multiplicity of his initials. He was also called 'Omnibus Bailey' from his having edited a periodical called the *Omnibus*. These names were given to him to distinguish him from Mr. Thomas Haynes Bayley, the sentimental song-writer, author of 'I'd be a Butterfly,' 'The Soldier's Tear,' &c. Dr. Charles Mackay became the literary and political editor of the paper in 1848, and in 1852 he took its entire management and control, in which position he continued till 1859, when he resigned. The late John Timbs was for many years on the editorial staff, and his familiar figure is well remembered in the old room at 198 Strand, where he sat with paste and scissors, undisturbed by the noises which surrounded him both inside and outside the house, for in this one room the whole business of the paper was at one time conducted. Here the young literary or artistic aspirant, who thought he saw in the new journal an opening for his hitherto unappreciated talents, had to explain his proposals before the eyes and in the hearing of rivals who were waiting for their turn. The place was open to all comers, and was at once the centre of managerial,

financial, and editorial affairs.   But the founder of the paper
received all who came with good-humour and generous
feeling, and never disregarded a useful hint or refused the
proffered assistance of a good man.

Herbert Ingram, the founder of the *Illustrated London
News*, was born at Boston, Lincolnshire, on the 27th of May,
1811.   He lost his father very early, and being sent to the
Boston Free School, he there obtained all the school education he ever received.   The course of instruction through
which he passed was of the most circumscribed character,
making his success in after-life all the more remarkable.
At the age of fourteen he was apprenticed to Mr. Jos.
Clarke, then a printer living in the Market Place, Boston.
His master soon found that he possessed industry, patience,
and perseverance in a high degree, qualities which un-
questionably lay at the root of his subsequent success in
life.   He was always ready to work all night when orders
were plentiful, and was unwilling to abandon anything he
began until it was entirely complete.   He established a
character for punctuality and trustworthiness, while he
carefully looked after the interests of his employer.   At the
expiration of his apprenticeship he came to London and
worked for about two years as a journeyman printer.   He
then settled in Nottingham, and commenced business as a
printer, bookseller, and newsagent.

It was at this time Mr. Ingram was struck with the
evident partiality of the public for *illustrated news*.   He
found such an extraordinary demand for the numbers of the
Weekly Chronicle containing the engravings of the Greenacre
murder that he set seriously to work on the scheme of an
illustrated newspaper, and put himself in communication
with Mr. Marriott, who was then the manager of the *Weekly
Chronicle*.   But at the outset it appeared impossible to overcome the difficulty of producing pictures quick enough and
in such numbers as would furnish forth a paper while the
news was fresh.   In the gradual development of the first
illustrated newspaper it was, however, found that the

draughtsmen and engravers of the day were fully equal
to the demands made upon them, and a system of quick
production was soon established which kept the paper on
a level with current events.

Mr. Ingram, who had settled in London before he started
the *Illustrated London News*, entered heart and soul into his
new enterprise. He had much to learn, and many things to
do that were neither easy nor pleasant, but he had the rare
faculty of picking out the right men to help him. It was
his wise policy to employ the best talent, and in order to
have it to pay its possessor munificently. He was brought
closely into connexion with the artistic and literary world,
by whom he was sincerely respected, and with whom his
dealings were uniformly marked by kindness and liberality.
Though he had not himself received the advantages of
literary or artistic culture, he was able to do much in
diffusing a knowledge and love of art amongst the people.
His enterprise helped to change the character of public taste,
and allured it into channels which were previously open only
to the wealthy and the refined. His practical knowledge as
a printer and newsagent were of infinite value in organizing
and conducting the varied details of newspaper business.
He was ever on the watch, and made opportunities where
other men would have been indifferent and inactive. When
a new Archbishop of Canterbury was installed the number
of the paper containing an engraving of the ceremony was
sent to every clergyman in England, and this was followed
by a large and permanent increase in the number of subscribers—the first large rise in the sale since the paper
began. At a much later date—long after the paper had
become firmly established—the French authorities stopped
the sale of the *Illustrated London News* in Paris on account
of some article reflecting on the Emperor Napoleon. Mr.
Ingram happened to be in Paris at the time, and he immediately showed that the old energy and perseverance of the
Nottingham newsvendor had not forsaken him. He used
great exertions to get the paper released, in which he at

length succeeded, and he himself afterwards went round in a cab and delivered the numbers to the various subscribers. When he was at Nottingham he walked five miles (and of course five miles back) to supply a gentleman with a single paper; and on one occasion he got up at two in the morning, and travelled to London to get some papers, the ordinary post not arriving soon enough to satisfy the curiosity of his customers. His exertions were rewarded by the sale of more than 1000 copies of that paper in Nottingham alone. This was probably one of the occasions which struck him so forcibly when the Nottingham public manifested such an eager interest in *illustrated news*.

Throughout his life Mr. Ingram was devoted to the interests of his native town, and in return the people of Boston, in 1856, elected him as their representative in Parliament. At the general election which occurred after the dissolution in 1857 he was returned again. Amongst other social and political questions in which he took an active interest he was prominent in the agitation for the repeal of the stamp duty on newspapers. He also exerted himself zealously for the repeal of the paper- duty, but he died before that important movement was brought to a successful issue. In 1848 Mr. Ingram started a cheap daily paper — the *Morning Telegraph* — upon which he spent a large amount of money. He was, however, before the time in this instance. The era of cheap daily papers had not begun, and after a time the new speculation was abandoned. He was one of the original shareholders of the *Great Eastern* steamship, and was on board the giant vessel when the accident occurred on her trial trip from the Nore to Portland Harbour. It is a remarkable circumstance that the dreadful catastrophe in which he lost his life happened on the anniversary of this accident on board the *Great Eastern*.

In 1860 Mr. Ingram visited America accompanied by his eldest son. They left Liverpool in the *North American* on the 9th of August, and landed at Quebec in time to witness, after traversing the Lower St. Lawrence, the knocking in of

HERBERT INGRAM, FOUNDER OF THE 'ILLUSTRATED LONDON NEWS.'

the 'last wedge' of the Victoria Bridge at Montreal by the Prince of Wales. They then went on to Niagara, where they stayed some days. From Niagara Mr. Ingram proceeded to Chicago, intending to cross the prairies, and to follow the Mississippi to New Orleans, and thence to New York, but more especially to Boston, which old associations of history had determined him to make the conclusion of his sojourn in the United States. He altered his plans, however, and decided to visit Lake Superior, and to prolong his stay in America, proposing to return to England about the end of October.

Mr. Ingram left Chicago at midnight on the 7th of September, accompanied by his son, in the *Lady Elgin* steamer, bound on an excursion up Lakes Michigan and Superior. Nearly four hundred persons were on board. The wind blew hard from the north-east, and a heavy sea was running, but no one thought of danger, and there was music and dancing in the saloon. Thirty miles from Chicago and ten miles from land, about two o'clock on the morning of the 8th, there came a sudden crash. The schooner *Augusta*, sailing at the rate of eleven knots an hour, had struck the *Lady Elgin* on the midships gangway, and then, having her sails set, and the wind blowing freshly, drifted off in the darkness. At first it was not thought that any serious damage had been done to the steamer, but those on board soon found that she was settling fast. The captain ordered parts of the woodwork of the vessel to be cut adrift to serve as rafts, and made such other provisions as the hurry would allow. In less than half-an-hour the hurricane deck floated off, and the hulk with the machinery went to the bottom with a tremendous noise. When the vessel parted all lights were extinguished, and the unfortunate passengers were left struggling amid the waves in total darkness. The steamer sank in three hundred feet of water, the sea was running high, and the land was ten miles away. Some of those who survived to see the dawn were drifted towards the shore on pieces of the wreck, and were drowned in the surf in the sight of hundreds of spectators. Out of 393 persons on board only 114 were saved. Among the drowned were Mr. Ingram and his son. The body of Mr. Ingram was washed ashore about sixteen miles from Chicago, and every effort was used to restore animation, but in vain. The body of his son was never found.

The citizens of Chicago were profoundly impressed by the melancholy fate of father and son, so far away from home and friends. Mr. Ingram's remains were escorted from the Brigg's House Hotel to the railway station by a procession of more than eight hundred of the British residents in the neighbourhood. The body was taken to Quebec and conveyed on board the *Bohemian* steamer, which arrived at Liverpool on the 2nd of October. From thence the remains were removed to Boston, and interred in the new cemetery at Skirbeck, about a mile from the centre of the town. On the day of the funeral all the shops and places of business in Boston were closed, the inhabitants filled the streets and followed the procession up to the gates of the cemetery. It was in every sense a public funeral, and afforded the strongest testimony of the respect in which the memory of the deceased was held by his fellow-townsmen. Two years afterwards, on October 6th, 1862, a statue of Mr. Ingram, raised by public subscription, was unveiled in the market-place at Boston. The life that began in the quaint old Lincolnshire town and ended amid the stormy waters of Lake Michigan, has now an enduring memorial standing not far from the spot where Herbert Ingram was born.

The *Illustrated London News* no sooner became an assured success than it was imitated. The *Pictorial Times* was the first competitor that entered the field, and a very strong literary staff was collected to contend for the new path that had been opened. Douglas Jerrold wrote the leading articles; Thackeray was critic and reviewer, in which capacity he reviewed Macaulay's *Essays* and Disraeli's *Coningsby;* Mark Lemon was dramatic critic, Peter Cunningham art critic, while Gilbert A'Beckett was the humorous contributor; the managing

editor was Henry Vizetelly, and Knight Hunt, author of the
Fourth Estate, afterwards editor of the *Daily News*, was the
sub-editor. One man who has since become famous as a journalist was amongst the artists employed on the new paper.
Those who only know Mr. George Augustus Sala as a brilliant
writer will be surprised to learn that he is also a facile draughtsman, and was on the artistic staff of the *Pictorial Times* in
1847. The *Pictorial Times* was continued for several years,
but it never achieved such a measure of success as to become
permanently established. A story used to be told in connexion with it which gave some countenance to the popular
belief that some of the sketches in illustrated newspapers
were evolved from the inner consciousness of the artists. I
cannot answer for the truth of the anecdote, but I know it
served to amuse the world of Bohemia at the time. When
the Queen and Prince Albert went first to Scotland, the
newspapers in recording the movements of the royal party
related, among other things (quoting a Scottish contemporary), that Her Majesty and the Prince had gone one day
to ' see the shearing.' The conductors of the *Pictorial Times*
seeing this, and being anxious to present their readers with
a perfect record of the royal doings, forthwith set an artist
to work to produce a pleasant pastoral scene, with a group of
shepherds *shearing their sheep* — not knowing that ' shearing '
in Scotland means *cutting the corn*, and forgetting for the
moment that sheep-shearing is not usually done in the
autumn.

Much energy and capital have been expended on several
other attempts to found pictorial journals in London, but
most of them failed to secure a profitable footing. *Pen and
Pencil* contained some capital cuts by Linton ; and the *Illustrated Times*, a threepenny paper, was well done. The
Illustrated News of the World, in addition to numerous woodcuts, issued portraits engraved on steel. The *Ladies' Newspaper* was started to fill a supposed void in journalism, but
was ultimately absorbed by the *Queen*, in which connexion it
still flourishes. The *Illustrated Midland News* was brought

out in Manchester, but it could not find in that city and its neighbourhood sufficient sustenance to subsist beyond a brief period. The *Illustrated London and Provincial News* in its title endeavoured to attract both town and country, but it only had a short career. While these different ventures were in progress, the *Penny Illustrated Paper* appealed to a lower stratum of the public with great success, and it has now a very large sale, having combined the *Illustrated Times* with its original title. In some of these enterprises the promoters appear to have been unable to shake off, in choosing their titles, the fascinating influence of the word 'illustrated.' A joint-stock company broke the spell, and started a paper with the very original title of the *Graphic* on the eve of the great war between France and Germany. It was a most favourable time for establishing a new paper, and the conductors handled the opportunity with great ability and success. The printing and general *get-up* of the *Graphic* are excellent, and it has earned for itself a wide popularity. The *Pictorial World* was started as a threepenny paper, and after existing several years at that price it became the property of a company and was raised to sixpence. During the Egyptian War it made strenuous efforts to obtain a footing on the same platform with the *Illustrated London News* and the *Graphic*. The large lithographic portraits published by the *Pictorial World* were very good. As the public taste improved under the influence of the pictorial press new fields were opened up for cultivation by the enterprising journalist. The *Illustrated Sporting and Dramatic News* addressed itself not only to the sportsman and actor, but also to that section of the public which finds amusement in the incidents and humours of the sporting world and the stage. It has deservedly obtained a good position. The last new comer on the journalistic stage is the *Ladies' Pictorial*, which has recently been enlarged and greatly improved. Its light and elegant contents are well suited to the tastes of its numerous patrons. All the existing illustrated papers in London have their publishing offices in

the ' Line of Literature,' as Fleet Street and the Strand have
been called.   In the streets and courts in the neighbourhood
are housed numbers of engravers and draughtsmen, who find
it mutually convenient to work in the vicinity of the head-
quarters of pictorial journalism.   Many of the same fraternity
consume the midnight oil in distant suburbs, their work
gravitating to the great centre in the morning.

All the countries of Europe, the United States, some of
the cities of South America, the Colonies of Canada and
Australia, have now their illustrated newspapers.   Some of
them supplement their own productions by reproducing the
engravings from the English papers, and many have attained
a high degree of artistic merit.   The American journals are
especially noteworthy for their excellent engravings.

CHAPTER IX.

How an Illustrated Newspaper is Produced—Wood-engraving—Box-wood—Blocks for Illustrated Newspapers—Rapid Sketching—Drawing on the Block—Method of Dividing the Block for Engraving—Electrotyping—Development of the Printing Machine—Printing Woodcuts—Machinery for Folding Newspapers—Special Artists—Their Dangers and Difficulties—Their Adventures in War and Peace.

IN describing the production of a modern pictorial newspaper, I take the *Illustrated London News* as the type of its class, because it was the first paper of the kind that was ever established. The art of wood-engraving, to which the illustrated newspaper owes its existence, has been fully described by competent authors. The best work on the subject is that produced by the late John Jackson in 1839; but since that date the resources of the art have been greatly developed, chiefly through the influence of illustrated newspapers.

The material used for wood-engraving is box-wood, which is preferred to all other kinds of wood on account of its close grain, hardness, and light colour. It admits of finer and sharper lines being cut upon it than any other wood, and great quantities are consumed in producing the engravings of an illustrated newspaper. According to Mr. J. R. Jackson, Curator of the Kew Museum, the box-tree is at the present time widely distributed through Europe and Asia, being found abundantly in Italy, Spain, Southern France, and on the coast of the Black Sea, as well as China, Japan, Northern India, and Persia. The box of English growth is so small as to be almost useless for commercial purposes. What is called Turkey box-wood is the best, and this is all obtained from the forests that grow on the

Caucasus, and is chiefly shipped at Poti and Rostoff. The forests extend from thirty to a hundred and eighty miles inland, but many of them are in the hands of the Russian Government and are closed to commerce. Within the last few years a supply of box-wood has been obtained from the forests in the neighbourhood of the Caspian Sea; but Turkey box is becoming dearer every year and inferior in quality. After the wood is cut in the forest, it is brought down on horseback to the nearest river, put on board flat-bottom boats, and floated down to the port of shipment. It arrives in this country either at Liverpool or London, chiefly the former, and is usually in logs about four feet long and eight or ten inches across.

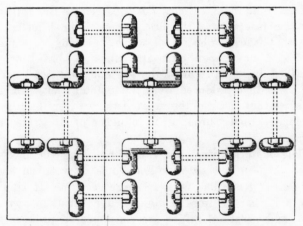

BACK OF A BLOCK, SHOWING THE WAY IN WHICH THE PARTS ARE FASTENED TOGETHER.

The wood intended for engraving purposes is first carefully selected and then cut up into transverse slices about an inch thick. After being cut, the pieces are placed in racks something like plate-racks, and thoroughly seasoned by slow degrees in gradually heated rooms. This seasoning process ought to last, on an average, four or five years; but the exigencies of trade seldom allow of so long a time. They are then cut into parallelograms of various sizes, the outer portion of the circular section near the bark being cut away, and all defective wood rejected. These parallelograms are then assorted as to size, and fitted together at the back by brass bolts and nuts. By this means blocks of any size can be made, and they possess the great advantage of being capable of being taken to pieces after a drawing is made, and distributed among as many engravers as there are pieces in the block. This invention of making bolted blocks was brought forward just about the time the *Illustrated London News* was started, when large blocks and quick engraving came to be in demand. In the days of the *Penny Magazine,* blocks were made by simply glueing the pieces of wood together, or they were fastened by means of a long bolt passing through the entire block.

The cut given on the opposite page represents the back of a half-page block of the *Illustrated London News,* and shows the way in which the bolts and nuts are used for fastening the different parts of the block together.

For the production of a pictorial newspaper a large staff of draughtsmen and engravers is required, who must be ready at a moment's notice to take up any subject, and, if necessary, work day and night until it is done. The artist who supplies the sketch has acquired by long practice a rapid method of working, and can, by a few strokes of his pencil, indicate a passing scene by a kind of pictorial short-hand, which is afterwards translated and extended in the finished drawing. The sketch being completed on paper, the services of the draughtsman on wood come into requisition, for it is not often that the drawing on the block is made by the same person who supplies the sketch. Sometimes the sketch to be dealt with is the production of an amateur, or is so hastily or indifferently done that it has to be remodelled or rearranged in drawing it on the wood. Faulty or objectionable portions have to be left out or subdued, and perhaps a point in the sketch that is quite subordinate, is brought forward and made to form

FACSIMILE OF SKETCH: SURRENDER OF SEDAN.

THE SURRENDER OF SEDAN.   FROM THE ' ILLUSTRATED LONDON NEWS,' SEPT. 17, 1870.

a prominent part of the picture. All this has to be done without doing violence to the general truth of the representation, and with due consideration for the particular conditions of the moment, such as the amount of finish and distribution of light and shade suitable for rapid engraving and printing.

An example of the adaptation of a rapid sketch occurs in the engraving of the surrender of Sedan, published in the *Illustrated London News*, September 17, 1870. This sketch, which carries with it the strongest evidence of being taken 'under fire,' came to hand a few hours before the engravings for the current week were to be ready for the printer. The cream or heart of the sketch, representing an officer waving a white flag over the gate of Sedan attended by a trumpeter, was taken for the subject, while the comparatively unimportant part of the sketch was left out. The drawing was rapidly executed and as rapidly engraved, and was ready for press at the usual time. I give a reduced copy of the engraving, together with a facsimile reduction of the original sketch, which will show the reader the way in which hurried sketches are sometimes adapted to the purposes of a newspaper without at all impairing their original truth.

Sometimes more than one draughtsman is employed on a drawing where the subject consists of figures and landscape, or figures and architecture. In such a case, if time presses, the two parts of the drawing are proceeded with simultaneously. The whole design is first traced on the block; the bolts at the back of the block are then loosened, the parts are separated, and the figure-draughtsman sets to work on his division of the block, while another draughtsman is busied with the landscape or architecture, as the case may be. Occasionally, when there is very great hurry, the block is separated piece by piece as fast as the parts of the drawing are finished—the engraver and draughtsman thus working on the same subject at the same time. Instances have occurred where the draughtsman has done his work in this way, and has never seen the whole of his drawing together. The double-page engraving of the marriage of the Prince of Wales in the *Illustrated London News*, March 21, 1863, was drawn on the wood by Sir John Gilbert at 198 Strand, and as fast as each part of the drawing was done it was separated from the rest and given to the engraver. Considering that the artist never saw his drawing entire, it is wonderful to find the engraving so harmonious and effective. Photographing on the wood is now in general use for portraits, sculpture, architecture, and other subjects where there is a picture or finished drawing on paper to work from.

The drawing on wood being completed, it passes into the hands of the engraver, and the first thing he does is to cut or *set* the lines across all the joins of the block before the different parts are distributed among the various engravers. This is done partly to ensure as far as possible some degree of harmony of colour and texture throughout the subject. When all the parts are separated and placed in the hands of different engravers each man has thus a sort of *key-note* to guide him in the execution of his portion, and it should be his business to imitate and follow with care the colour and texture of the small pieces of engraving which he finds already done at the edge of his part of the block where it joins the rest of the design. The accompanying cuts represent a block entire and the same subject divided.

Though this system of subdividing the engraving effects a great saving of time, it must be admitted that it does not always result in the production of a first-rate work of art as a whole. For, supposing the subject to be a landscape with a good stretch of trees, the two or three engravers who have the trees to engrave have, perhaps, each a different method of rendering foliage; and when the whole is completed, and the different pieces are put together, the trees perhaps appear like a piece of patchwork, with a distinct edge to each man's work. To harmonise and dovetail (so to speak) these different pieces of work is the task of the superintending artist, who retouches the first proof of the engraving and endea-

A BLOCK BEFORE IT IS TAKEN TO PIECES.

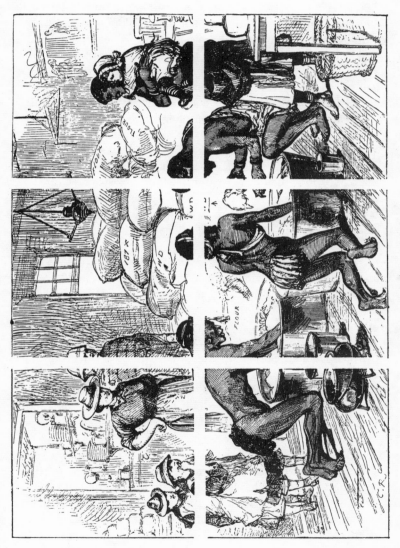

THE SAME SUBJECT DIVIDED.

vours to blend together the differences of colour and texture. This is often no easy task, for the press is generally waiting, and the time that is left for such work is often reduced to minutes where hours would scarcely suffice to accomplish all that might be done. Or the block to be engraved may be a marine subject, with a stormy sea. In this case, like the landscape, two or three engravers may be employed upon the water, each of them having a different way of representing that element. Here it is even more difficult than in the landscape to blend the conflicting pieces of work, and requires an amount of ' knocking about' that sometimes astonishes the original artist. All this is the necessary result of the hurry in which the greater part of newspaper engravings have to be produced. When the conditions are more favourable better things are successfully attempted, and of this the illustrated newspapers of the day have given abundant proofs.

It is obvious that when a block is divided and the parts are distributed in various hands, if any accident should occur to one part the whole block is jeopardised. It is much to the credit of the fraternity of engravers that this rarely or ever happens. I only remember one instance of a failure of this kind within my own experience. An engraver of decidedly Bohemian character, after a hard night's work on the tenth part of a page block, thought fit to recruit himself with a cheering cup. In the exhilaration that followed he lost the piece of work upon which he had been engaged, and thereby rendered useless the efforts of himself and his nine compatriots.

When the block is finished the parts are screwed together by means of the brass bolts and nuts at the back of the block. It is then delivered to the electrotyper, who first takes a mould of the block in wax, which mould is then covered with a thin coating of blacklead, that being a good conductor of electricity. The mould is then suspended by a brass rod in a large bath filled with a solution of sulphate of copper and sulphuric acid. A strong current of electricity, obtained from a dynamo-electric machine close at hand, is conducted to the wax mould in the bath and also to a sheet of copper which is placed near the mould. The electricity decomposes the copper and deposits it in small particles on the mould, on which a thin coating of copper is gradually formed, producing an exact facsimile of the original engraved block. This copper reproduction of the woodcut is filled in at the back with metal, mounted on wood, and is then ready for the printer, who has his 'overlays' all ready, and the business of printing begins.

There is nothing more wonderful in the history of printing than the rapid development of the printing machine and the extraordinary increase of its productive power. The ordinary press, though greatly improved, was found quite inadequate to the demands made upon it ; and, the attention of practical men being directed to some more rapid means of production, the steam printing machine was invented. As early as 1790 Mr. W. Nicholson obtained letters patent for a machine very similar to those since in use ; but it was not till 1814 that any practical use was made of the steam printing machine. In that year a German named König constructed a machine for the *Times* newspaper, which worked successfully ; but, though highly ingenious, the machine was very complicated, and it was soon superseded by the invention of Messrs. Applegarth and Cowper, possessing several novel features. This machine, again, was replaced by another where the type was arranged vertically. Then came Hoe's American machines, and finally the Walter Press, the principle of which last invention has, in the Ingram Rotary Machine, been successfully applied to the printing of cheap illustrated newspapers. By the old 'two-feeder' machines the engravings were printed on one side of the sheet, and, by a second printing, the type on the other side. They turned out 1500 impressions of the engravings in an hour, while the type side was printed (by a six-feeder American machine) at the rate of 12,000 impressions an hour. The *Penny Illustrated Paper* is printed by the Ingram

Rotary Machine at the rate of 6500 an hour. It prints both sides of the sheet at once, cuts each number to its proper size, folds it, and turns it out complete. It occupies no more space than an ordinary perfecting machine, and only requires four men to attend to it, while thirty men and five 'two-feeders' would be required to do the same amount of work by the old system.

If a block be well engraved and carefully used in printing there is practically no limit to the number of impressions that may be taken from it. The blocks in the Christmas number of the *Illustrated London News* of 1882 had 425,000 impressions taken from them, and they are still good for a new edition of the like number.

After the paper is printed each sheet is neatly folded by folding machines, which fold the entire edition in a few hours. One double-action folding machine will fold fifty sheets in a minute. As it is found that machinery for folding newspapers works much better at a moderate speed, in the case of the Ingram Rotary Machine it has been arranged in duplicate, so that each folder only works at half the speed of the printing machine. The folding machine completes its work by inserting the paper in its cover; but as the *Illustrated London News* has not sufficient space for machines to carry out the whole of this part of the business, a number of women and girls are employed, whose nimble fingers supplement the work of the folding machines.

In these days of electric telegraphy Puck's notion of putting 'a girdle round about the earth in forty minutes' is not so very far from being realised. The London citizen as he sips his coffee at his villa in the suburbs runs his eye over the pages of his morning paper, and reads of events that took place yesterday many thousand miles away. Before he starts for business he is informed of what is passing on every side of the inhabited earth. This rapid transmission of intelligence is somewhat damaging to the illustrated newspaper, for by the time it can publish sketches

THE EVE OF A BATTLE : NEWSPAPER CORRESPONDENTS SLEEPING ON THE FIELD.

of interesting events in far distant countries the freshness
of the news is gone, and the public mind is occupied with
later occurrences. Until some method is invented of sending
sketches by electricity the pictorial press must endure this
disadvantage, but in the meantime it spares no pains to
overtake the march of events. Wherever there is any
' moving accident by flood or field ' the ' special artist ' of
the illustrated newspaper is found ' takin' notes.' No event
of interest escapes his ever ready pencil. He undergoes
fatigues, overcomes formidable difficulties, and often incurs
personal danger in fulfilling his mission. On the eve of a
battle he will sleep on the bare ground wrapped in a blanket
or waterproof sheet, and he will ride all night through a
hostile country to catch the homeward mail. He is equally
at home in the palace and the hovel, and is as ready to
attend a battle as a banquet. He thought nothing of
stepping over to China to attend the nuptials of the celestial
Emperor ; and on that occasion extended his travels until
he had completed the circuit of the globe, winding up with
a run on the war-path among the American Indians. He
assisted at the laying of the telegraph cable between Europe
and America, and diversified his labours, and showed the
versatility of his powers by taking part in an impromptu
dramatic entertainment which he and his comrades got
up for the occasion, and which they appropriately called
'A Cable-istic Extravaganza.' He was at the opening of
the Suez Canal, and he passed with the first railway train
through the Mont Cenis tunnel. In pursuing his vocation
the special artist has to encounter the perils of earth, air,
fire, and water. Now he is up in a balloon, now down in a
coal-mine ; now shooting tigers in India, now deer-stalking
in the Highlands. Dr. Schliemann no sooner announced that
he had discovered the site of Troy than the special artist was
down upon the spot at once. He is found risking his life
in the passes of Afghanistan, and in Zululand assisting at
the defeat and capture of Cetywayo. Now he is at the bom-
bardment of Alexandria, and now facing the savage warriors

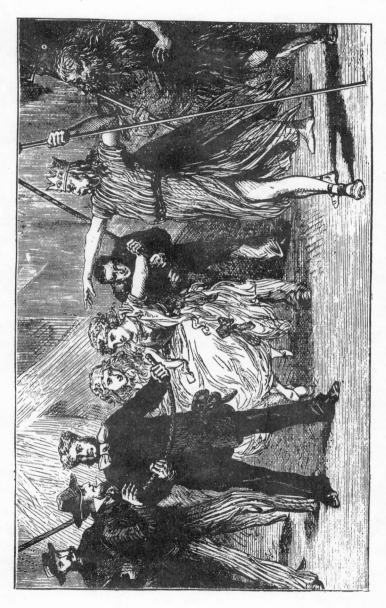

A CABLE-ISTIC EXTRAVAGANZA, PERFORMED BY NEWSPAPER CORRESPONDENTS ON BOARD THE *GREAT EASTERN*, AT SEA, JULY, 1866.

of the Soudan at El-Teb and Tamasi. At the present time
(November, 1884), he is on his way up the Nile with the
expedition for the relief of General Gordon at Khartoum,
and he is in India with the Boundary Commissioners exploring the dangerous passes of the Afghan frontier. In
peace or war the special artist pursues his purpose with
stoical self-possession in spite of cold, hunger, and fatigue.

The special artist may be said to have commenced his
career with the Crimean War. While the signs of the
coming storm were yet distant the *Illustrated London News*
sent the late Mr. S. Read to the expected scene of action,
and during the whole course of the war special artists were
on the shores of the Black Sea and in the Baltic to chronicle
the great events of the time. The world had scarcely forgotten Balaklava and Inkerman when the war between
Italy, France, and Austria broke out. Solferino and
Magenta were fought, Garibaldi conquered Sicily, and
wherever the interest was greatest there the special artist
was found. Special artists went with the contending armies
when Denmark opposed herself single-handed to the united
forces of Prussia and Austria, and delineated every important incident of the campaign. When the present Emperor
of Germany was crowned King of Prussia at Königsberg
special artists travelled to that ancient city to furnish
sketches of the ceremony. The gigantic civil war in
America, and the brief struggle between Prussia and
Austria in 1866, gave active employment to the special
artist; and when a British force advanced into Abyssinia
a special artist was with that most romantic expedition,
and sent home numerous sketches of the remarkable scenery
of the country, as well as of all the principal events of the
campaign. The assault on Magdala, the dispersion of King
Theodore's broken army, the customs and dwellings of the
people, were all noted and illustrated. When the great war
of 1870, between France and Prussia, broke out, the illustrated newspapers had special artists on both sides, who
encountered all sorts of hardships, and passed through all

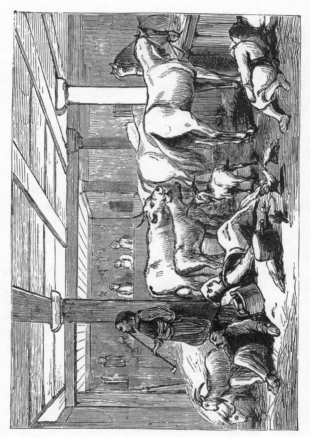

HEADQUARTERS OF SPECIAL ARTIST IN ASIA MINOR, 1877.

kinds of adventures in fulfilling their duties. Besides being frequently arrested as spies, and undergoing the privations of beleagured places, they had also to run the risk of shot and shell, and sometimes they were obliged to destroy their sketching materials under fear of arrest. One of them was in custody as a spy no less than eleven times during the war. The danger of being seen sketching or found with sketches in their possession was so great that on one occasion a special artist actually swallowed his sketch to avoid being taken up as a spy. Another purchased the largest book of cigarette papers he could obtain, and on them he made little sketches, prepared in case of danger to smoke them in the faces of his enemies.

The following extract from a letter I received from a special artist during the war, will give some idea of the trouble and danger of sketching :—

'Of the trouble I have taken to get these sketches you can have no conception. The plan I have been obliged to adopt is this. I walk about quietly, apparently noticing only the goods in the shop-windows. When I see anything, I make memoranda on small bits of tissue paper, perhaps in a café, or while appearing to look at the water from the top of a bridge, or on the side of an apple, with a big knife in my hand pretending to peel it. These little mems I roll up into pills, place them handy in my waistcoat pocket to be chewed up or swallowed if "in extremis." When I get home at night, first making sure that I am not overlooked by way of the window, I unroll these little pills, and from those mems make a complete outline on a thin piece of white paper. Then I paste these sketches face to face, trim the edges, and it looks like a plain piece of paper, but hold it up to the light and the sketch shows. So I make memoranda all over it,—the times of trains starting, prices of articles, or extracts from newspapers. When I get to a place of safety, I soak these pieces of paper in water, pull the sketches apart, and from them have made the sketches I have forwarded to you. If I could not get into a place of safety to make the sketches, I don't know what I should do, in fact I don't think I could do anything, for I would not, for any consideration *be found making a sketch, nor with a sketch in my possession ;* nor should I dare post a sketch at the " Bureaux de poste," but I might get it into a street box.'

Another special artist being at Metz, found himself in the midst of a population infected with what he called the ' spy-fever.' About a dozen English newspaper correspondents were there, and they became a united body through persecution. There was always about a fourth of their number in prison, and what most persons would have considered to be clear evidence that they were not spies, was in the minds of the French clear evidence that they were. If they were told that the correspondent of an English newspaper could not possibly be a spy, the reply was that that was just the character that a *cochon* of a Prussian spy would assume. The townspeople of Metz became quite wild when they heard of the French defeats at Wörth and Forbach, and when they saw an artist sketching the Emperor's carriage, they pounced upon him as a Prussian spy, and he and his companions were marched off in custody, amid the hootings of the mob. The following account of this affair is extracted from the *Illustrated London News* of August 20, 1870 : ' Three of the representatives of London papers, Mr. Simpson, Mr. Henry Mayhew and his son, went to the railway station, having heard a rumour that the Emperor was about to start for the front, and also that a train full of the wounded was expected to arrive. At the station they met Mr. Stuart, another newspaper correspondent, who had just come from Italy, having travelled all night. They found the Emperor's carriage and horses waiting to be forwarded by a train on the railway towards St. Avold. Our artist thought it would be doing no harm to employ the few minutes of his waiting at the station in making a slight sketch of the carriage and horses, which might be useful as materials for an illustration of some future scene where the same equipage might figure. He took a small sketch-book

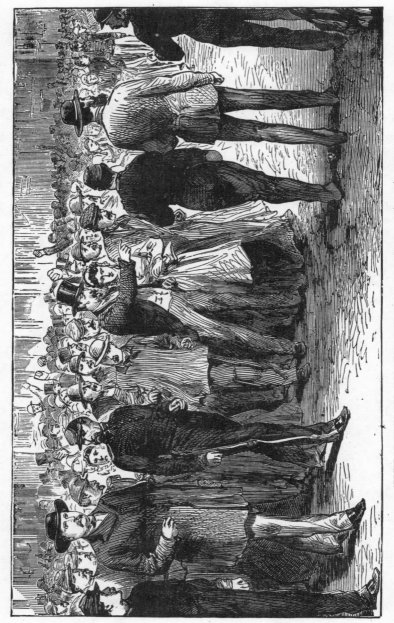

ARREST OF NEWSPAPER CORRESPONDENTS AT METZ, DURING THE FRANCO-GERMAN WAR.

and pencil out of his pocket and quickly finished this little drawing. There was no attempt at concealment; he even showed his sketch to one of the bystanders who was close to him, and who seemed to watch his movements with some curiosity. Mr. Simpson then rejoined his three English companions, but had scarcely done so before they were surrounded by a large party of artillery soldiers, who wore undress jackets and had not their arms with them. They were taken into custody, each one placed between two soldiers, and thus were marched through the streets of Metz to the Place de la Cathedral. A mob of people followed, increasing as they went on, and reviling the foreigners as "Sacrès Prusses," or "Cochons de Prusses," threatening vengeance upon them, which might probably have been taken if their violence had not been restrained by the presence of the soldiers. The whole party were then brought into the guard-room, where several persons came forward as their accusers to denounce them as spies of the enemy, lurking about Metz with a hostile and insidious purpose. The chief evidence against one of them was that he had bought three copies of a Metz local newspaper; another was suspected because he had been seen four days successively in the same cafè, "and always sitting in the same seat;" a third could be no true man, because, while he said he belonged to a London paper, he confessed that he had just come from Florence. The main charge against Mr. Simpson was that he did not lodge at an hotel, but in a private house. These particulars were repeated to the crowd outside, which filled the whole Place, and was in a state of raging fury; till at last the officers in charge made their appearance and commenced a more regular examination. Our artist produced his passport, which was approved as in due order ; but his little sketch-book, with its scraps of notes and bits of outline, seemed to contain matter for serious investigation. In spite of his awkward and rather alarming position, he was struck with the absurdity of viewing such innocent scrawls as proof of heinous guilt. He endeavoured, however, with the assistance of Mr. Mayhew, to explain what they were, and to persuade the officers that they could do no harm. After a tedious detention, they were permitted to write a note to a friend, who instantly went to the Provost-Marshal, and at once got an order for their immediate release. Their private letters and papers were examined. Several other persons, Frenchmen as well as foreigners, including one who was the artist employed by a Paris illustrated paper, were arrested at Metz on the same day; and more than one of them suffered rough usage at the hands of the mob. On the next day they were all ordered to leave the town.' The following is a facsimile of the sketch that produced all this commotion.

7ᵗʰ augᵗ 1870.

THE EMPEROR'S CARRIAGE AT METZ.

The same artist who made his sketches into pills, being at Bremerhafen, found himself so watched and dogged by the police and others who had observed he was a stranger, that he could not make the sketch he wanted. After much walking about he at length returned to the place where he desired to sketch, and sitting down at the edge of the harbour he began to draw lines with his umbrella on the mud, as if in a fit of abstraction, and soon had sketched in this way the principal points of the scene before him. This he repeated several times, until the view was fixed in his memory, when he retired to the railway-station, and there, unobserved, committed the scene to his sketch-book. On another occasion, in the neighbourhood of Mezières, he was driven at nightfall to seek a lodging in a very lonely and villainous looking inn. The occupants of the place looked upon him with evil eyes, and dreading lest one more should be added to the numerous graves already near the cabaret, he betook himself to a neighbouring wood, where he spent the whole night surrounded by the carcases of dead horses. At Lyons he penetrated into the theatre where the people were storing corn and flour in anticipation of a siege. He had made some hasty notes in his sketch-book, when he was observed and obliged to retreat, followed, however, by several men. He had noticed an umbrella shop round the corner in the next street, and into this shop he rushed, seized an umbrella, opened it, and kept it expanded between himself and the door, as if examining the quality of the silk, while his pursuers ran past, when he demanded the price of the umbrella, paid the money, and walked off, glad to escape at so small a cost. Sometimes his adventures had a more amusing termination. When the spy-fever prevailed very strongly both in France and Germany, he was one day looking into a shop-window when he became conscious that he was watched by two officers. ' Now,' thought he, ' I am in for it again, and shall certainly be arrested.' This feeling was confirmed as one of the officers advanced towards him, and raising his hand as if to seize him by the collar, addressed him thus : ' Permit me, monsieur, to adjust the string of your shirt collar, which has escaped from behind your cravat.'* This gentleman was somewhat old-fashioned in his costume, and during his wanderings was sometimes mistaken for a sea-captain. He had even

---

* This incident was illustrated in *Punch,* and lest I should be accused of using up old material, I must explain that the hero of the adventure, on his return to England, told the story to one of the *Punch* artists, who made a sketch of the incident, which was afterwards published.

received confidential proposals to discuss the question of freight.

The *Illustrated London News* had five artists in the field during the Franco-German war: W. Simpson, R. T. Landells, G. H. Andrews, C. J. Staniland, and Jules Pelcoq. From the fact of Landells being already known to the Crown Prince of Prussia and several of his staff, it was settled that his destination should be Germany, and I remember that before his departure he expressed to me just the slightest shade of discontent that he should be selected to go on what he thought would be the losing side. He was destined, however, to be present at the proclamation of the German Emperor in the palace of Versailles, and he was one of the first to enter Paris after it capitulated to the German army. Soon afterwards he very nearly experienced the unpleasant consequences of being taken for a German spy. Landells himself was of a dark complexion, and might very well have passed for a Frenchman, but on the occasion referred to he was in the company of a brother artist (Mr. Sidney Hall, of the *Graphic*), who, being fair, might easily be mistaken for German. The excited mob of Paris had just vented their rage on a suspected spy by drowning him in the Seine, and the two special artists were loitering on the outskirts of the crowd, when Mr. Hall imprudently took out his sketch-book, which was no sooner perceived than a cry was raised of ' Prussian spy !' and they too would probably have been pitched into the river had they not managed, with great difficulty, to escape from the crowd.

When the German armies were closing round Paris M. Jules Pelcoq consented to be shut up in the devoted city for the purpose of supplying the *Illustrated London News* with sketches. During the hardships of the siege he was quite unable to obtain fuel to warm his apartment, and was compelled to retire to bed, where, wrapped in a blanket, he finished up the rough sketches he had made out of doors, which were then photographed and sent off by balloons to London. These balloons were regularly despatched during

NEWSPAPER CORRESPONDENTS ON THEIR WAY TO THE FRONT.—SISTOVA, 1877.

the prevalence of winds that would carry them to the provinces unoccupied by the Germans. They were followed by Prussian light cavalry as long as they were in sight, and some were captured. Afterwards, as the city became more closely invested, and the danger increased, the precaution was taken of despatching the balloons at night, and the time fixed on was kept concealed from all save those immediately concerned, in order to avoid, as far as possible, the chances of its being communicated to the enemy, and thereby exposing the aëronauts to the fiery rockets and other projectiles with which the Germans were prepared to favour them. The railway-stations were generally chosen as the starting-places, for they not only offered large open spaces in which to fill the balloons, but, being situated away from the centre of Paris, there was less risk, in ascending, of coming in contact with buildings.

To provide against the loss of sketches so sent, photographic copies were despatched by other balloons. In some cases two, and even three, copies of the same sketch reached my hands by balloon-post during the German investment of Paris. Considering the danger and difficulty of this mode of communication, the intercourse between the *Illustrated London News* and its artist in Paris was kept up pretty regularly during the whole siege.

The requirements of special artists when on the 'war path' vary according to circumstances. Mr. Simpson, in France during the Franco-German war, found no scarcity of food, but could seldom get a bed to sleep in. On the other hand, Mr. Melton Prior, in South Africa and other hot countries, found that he was never sure of obtaining either food or drink. During the war in Herzegovina in 1876 the newspaper correspondents had to rough it pretty considerably. Sometimes, when the special artist got to a resting-place for the night, he would have to work up his sketches by the light of a single candle, which he kept in an upright position by holding it between his feet as he sat on the ground, while the correspondent of a London 'daily' scribbled his notes beside him. The difficulty of obtaining sleeping accommodation was experienced by

SKETCHING UNDER DIFFICULTIES.   HERZEGOVINA, 1876.

another artist in Servia, who was obliged one night to go to rest in a sort of diligence or covered waggon which stood in the inn yard. It was the only 'spare bed,' and the tired 'special' was very glad to coil himself up within its recesses. These hardships, however, belong to the past. Just as the combatants in modern warfare fight their battles with the most scientific weapons, so the newspaper correspondent now goes to the field armed with the latest appliances against cold, fatigue, hunger, and thirst. He provides himself with an abundant supply of tinned meats and champagne, plenty of clothing, the latest improvements in saddlery; and when he arrives at the scene of action he buys as many horses as he wants for himself and servants. Acting on the experience of former campaigns, Mr. Prior was able in the Zulu War to travel much more comfortably than any member of the staff, not even excepting Lord Chelmsford himself. 'I had then no fewer than five horses: two in the shafts of my American waggon, one for myself, one for my servant, and one spare horse. I followed the army through all its marches in my travelling carriage, and on the eve of the Battle of Ulundi I was the only man who had a tent; all the others lay down in the open.'

While recording the progress of events—the deeds of war mingling with the works of peace—the pictorial press is not unmindful of what is done in the cause of humanity. One of the recent experiences of the special artist was in making a journey across Siberia in search of the survivors of the crew of the American exploring ship *Jeanette.* Mr. J. Gordon Bennett, the proprietor of the *New York Herald,* having

THE SPARE BED.

sent out a commissioner to search for the missing expedition, he was joined by the special artist of the *Illustrated London*

SPECIAL ARTIST'S TENT.

News. They had before them a journey of two or three thousand miles, and they travelled in one of the covered sledges used in Siberia in the winter time. It was their travelling carriage by day and their sleeping apartment at night. Sometimes they had to turn out and defend themselves from the wolves which followed them over the snowy waste. The artist on this occasion was Mr. Larsen, of Copenhagen, who proved himself a first-rate special.

When the effects of a deadly climate are added to the usual chances of war, the courage and endurance of the newspaper correspondent are doubly tried. The 'specials' of the principal London journals joined the Ashantee expedition with as much alacrity as if they had been going to a review in Hyde Park. Among them was Mr. Melton Prior, the artist of the *Illustrated London News*, who landed at Cape Coast Castle before the arrival of the British troops, marched with them to Coomassie, and remained in that place till it was destroyed by the victors. But the long march in such a climate had exhausted the strength of many, and the special artist was among the number. On nearing Coomassie he could no longer trust to his own unaided powers of locomotion, so he laid hold on the tail of a mule which he saw ambling before him, and so was helped forward. The gentleman who was riding the mule turned round, when it proved to be Sir Garnet Wolseley himself, who, in answer to the exhausted artist's apologies, good-humouredly told him to 'hold on !'

While coolness and courage are indispensable qualifications for the special artist, if he can sometimes accomplish a little harmless dissimulation he finds it very useful. In 1877, during the war between Russia and Turkey, a special artist overcame the difficulties he encountered in getting to the front by assuming the character of a camp-follower, and professing to sell composite candles, German sausages, Russian hams, dried fish, Dutch cheese, &c., and when passing Cossacks became importunate they were propitiated with a candle or two, a slice of cheese, or a packet of

NEWSPAPER CORRESPONDENTS STARTING FOR SIBERIA.

Roumanian tobacco. In like manner the artist who went to the port of Ferrol to accompany Cleopatra's Needle to London shipped on board the tug *Anglia* as a coal-trimmer, and signed the usual articles as one of the crew, there being no room for passengers. After the successful voyage of the tug the artist left her at Gravesend, being anxious to bring his sketches to head-quarters; but until he was legally discharged from service he ran the unpleasant risk of being taken up for absconding from his ship.

Not the least of a special artist's troubles is to get his sketches sent home without loss of time. Mr. Simpson, who has had a large and varied experience as a special artist, having been all round the world in that capacity, gives it as his opinion that the first duty of a special correspondent when he arrives at the scene of action is to find out the post-office, if he happens to be in a part of the world where such a civilised institution exists. He should take care to post all his packets himself, and never trust to any one else. He says, 'In all my various travels I never lost a packet but once, and that was during the week's fighting at the time of the Commune in Paris. There were three sketches in the packet. I was very dubious about letting them out of my hands, but I had been all the week with the correspondent of the *Times*, who had spent a considerable sum of money upon messengers to get his letters taken through the lines outside Paris and off to London. I ventured to let my packet go with his, thinking it was safe, but neither of them ever reached their destination.' In connexion with this subject I may quote the following story related by Mr. Prior to the editor of the *Pall Mall Gazette*:—'I remember one time when I was attached to Mehemet Ali's head-quarters in Bulgaria during the Russo-Turkish war. The Turkish censor stopped no fewer than six weeks of my sketches. Things were getting desperate. Our people were telegraphing out to know whether I was alive or dead; and, finding that something must be done, I determined to see the thing through or leave the camp. It so happened that I had

CAMP OF THE 'TIMES' AND 'ILLUSTRATED LONDON NEWS' CORRESPONDENTS ATTACKED BY WOLVES. BULGARIA, 1877

been the witness of some peculiarly atrocious deeds perpetrated by Turks upon Bulgarians, so I set to work and drew half-a-dozen faithful representations of the sufferings which I had witnessed. Armed with these I went up to the censor's office and asked that they might be stamped for transmission home. The censor looked at the first and said it was ridiculous. Couldn't pass that; no such atrocities had ever been committed; and so forth. The second was condemned in the same way, and so on until the last was reached. When he had rejected that also I said to him very deliberately, " You are going to pass every one of these sketches !" " On the contrary," said he, " I am going to tear them up." " If you do," said I, " I shall draw not only six but twelve pictures worse than these, and send them home by my own messenger." " I will have him arrested then," said the censor. " Very well, then, in that case I shall leave the camp at once, and in London I will draw twenty pictures all worse than these, and they will all be published, so that people may see the real truth about how you are behaving here." The censor, like a sensible man, saw that it was no use carrying things with too high a hand, and came to terms. He admitted he had stopped all my sketches, promised to do so no more, and I left him with my atrocity pictures in my pocket, assuring him that the first sketch of mine that he stopped again the whole series should go to London by the next steamer. I never had any more trouble with him in that respect, though he paid me out by having me arrested some months later.'

During the Franco-German War Mr. Simpson often proved the advantage of his plan of always posting his sketches himself. At the fall of Strasburg he was in the advanced trench when the white flag was displayed from the tower of the cathedral. It was late in the evening when he got home to bed, but he was up with the first streak of dawn finishing his sketch of the historical event he had witnessed the day before. He then walked five miles to General Werder's head-quarters to post the sketch. He wasted no time in trying to get a horse or carriage, in which he might have failed, nor would he trust the packet to a messenger. He knew that the slightest delay would postpone the publication of the sketch for a whole week. The sketch arrived in time, as he had calculated, for the next publication, and he had the satisfaction of knowing that on this occasion, as on many others, his promptitude and energy had well served the interests of the journal he represented.

A special artist has to encounter many troubles and vexations apart from the dangers and difficulties of war time. When Mr. Simpson was at Brindisi, on his way to the opening of the Suez Canal, wishing to sketch the town and fortifications, he ensconced himself in a snug corner, well sheltered from the 'Bora,' or cold wind that was blowing, and had settled down comfortably to work, when he was interrupted by a man who addressed him in Italian, a language Simpson did not understand. He, however, made out that the man's 'padre' or master would not like Simpson to be there; but the latter replied in plain English that he cared nothing for his 'padre,' that he had the permission of the Commandant to go where he pleased, and so he went on with his sketching. After much unintelligible talk the man attempted to stop the sketcher's view by standing between him and the town, but finding the sketching went on just the same, he suddenly went away and then returned with a gun, pointing it in a threatening manner towards Simpson, who thought the gun was perhaps not loaded, or at all events that the man would never be such a fool as to shoot him, so he merely gave a majestic wave of his hand and went on with his work. The man's rage then increased to such a degree that he seized the butt end of his gun, uttering a volley of curses, and from the word 'testa' Simpson supposed the man wanted to smash his head. However he never flinched, and the man, lowering his gun, muttered something about the 'Cani,' and went off again. Presently he returned dragging with him a huge dog. Simpson felt more afraid of the dog than the man, but it turned out that the dog had more sense than his

master and refused on any terms to attack the artist. He
bolted, the man after him, and Simpson then armed himself
with two stones in case the attack should be renewed, resolving, like Tell when he devoted one of his arrows to Gessler,
that one stone should be for the dog and the other for his
oppressor. The man however could not get the dog to
return to the attack. He had exhausted the whole of his

NEWSPAPER CORRESPONDENTS' HUTS ON THE BATTLE-FIELD OF KACELJEVO, 1877.

resources, and was evidently astonished and annoyed to find
he had failed to frighten the artist, so he finished off with a
torrent of curses and then gradually calmed down. He
remained watching the completion of the sketch, and then
obligingly favoured the artist with some criticisms on his
work. He pointed out that a ship in the harbour had been
forgotten, and could not understand that it had been purposely left out because it interfered with one of the principal
buildings. In this instance it was perhaps best for both

parties that they did not understand each other's language; but the special artist is occasionally placed at a disadvantage by not understanding the language of the country where he happens to be. However it rarely leads to more than a temporary embarrassment, and is often the cause of more amusement than vexation. Mr. G. H. Andrews on one occasion desired to have a couple of eggs for breakfast, but could not make the maid of the inn comprehend his meaning. He tried all he knew of French, Flemish, and German, but the girl shook her head. At length a bright idea struck the artist. He drew from his pocket a pencil and note-book, and sketched a couple of oval forms, meaning them for eggs, and explained by gestures that *that* was what he wanted. The girl's face brightened at once when she saw the sketch, and with a nod of intelligence she tripped away. In a few minutes she returned and presented the hungry artist with —*a pair of spectacles !*

The late Mr. S. Read, who was one of the first special artists employed on the pictorial press, travelled much abroad, yet he knew little or nothing of any language save his mother tongue. Germany, Italy, Austria, Spain, France, Belgium, Switzerland, were all visited by him, and he got on very well without speaking the language of any of those countries. He was a man of genial humour, accustomed to make the best of everything, and not easily put out by trifles. He was once travelling in the south of France when a fellow-passenger in the train accosted him in French, and was much surprised to find he was not understood.

'Vat!' said the Frenchman; 'you travel and speak no French! Speak you German?'

'No.'

'Nor Italian?'

'No.'

'Spanish?'

'No.'

'Ah, mon Dieu! you travel and speak noting!' and with a pitying grimace and shrug of the shoulders he looked round at the other passengers. Presently our artist took his revenge. As they were passing a town with a ruined castle on a hill he said, with much fervour, addressing the Frenchman,—

'How beautifully that old tower is relieved by the dark foliage! What a splendid contrast is the cold grey of the hill behind! How harmoniously the distance is blended with the middle distance, and the middle distance with the foreground, by means of the bridge across the river!' The Frenchman staréd, stammered, and confessed he did not comprehend.

'What!' said our artist; 'you travel and do not understand English!'

'Ver leetle.'

'Do you speak Scotch?'

'Non, m'sieur.'

'Nor Irish!'

'Non.'

'Welsh?'

'Non.'

'Suffolk?'

'Non, non, m'sieur.'

With an exact imitation of the Frenchman's contemptuous shrug our friend turned to their fellow-travellers amid the loud laughter of those who understood the joke.

When the special artist exercises his vocation at home, though he lacks the excitement of danger, he meets with many amusing incidents. An artist who attended the meeting of the British Association at Lincoln many years ago desired to sketch the house which was reputed to have been the residence of John o' Gaunt, and asked the waiter at the hotel if he could direct him to it. 'Johnny Gaunt, Sir?' said the waiter, evidently puzzled; 'I don't know him, Sir, but I'll inquire.' In a few minutes he returned and said he had inquired at the bar, but that no such person as Johnny Gaunt resided thereabouts. Another, who was something of a wag, was once making a sketch in the heart of St. Giles's;

there were no School Boards in those days, and numbers of idle street boys surrounded our sketcher, performing all manner of bewildering gymnastics. Not at all disturbed, however, he amused himself by asking his young friends numerous questions, all of which were answered with rapid pertness. At last he inquired of one active imp if he could read. 'No, I can't read,' said the young gentleman, 'but I can stand on my head and drink a quartern o' gin.'

The methods pursued by special artists in obtaining their sketches are as various as the methods of painters in producing their pictures, or of authors in writing their books. One man uses a very small sketch-book, another prefers a large one, but they all require to supplement their hurried sketches with marginal notes. When there is not time to sketch a complete cow, it is good to write underneath the sketch, 'This is a cow.' Many events have to be sketched that last only a few minutes, and in such cases some little mistakes will occur even with old practitioners. Literary correspondents are liable to the same misfortune. At a certain royal marriage in St. George's Chapel, Windsor, the Lord Chamberlain obligingly sent a gentleman to attend the members of the press, and inform them as to the name and rank of the distinguished guests as they entered the chapel. The correspondents courteously allowed the artists of the pictorial press to take front places, so that some of their number were unable to see what was going on, and had to trust to their comrades for information. When the Duke of A——, in full Highland costume, entered the chapel, there was a general inquiry, 'Who is that?' 'That,' said the gentleman from the Lord Chamberlain's department, 'is the Duke of A——, the great Mac Callum More.' 'Who is it?' cried some of the gentlemen in the background, and the name was passed on, but by the time it reached the outer fringe of correspondents it was changed into 'The Duke of A—— with the Great Claymore,' and under that style and title his grace's name figured in at least one newspaper next day.

A A

What may be called the shorthand notes for a sketch are sometimes difficult to make out without explanation. On one occasion a sketch was under consideration, when the editor made certain suggestions to the artist, who was very good natured, and of a most pliant disposition. 'I think, you know,' said the editor, 'if you were to add two or three more figures in the foreground it would improve the composition and help to detach the principal group from this windmill.' 'Well, the fact is,' replied the artist, 'what you call a windmill I intended for a man on horseback, but if you think it will come better as a windmill I'll alter it with pleasure.'

THE SPECIAL ARTIST ON THE ROAD.

CHAPTER X.

Artists who have assisted in founding the Pictorial Press—Sir John Gilbert, R.A., G. H. Thomas, and others—Wood-Engraving and its Connexion with the Pictorial Press—Other Methods of producing Illustrations—Wood-Engraving in England before and after Bewick's time—Its wide Diffusion owing to the kindred Art of Printing—The resources of the Art developed by Pictorial Newspapers—Conclusion. Newspapers a Necessity of Civilised Life—The *Acta Diurna* of the Romans—Early Newspapers in Venice, Germany, and the Low Countries—List of Illustrated Newspapers published Abroad.

THE establishment of the pictorial press as an English institution was greatly aided by the active co-operation of many distinguished artists, the very foremost in this connexion being Sir John Gilbert. Other Royal Academicians and eminent painters have drawn on wood for the illustrated newspapers, but Gilbert stands out pre-eminently the great popular illustrator of the Victorian era. He it was who first gave a distinctive character to the illustration of news. He seemed to possess an inborn knowledge of the essentials of newspaper art, and could express by a few freely drawn lines and touches the hurried movement of street crowds or the state and dignity of Court ceremonies. Whether he had to draw a knight in armour or a gentleman in a paletôt he did it in a way exactly suited to rapid engraving and printing. The feeling which, in his pictures, makes him delight in battle-fields, blazoned banners, velvet and gold, made his drawings on wood brilliant in handling and always picturesque. It was most fortunate that the commencement of his career was coincident with the foundation of the pictorial press. William Harvey and other artists were already in the field, but Gilbert's style was better adapted to newspaper work. His quickness and versatility made him just the man that was wanted. Harvey had drawn some of the subjects published in the *Observer*, but his style was not suited to the illustration of current events. Nothing came amiss to Gilbert, who supplied the pictorial press for twenty years with a constant succession of effective drawings, embracing all kinds of subjects, and he never failed in that most essential quality of a newspaper artist—*punctuality*. It is as the popular illustrator that the name of Gilbert stands at the head of that numerous band of artists who contributed to the foundation of illustrated journalism in this country.

The late George H. Thomas was not less successful than Gilbert in the spirit and vigour of his drawings. His bold and eminently artistic pencil alternated with Gilbert's in portraying the exciting events following the revolutionary period of 1848–49. His contributions to the *Illustrated London News* during the Crimean war were marked by great force and truthfulness, and procured him the notice and patronage of her Majesty Queen Victoria. Mr. Thomas's premature death in 1868 was a great loss to the world of art in general, and to the pictorial press in particular.

It is remarkable that many of our distinguished artists should have begun their careers as engravers or draughtsmen on wood. The production of works in black and white, whether as engravings or drawings, is no doubt good artistic practice in the study of light and shade, and the young artist who draws on wood as a means of helping him to live while he is waiting for fame, is at the same time pursuing a useful branch of his art education. Luke Fildes, A.R.A., Birket Foster, W. Small, R. C. Woodville, C. Gregory, A.R.A., and many others began in this way, and among deceased artists occur the names of S. Read, E. Duncan, and F. W. Topham. The two last were both engravers. All these men have done good work on the pictorial press, and some of them first won distinction through its medium. Both the *Illustrated London News* and the *Graphic* may claim to have done good service to art and artists in this respect. Their pages have always been open to young artists of ability, and while they have helped forward struggling genius they have opened up new sources of enjoyment to the general public.

The pictorial press has hitherto been mainly dependent on the art of wood-engraving for its illustrations, but latterly several inventions have been used, not unsuccessfully, in the production of blocks in relief, to be printed in the same manner as woodcuts. The great improvements that have been made in surface printing render it probable that in the future these *process* blocks may be extensively used in illustrated newspapers. They are recommended by their cheapness and rapid production; and as the intermediate process of engraving is dispensed with, they retain the exact touch of the artist, and are not liable to be mutilated by careless or hasty engraving. It may be said of all these inventions, however, that they are best suited for slight sketches, and should not be applied to the production of highly-finished subjects. For the latter there is nothing better than a woodcut, which, when well executed and carefully printed, has a richness superior to any other method of engraving. But in the present day competition is so great and the march of events is so rapid that cheapness and rapidity of production will override artistic excellence, and *process*-engraving, as it is called, will probably be the method adopted for the *daily* pictorial press, the era of which is approaching.

Wood-engraving, as an art, scarcely existed in this country before the time of Thomas Bewick. To him we owe its revival, and he was thus indirectly concerned in the creation of the pictorial newspaper. Though we have seen that the *Grub Street Journal* and the *Observer* on a few occasions used copperplate illustrations, it is perfectly certain that an illustrated newspaper, properly so-called, never could have existed but for the art of wood-engraving. It was an essential agent in bringing into life this novel offspring of the printing press, just as it assisted in the birth of the old 'block books.' When Caxton brought the art of printing into this country the woodcuts printed at his press were probably executed by the printers whom he brought with him. His successors illustrated their books in the same way, and even after wood-engraving was practised in England as a distinct profession many of the illustrations in books and pamphlets were the work of printers. When something of superior design and finish was wanted, ready-made woodcuts were procured from Nuremberg or Lyons, then the chief marts for such productions. The blocks so obtained were sometimes used without much regard to the book in which they were printed. Cuts originally designed for an edition of *Ovid* appeared in the Bible, and no notice was taken of this mixture of sacred and profane things. Albert Dürer's influence on the art of wood-engraving was very great, but it never extended to this country. Hans Holbein, who came to England two years before Dürer's death, made a few designs for the wood-engravers during his long residence here. His transient use of the art, however, did not raise it to a better condition, and printers continued to be the chief producers of woodcuts. In the time of Queen Elizabeth there flourished a printer and engraver of the name of John Day, who took for his mark an emblematic device of the day-spring of the reformed religion, with the motto, ' Arise, for it is Day.' The best illustrated books of that period were produced by him. About this time the art was rapidly declining in other countries, but in England it was in a better condition than at any previous period. It soon, however, declined in this country also, but was kept alive by Edward Kirkall, John Baptiste Jackson, and others, until it was revived by ·Thomas Bewick.

The low condition of the art of wood-engraving in this country was chiefly owing to the want of good designers, and it was not until a man arose who possessed the power to *draw* as well as to *engrave* that an English school of wood-engraving was created. Bewick possessed the artistic faculty as a direct gift from nature ; and though it was from accidental circumstances that he was led to exercise this innate power in drawing and engraving on wood, he soon discovered of what the art was capable, and devoted his chief attention to it. He drew such things as he understood and had studied from nature, and thoroughly comprehending the scope and power of wood-engraving, he was able, with little labour, to produce the best results.

At the time of Bewick's death, in 1828, England had scarcely recovered from the exhausting wars of Napoleon, trade was stagnant, and taxation was heavy. The mass of the people had no money to spend on such luxuries as illustrated books, and the enterprise of publishers was confined to the production of the well-known 'Annuals' of that day; but they were illustrated with steel engravings, and were only purchased by the wealthier classes. Such works as *Robinson Crusoe* and the *Pilgrim's Progress*, for which there is always a demand, were illustrated by Cruikshank and Harvey. There was *Northcote's Fables*, on which all the best engravers of the day were employed; but it was not until the Society for the Diffusion of Useful Knowledge began its operations, and Charles Knight took the lead in illustrated literature, that wood-engraving began to be extensively used. The art was so little known that when the woodcuts of the *Penny Magazine* began to attract attention a nobleman of that day spoke of them as the productions of a new art. Illustrations were so seldom used that the preparation of even a small woodcut was of much moment to all concerned. I have heard the late William Harvey relate that when Whittingham, the well-known printer, wanted a. new cut for his 'Chiswick Press' series, he would write to Harvey and John Thompson, the engraver, appointing a meeting at Chiswick, when printer, designer, and engraver talked over the matter with as much deliberation as if they were about to produce a costly national monument, and after they had settled all points over a snug supper, the result of their labours was the production, months afterwards, of a small woodcut measuring perhaps two inches by three. At this time only about a dozen persons, besides Bewick's pupils, were practising the art of wood-engraving in England, and in France the art was so low that a few years later the

blocks for the *Magazin Pittoresque* were sent from Paris to
London to be engraved.   In Germany, the cradle of the art,
it languished as in other countries, while in America, a
country which is now taking a leading part in the cultivation
of wood-engraving, the art was almost unknown as a native
production.   It is now in use all over the civilised world,
and there is scarcely a capital city without its newspaper
illustrated with woodcuts.   It has even penetrated to the
sunless regions of ice and snow.   In the Library of the
South Kensington Museum there is a book with illustrations
drawn and engraved on wood by Esquimaux !

   The cause of this wide diffusion and extended employment of the art of wood-engraving is undoubtedly its close
alliance with the kindred art of printing.   No other method
of engraving lends itself so easily to the rapid productions of
the printing-press.   From the earliest days of printing the
two arts have advanced hand in hand, aiding in the growth
of knowledge and the spread of civilisation.   The application
of steam to the art of printing revolutionised the world of
typography, and wood-engraving was not slow in adapting
itself to the new conditions.   The advancing spirit of education created a demand for cheap knowledge.   Penny maga-
zines and pictorial newspapers came into existence.   The
steam printing-press spread them far and wide, and wood-
engraving since the time of Bewick has shown that it pos-
sesses capabilities which that genuine old artist would have
rejoiced to behold.

   In tracing the origin and progress of the pictorial press I
have confined my researches to British journalism, but the
subject might be widely extended.   From the days of the
Acta Diurna of the Romans something in the shape of a
newspaper appears to have been a necessity of civilised life.
Soon after the invention of printing small news-sheets appeared in various towns of Germany and in Venice.   In the
Low Countries an illustrated war gazette was published as
early as 1605.   It was called the *Niewetijdinghe*, and it was
the precursor of the *Gazette van Antwerpen*, which survived

till 1805. During the Spanish and Austrian rule in Belgium each town had its privileged newspaper. As the printers of those days were well acquainted with the art of wood-engraving, it is not unlikely that some of these early newspapers contained illustrations. The earlier newspapers of Holland were chiefly devoted to commercial intelligence, and afforded little scope for illustration, but illustrated broadsides were not uncommon. In Germany the first regular newspaper appeared in 1615, when the art of wood-engraving had greatly declined; and when the physician Renaudot started the first newspaper in France, in 1631, if the idea of illustrating it had occurred to him he would have had to rely on his printer for the production of the woodcuts. As, however, the low condition of illustrative art in the seventeenth century did not deter English printers of 'News-books' from seeking such pictorial aid as they could obtain, it is highly probable their Continental brethren did the same, however insufficient might be the means at their command.

When the history of our own age comes to be written the pictorial newspapers will form an inexhaustible storehouse for the historian. The following list of cities in Europe, America, and the English colonies, with the names of the illustrated newspapers published by them, will convey some idea of the extent to which pictorial journalism has spread during the last forty years:—

PARIS:

L' Illustration.
Le Monde Illustré.
L' Univers Illustré.
La République Illustrée.
La France Illustrée.

BERLIN:
Deutsche Illustrirte Zeitung.

STUTTGART:
Uber Land und Meer.
Das Buch für Alle.

LEIPZIG :
  Illustrirte Zeitung.

VIENNA :
  Neue Illustrirte Zeitung.

MILAN :
  L' Illustrazione Universale.
  L' Illustrazione Italiana.

MADRID :
  La Illustracion Espanòla.

BARCELONA :
  La Illustracion Catòlica.

WARSAW :
  Klosy.
  Tycodnik Powszechny.

AMSTERDAM :
  De Hollandsche Illustratie.

ST. PETERSBURG :
  Universal Illustration.

COPENHAGEN :
  Illustreret Tidende.

CHRISTIANA :
  Nu Illustreret Tidende.

NEW YORK :
  Harper's Weekly.
  Harper's Bazaar.
  Frank Leslie's Illustrated Newspaper.
  Spirit of the Times.
  The Daily Graphic.
  Illustrirte Zeitung (printed in German).

WASHINGTON :
  Illustrated Washington Chronicle.

MONTREAL :
  Canadian Illustrated News.
  Le Monde Illustré (French).

SYDNEY:
  Illustrated Sydney News.
MELBOURNE:
  Illustrated Australian News.
  Australian Sketcher.
MEXICO:
  Revista Universal.
MONTEVIDEO:
  La Illustracion Uruguaya.
RIO DE JANEIRO:
  A Illustração.
CAPE TOWN:
  South African Illustrated News.

THE END.

London Printed by STRANGEWAYS AND SONS Tower Street Upper St Martin's Lane